The Dreamers of Allianz
A Novel

By
Antonio Chiareli

Copyright © 2007 by Antonio Chiareli

The Dreamers of Allianz
A Novel
by Antonio Chiareli

Printed in the United States of America

ISBN 978-1-60477-064-3

All rights reserved solely by the author. The author guarantees all contents are original and do not infringe upon the legal rights of any other person or work. No part of this book may be reproduced in any form without the permission of the author. The views expressed in this book are not necessarily those of the publisher.

Unless otherwise indicated, Bible quotations are taken from the MacArthur Study Bible, New King James Version. Copyright © 1997 by Word Publishing, and the NIV Study Bible, Copyright © 1995 by Zondervan.

Imagine
Words and Music by John Lennon
© 1971 (Renewed 1999) LENONO.MUSIC
All Rights Controlled and Administered by EMI BLACKWOOD MUSIC INC.
All Rights Reserved
International Copyright Secured. Used by Permission

www.xulonpress.com

MARCH '08

To Elizabeth,

Hoping we will make a difference as God calls and equips us.

In Christ,

[signature]

For my dearest Teresa
and our three princesses, Isabella, Luisa, and Bianca.

"For when absolute, hateful tyranny looks and feels right to all but a small and almost invisible minority, it takes an absolute, righteous God to sovereignly move again in history to reclaim His Name and His Word, and through the few gloriously and lovingly liberate humanity for Himself."

Contents

Author's Preface xi
Prologue: Imagine… xv
Part I: The World Under Allianz **19**
    One: The New World Order 21
    Two: The Birth and Focus of the Resistance 33
    Three: World Language and the Cognit Implant
        Protocol 39
    Four: Society, Culture, and the CyberSat System 45
    Five: The Metaphysical Path of Transcienz 51
    Six: Transcienz Dream States 57
    Seven: Population and Environmental Pressures 61
Part II: The Dreamers and the Struggle **65**
    Eight: Growing Angst 67
    Nine: Morning Routine 77
    Ten: Change in the Air 83
    Eleven: Friends and Dreams 91
    Twelve: Zeke at Risk? 101
    Thirteen: Shopping? 107
    Fourteen: Psychology? 113
    Fifteen: Word of Vanishings 119
    Sixteen: Zeke and Alyssa 123
    Seventeen: Dariah's Plan Conceived 129
    Eighteen: A Foreboding Message 133
    Nineteen: The *Evangel* 137
    Twenty: On to the Brethren Gathering 145
    Twenty-One: Allianz Repression 151

Twenty-Two: Danger 157
Twenty-Three: Preparation 161
Twenty-Four: The Play and the Siege 165
Twenty-Five: Dariah's Discovery 173
Twenty-Six: Resisting and Spirit-Sealing 179
Twenty-Seven: Liberation? 185
Twenty-Eight: Baptisms 191
Twenty-Nine: Reality Check and Dreaming Isaiah 195
Thirty: Horn's Strategy 203
Thirty-One: Andrus' Counsel 209
Thirty-Two: Uncertainties 213
Thirty-Three: *Les Invalides* II 219
Thirty-Four: Horn and Dariah Meet Again 221
Thirty-Five: Estrangement 227
Thirty-Six: More Vanishings 233
Thirty-Seven: Confrontation 237
Thirty-Eight: The Great Allianz Directive Revealed 241
Thirty-Nine: Christensen's Despair 247
Forty: Strange Last Day 253
Forty-One: Fateful Showdown 257
Forty-Two: Fleeing the Tempter 267
Forty-Three: No Word 277
Forty-Four: The Great Escape 281
Forty-Five: Crashed? 287
Forty-Six: Horn's Great Ambitions 291
Forty-Seven: Christensen Feared Dead 295
Forty-Eight: Alyssa Arrives 299
Forty-Nine: Zeke and Alyssa Captured 303
Fifty: Safe at Last? 307
Fifty-One: Leaving Home 317
Fifty-Two: Dariah Recommits 323
Fifty-Three: Rendezvous with Dr. C 325
Fifty-Four: At the Slovak Monastery 329
Fifty-Five: Morph-ship Ride to Croce Cavern 337
Fifty-Six: Horn and Dariah in North Africa 343
Fifty-Seven: Anxiously Waiting 347
Fifty-Eight: Andrus' Warning 349

Fifty-Nine: What's a *Sociologer*? 355
Sixty: Inside the Great Catacombs Project..................359
Sixty-One: Analyzing Allianz..363
Sixty-Two: Rejoined 367
Sixty-Three: Horn Denied 371
Sixty-Four: "The One Sent" 375
Sixty-Five: Allianz Unleashed 381
Sixty-Six: Reunification Interrupted................................385
Sixty-Seven: Out of Damascus 389
Sixty-Eight: The Red Monastery Attacked.....................391
Sixty-Nine: Going Underground......................................397
Epilogue: Dariah's Conversion **401**
Allianz Timeline **407**
Cast of Main Characters **409**
Allianz Glossary **413**

Author's Preface

Dreams and imagination have been a part of our common human experience since time immemorial. They are important themes in this story, as well. In them lie our brightest hopes, our deepest joys, and our most terrifying fears. When I first formulated the basic idea for this project, early in 2001, I began to imagine and reflect upon the troubling specter of a world almost entirely devoid of the presence of God and the impact of His Word. I also dreamed about how God, in His sovereignty, might choose to reclaim Creation for Himself given such a scenario. The result of my musings is **The Dreamers of Allianz**, a fictional account of the global underground Church in the not-too-distant future, though perhaps not as imaginary as one might think.

Angelo Croce, better known as "Dr. C," narrates this story from the vantage point of heaven. A former professor of sociology, Dr. C grew deeply committed to a global, faith-based resistance movement, known as the "Community of Brethren Resistance," which he was instrumental in organizing, soon after the "Great Digital Meltdown." In this story, the Resistance struggles against a post-digital world system whose culture and social structure have been completely transformed, for evil ends, by the advent of the "Cognit Forehead Implant." Seemingly powered by occult forces, this strange, new technology divides the world's human inhabitants between a vast implanted majority and non-implanted minority – respectively, the privileged many and the persecuted few.

In reading this novel, you will come across such terms as, "The Name," "Spirit-sealed," "*Evangel*," and others, which will likely sound unusual from the perspective of mainstream Christianity. Moreover, nowhere in this narrative will you find the label "Christian," much less a denominational identification being applied to any particular group. These are purposeful editorial alterations meant for effect, as they reflect a process of acute change in all things religious by the time the story's plot begins, including a significant degree of estrangement worldwide from the real essence of the One true and living God.

My simple hope in writing this novel, is to assert that God takes His Word for this world seriously, and so should we. I wish to convey the continued centrality and importance of His entire Message for the living faith which I and untold numbers of other Believers around the world have come to know, through Jesus Christ, His son and our Lord. The consequences, to our faith and to the Church, of somehow losing access to His Word – far-fetched as that may seem – could only be dire. We must cherish, teach, and apply it while and wherever we still enjoy the privilege of having it before us. I also want to challenge the reader to awaken to a keen realization of what his or her place in Allianz might be – as privileged or as persecuted – even if our actual individual or collective futures be only remotely related to the premise and development of this story. Again, I want to remind the reader that this book is a work of fiction. Although there is much here that points to truth, the entirety of the story that follows is a figment of my own imagination, and is thus not an attempt at prediction or prophecy.

Finally, this book is divided into two main parts. In Part I, I lay out the framework for the story, offering an introductory overview of the new world order. This material briefly provides the reader with key pieces of the Allianz world system mosaic. In Part II, I develop the more extensive story plot and its conclusion, though not yet the final one for the world under Allianz and its inhabitants. For the benefit of the reader, an "Allianz Timeline," a "Cast of Main Characters," and an "Allianz Glossary" have been included at the end of this volume, as helpful reference material.

I must conclude with a word of eternal gratitude to Almighty God, Whom I felt faithfully energizing me throughout the writing process, and Who deserves all the glory for the inspiration, materialization, and impact this novel may make upon its audience. I am also indebted to my parents and sisters, who through selfless nurturing gave me my earliest glimpse into enduring, unconditional love. They have helped to shape me and to unleash my creative energies. I owe many thanks, as well, to the local and universal "Community of Brethren," of which I am a part, for their availing prayers and encouragement. Here, I especially want to acknowledge the faithful contributions and support of Mrs. Julia Morris and of Michal and Viera Kliman throughout the entire writing of this book. Thanks also to Fred Morgan and Walton Padelford for their helpful feedback on early versions of the manuscript. I want to acknowledge and thank Teresa Chiareli and Julianna Bienert for their invaluable editing work, and Jack Walton and Linda Cabibbo, of Xulon Press, for their expert support. I am grateful to Union University for making possible years of intercultural research, which served to enhance this project, and to Covenant College for affording me the privilege of continuing to pursue my calling in innovative, creative, and scholarly ways. Last but never least, I want to give thanks with all my heart to my precious wife and daughters, who have lovingly inspired me simply by being who they are in Christ and in my life, and to whom I dedicate this, my debut novel.

Humbly by His Grace,
Antonio A. C. P. Chiareli, Ph.D.
Lookout Mountain, summer 2007

Prologue: Imagine…

Looking back, I never could have imagined how strangely prophetic the famous lyrics to John Lennon's song, "Imagine," would really have turned out to be. Unlike anything man ever penned artistically to spur on generations of dreamers to a new vision of society, Mr. Lennon's poetry ironically stood as a presage about the dark reign of **Allianz**, the abominable world order. Indeed, humanity's mass assimilation into the greatest deception of the 21st century began much like the utopian imaginings of a cultural prophet…

Imagine there's no heaven,
It's easy if you try,
No hell below us,
Above us only sky,
Imagine all the people living for today...

Imagine there's no countries,
It isn't hard to do,
Nothing to kill or die for,
No religion too,
Imagine all the people living life in peace...

Imagine no possessions,
I wonder if you can,
No need for greed or hunger,
A brotherhood of man,

The Dreamers of Allianz

Imagine all the people
Sharing all the world...

You may say
I'm a dreamer, but I'm not the only one,
I hope some day you'll join us,
And the world will live as one

- John Lennon

But dare we really imagine...the world under Allianz? I wonder if you can... No sovereign countries, no true religion, no notion of heaven or hell, nothing to truly possess, pacified masses with no passions to die for, an eager invitation to join a unified brotherhood of man, a world of dreamers living for today...

Greetings. My name is... Well, for security purposes – yours, not mine any longer – let me simply say that my students used to call me, "Dr. C." The story I have been commissioned to tell may strike some as a fantastic tale. Indeed, I would not be exaggerating if I told you that aspects of this account are truly out of this world. Yet, I beseech you, my dear friend, to consider it soberly, for it ought to be received as a warning to you about the struggle that is to come when Allianz rises. This story comes at great cost to so many. But if you are reading this, then I am encouraged, for I have succeeded in telling it, and others have faithfully accomplished its transmission – for lack of a more fitting descriptor – backwards in redemptive history, as was intended, for the time is short indeed.

You can trust me in its careful account, for I have been allowed to witness it in its entirety, although I am precluded from explaining to you just how. And I admit, you might not fully understand it if I were to attempt such an illumination. What I can tell you is that you will eventually find out about me, and where I do fit into this epic tale. That is, of course, if you persevere. Oh, another thing. I happen to know who the victors are in this story, and I can barely hold back from telling you, either. But then again, the mere fact that you can come to know this chronicle should be most revealing and reassuring.

I should say that this is not yet a story of complete victory. Rather, it is one of fatefully unavoidable historical process. The colliding forces herein are dramatic and beyond the complete grasp of the natural, empirical world. In the course of this narrative, you will no doubt realize exactly what I mean. For now, suffice it to say that all of us who have once lived and moved on the surface of the earth have experienced these forces…some for evil, some for good. They are eternal, really. And who could ever hope to escape either of them while living? For good and evil truly exist to constantly affect each of us from birth 'til death, and one of them for infinite eternity. Believe me, I ought to know a thing or two about it.

Beware, though. For as the time of great repression and distress draws near, these timeless, inimical powers – human, institutional, and spiritual – will fantastically oppose each other in greater and more bizarre intensity. And for a while, a part of humanity will know what evil at its most perverse really looks and feels like. Many who oppose it will lose heart and grow faint while under the weight of terrible devastation. However, countless others, who will unknowingly give themselves over to great abomination, will be allowed to lose their ability to recognize evil for what it truly is…perhaps to their own good fortune, short-lived as it may ultimately be. But there will yet be others who will be chosen, and will accept their fate and become mighty instruments in the enemy's ultimate and systemic demise. For when absolute, hateful tyranny looks and feels right to all but a small and almost invisible minority, it takes an absolute, righteous God to sovereignly move again in history to reclaim His Name and His Word, and through the few gloriously and lovingly liberate humanity for Himself.

If I have not lost you yet, I urge you now to let yourself imagine… Sit back and join me as we gaze into the history of your not-so-distant future, and as I recount the story I have been privileged to watch and know experientially, at least in part, about the world under Allianz, about the dreamers – of one sort or another – and about the happenings that ushered in the darkest times to come…

One more thing… The words to that famous twentieth century song I refer to above beckon us to imagine a new world, an alternate reality. As the one offering the invitation, Mr. Lennon had to know in his heart that, as things go, once given and accepted the invitation to imagine which he freely extends leaves his control, and the imagination of the one being beguiled grows its own wings and flies away in unpredictable and almost always unknowable directions. Many may grasp it and truly dream. Others might capture it, co-opt it, and exploit it for their own empowerment and for the subjugation of humanity. That's always the risk, I suppose, but also the thrill of our divinely given, human ability to imagine. But I've got a distinct feeling that this former member of the Beatles fully understood the potential impact of words, the consequences of imagination taken flight, and the construction of a reality few have the power to contest.

And lastly as we begin, for those of you who have held out no hope for sociologists, let me just say that, thankfully, we did get a few things right. And perhaps to your surprise, there are a host of others like me here, where we continue to exist beyond common time and dimension, in ecstatic, holy fellowship and community.

Now to Him Who sits on His majestic throne, be honor, and glory, and power, forever and ever! Amen.

**Yours truly in the Resistance,
"Dr. C"**

Part I

The World Under Allianz

One

The New World Order

Like an utterly devastating, worldwide tsunami, the sudden viral attack on the binary technological superstructure had proven to be the final and most perfect virtual storm. Every last byte and stringed line of command in its path had been wiped out, until nothing was left but contorted, unrecognizable digital debris, afloat in a dark, vast, and silent cyberspace. It was as if an invisible, global tidal wave had swept up and all but obliterated the very sustaining marrow of our fully digitized human civilization. Life as we had come to depend on all over the earth had met an abrupt end at the stroke of midnight, Paris time, in the first moments of the year which was to exalt, of all things…humanity's great technological achievements. Inexplicably and without warning, and ironically by the precision of the world's digitized time-keeping instruments, the tides permanently went out on the fragile digital era.

Of what had become our great, ordered pillars of knowledge, finance, technology, and social control, in the once seemingly untouchable global information society, only the hollowed out hardware shell had remained, as if a virtual hydrogen bomb had been detonated. Literally overnight, human culture had been forcibly propelled into a techno Dark Age, rendering even the brightest scientific minds helplessly dismayed and confounded. The global chaos that Y2K had promised and failed to execute decades earlier had finally been delivered in the form of a wireless, part electronic, part electromagnetic, viral intruder, known as the **Minotaur Virus**.

This mysterious global attack was fulminating, and was executed with such unrelenting, destructive intensity that it simply overwhelmed the self-assured and costly defensive apparatus that the world's electronic warfare sages had constructed to thwart terrorist mayhem targeting the digital gridiron. But this time, our weakest links were targeted first. The totality of our massive constellation of aged, unprotected satellites came crashing down, one by one, like brilliant stars falling from the sky. It seemed like the whole earth trembled. As in a long feared apocalyptic nightmare, instant worldwide panic and pandemonium ensued after the **Great Digital Meltdown (GDM)**.

Yet, upon this sudden and dramatic ending to the once promising digital age, what had been thought to unavoidably devolve into a long, drawn-out, "Mad Max-like" scenario was instead astutely averted within a short year's time. A surprisingly timely confluence of cunning political genius and innovative technological renaissance, top-secretly developed for just such a catastrophic scenario on the earth, saved humanity from its dreadful and all but certain undoing. In an historic – and in the eyes of the masses, heroic – "final act," the long-ineffective and corruption-prone **United Commonwealth Organization (UCO)** reluctantly conceded a new world order, devised by its own power-elite group, led by the organization's last sitting Secretary General.

This global political reorganization – nothing short of an international coup – would ultimately come to be touted as having rescued all of humanity from the brink of self-destruction, as the world's population at best faced a kind of elemental existence, and at worst a likely all-against-all demise in GDM's aftermath. As in a well-scripted, triumphant geopolitical dramatization, our human civilization had somehow been reinvented only one year after the calamitous GDM, which came to mark the literal calendric "restart" point of global society's history.

Despite a relatively short period of sweeping and often turbulent political reformation and military reorganization, by the new calendar year, GDM-1, the entire world had become reunified. This process culminated in the formation of the **Allianz Federation**, a single, hegemonic world government. Allianz, as it came to be commonly called, thoroughly supplanted all other forms of governance. As this new world system established itself, and for a time greatly thrived, its very equilibrium became inextricably dependent upon the worldwide expansion and dominance of the new **Cognit Technological Protocol**. Sustaining and integrating the entire Allianz empire, was the expansive and increasingly powerful network of new-generation satellites, known as **CyberSat**, visible only with the aid of telescopes. Over time, this dependence came to signify Allianz's greatest strength, but also its most delicate vulnerability.

Headquartered in the capital district of Paris, Province of France, from its inception in the provisional mandate year, GDM-1, the Allianz Federation had been exercising sovereign political authority over all global provinces. Prior to that, these regions had been autonomous nation states for several decades and, in many cases, centuries. A ten-member **Council of Regents**, presiding over a **General Parliament** made up of two hundred **Allianz Nobles**, carried out the regency of the entire Federation from the **Allianz Palace**, overlooking the Seine River, whose serpentine flow divided the Parisian district.

Above the grand entrance archway of the Federation's Palace, the words "Liberty, Equality, and Fraternity," written in **Allianzi**, the new official world language, were prominently inscribed. Paradoxically, this promising motto obscured the fact that democratic principles once fervently championed across the globe had suffered critical setbacks. For nearly a decade now, the Federation had been successfully litigating in the **Supreme Juris Court** against what it deemed to be inherent flaws in that old form of representative governance. Formerly democratically elected Heads of State, who had ruled in the now superceded world order, were systematically being indicted and prosecuted for alleged corruption and, in some instances, high treason against the Allianz Federation.

Since transitioning out of his high post as the Secretary General of the now defunct UCO, Mr. Adammus Horn, the Federation's bright and ambitious **Allianz Prosecutor General**, had been tirelessly bringing to trial numerous high-profile legal cases involving former world leaders. Defendants were being charged with blatant and scandalously fraudulent governing practices, which had allegedly been responsible for intense political upheaval all over the world in the period that immediately preceded the establishment of the Federation. Through Horn's demagoguery, charismatic style, and astute powers of persuasion, billions across the globe had been clamoring for justice to be done against such vilified rulers. In the process, hundreds of former world leaders and their cabinet members were being duly tried in the highest court, the majority of them being found guilty and indefinitely detained in Federation prisons.

On one particular afternoon in the early spring of GDM-13, following another significant trial event, the assembled press met outside the Court's building for a highly anticipated, but disappointingly brief official pronouncement by Mr. Horn, himself. From the steps of the imposing government edifice, the Prosecutor General proudly stated:

"Ladies and gentlemen of the **Allianz Federation Press**... Vigor to Allianz. It is my great privilege to announce to you that, today, our beloved Federation has come a giant step closer to achieving our preeminent goal of being totally purged from the lasting and poisonous effects of institutional corruption and disorder, under our former and dishonorable political system. At long last, defiled and deceitful world democracy breathes her final, dying breath."

"Mr. Prosecutor General!" cried a press delegate, who inquired, "Can you tell us when these defendants and the other long held political detainees will finally be sentenced?"

"All sentencing hearings are being held privately. It would be imprudent of me at this point to offer any further details on these proceedings and on their particular outcomes. We will not allow these highly sensitive cases to be tried in the media. However, you can be assured that the press will be summoned when the Federation is prepared to make such information available to the public," Horn

The Dreamers of Allianz

said, skillfully evading the question. In vain, the reporters pushed for further comments.

"Mr. Prosecutor! Mr. Prosecutor! One more question, please!" they all shouted, as one reporter near the back of the sizeable press assembly asked loudly, "Can you comment on the latest crackdowns on this worldwide religious **Resistance movement**? What about its remarkable growth in some areas of the American Province?"

"Thank you all very much. I will take no further questions at this time...Vigor to Allianz!" Horn exclaimed, as he waived and turned away from the press crowd, and hastily climbed back up the marble steps. Visibly upset, he dashed toward the Court's grand entrance doors. In just seconds, he had disappeared behind a quickly formed line of homogenously uniformed policemen, who barred the press' access into the building.

"Get me the American Marshall on my Visual...immediately!" the angry Horn ordered his newest clerk. Horn's long, black coat flared behind him, revealing his tall, slender build, as he moved hurriedly across the interior of the Court building's stately rotunda.

"Yes, Mr. Horn, right away, sir," the attractive young woman replied. "May I also remind you, Mr. Horn, that you're scheduled to speak to the Environmental Caucus at Versailles in exactly two hours?" she added, trying to cover all her bases with her new and terribly exacting boss.

"Cancel it."

"Sir?"

"You heard me, Ms. Price. Cancel my appearance," Horn said sternly, then adding, "I can't think of a single reason right now why I would want to stand before three-hundred pushy, entitled, alfalfa-sniffing, and bird-food-eating, naturalist pricks, who just want their ears tickled, as if it were Allianz that needed them, instead of the other way around."

"Uh, yes, Mr. Horn," answered the perplexed young assistant, struggling in her petite frame not to lag behind Horn's frantic pace. "Any alternate plans, then, while we're looking at your schedule?" she asked, now gasping.

"Dinner... Have dinner with me, Ms. Price," he said, abruptly turning around to face the exasperated-looking young woman.

"I beg your pardon?"

"Dinner. Tonight. Eight o'clock. *Le Procope*," Horn's favorite and still the oldest restaurant in all of Paris, founded in 1686, and frequented by the 18th century emperor, Napoleon, himself.

"Uhh...yes, sir," she awkwardly replied, not knowing how else to respond to the completely unexpected request by her superior.

Horn's predatory instincts were always heightened when political dissidents challenged his authority and forced him to assert his power. And in light of the press' aggravating allusion to the growing threats by the Resistance movement, this young woman was just going to be Horn's next, unsuspecting victim. Late that very evening, the helpless clerk would be the one to pay the price for his self-perceived, slight public humiliation. For Horn, however, the outcome of his forceful overture toward her would simply be considered as political collateral damage; a fringe benefit of his political immunity – or rather, impunity – under the **Allianz Code**.

Upon close and critical examination, it was becoming increasingly evident that for years now the entire world had been moving on a fast track toward a form of supposed benevolent totalitarianism, unlike anything humanity had ever seen. But many throughout the globe were distracted, still dealing with the horrendous aftermath of another serious development.

For nearly a decade, a strange but almost always lethal form of skin cancer had been rapidly devastating the majority of the world's geriatric population. Fully a quarter of the world's inhabitants ultimately perished, out of a total population of nearly nine billion before this cataclysmic cancerous plague hit. A marked and ever-worsening depletion of the atmosphere's protective ozone layer had created peculiarly harmful and virulent effects that disproportionately affected the aged population, perhaps due to this cohort's loss with age of natural biological defenses against the unfiltered sunrays. Consequently, very few people over 50 years of age had survived it unharmed – I, myself, was among the fortunate few who narrowly escaped what seemed like the worst of fates. For this very reason, world government positions had largely been left in the hands of a much younger generation, which had grown up with weaker ties to once dominant, pre-Federation-period cultural norms, beliefs, and traditions. But could a twisted plot by the Federation have wickedly stood behind this terrifying devastation on the earth? What about the unleashing of the mysterious Minotaur Virus? Could the masterminds behind the new world order have unthinkably been responsible for it as well? Some anti-Federation critics feared as much on both counts.

By mid GDM-2, the Allianz Federation had begun an ambitious worldwide campaign for achieving its goals of universal conformity with the Allianz Code. Universities and trans-global businesses had since then become inundated with the rather successful **"Imagine"** government propaganda and its iconic, golden telescope. The worldwide diffusion of this campaign had been facilitated by the use of the pre-existing, inter-provincial platforms of academic and corporate knowledge sharing. In fact, well before the advent of the Allianz Federation, the global stage had already been set for the rapid spread of seductive "one-world" ideologies, due to an ever-accelerating globalization trend that was well celebrated by the turn of the 21st century. This tactic was key, especially in reaching the population's under-forty cohorts, whose political support was being avidly sought after by the central government.

According to the system's main existing law enforcement directive, an **Allianz Federation Marshall**, in charge of overseeing the governance of each province, in place of the former Office of the President, functioned also as the top commander of law enforcement. Each Marshall was thus charged with commanding and coordinating battalions and sub-units of troops, known as **cogs**, who constituted the primary **Allianz Federation Police Force**. Their main duty was to uphold and fully enforce the Allianz Code. The Code, unanimously approved by the General Parliament and adopted by the full Council of Regents, as the Federation became permanently instituted in GDM-2, carefully outlined core universal values and sanctions for the Federation and society as a whole, along with the essential privileges and obligations of its billions of citizens across the globe.

The Dreamers of Allianz

Since GDM-12, the use of force had intensified considerably as a means of social control against an as-of-yet peaceful, faith-based Resistance movement found in small pockets throughout the world. Generally known as the **Community of Brethren**, this movement was loosely structured, which facilitated their operations and mobilizations throughout many global provinces, including the American Province, where the Resistance had become especially strong, in the South and Southeast regions.

In the American South, a fast growing assembly of men, women, and children of the Resistance had been defying the Allianz Code, at great peril to themselves. They called themselves, the **Children of the Promise** group, and their apparent effectiveness in indoctrinating dissidents against the Allianz Code was becoming an increasingly difficult problem to ignore. They were a growing embarrassment to Commander Misha Dariah, the American Province Marshall. Through masked maneuvers by her **Secret Cog Units**, her administration had been closely watching and collecting intelligence on this and numerous other Resistance cells. Dariah urgently sought to develop a strategy for just how to decisively deal with the growing threat of disorder, which they decidedly represented.

"Commander," reported a cog Colonel, during a debriefing at the HQ in Washington, D.C., "our sources have detected unusually high recent activity by some movement cadres in the South and Southeast, and we believe they are making preparations for imminent and significant **Brethren Gatherings** in these regions."

"Give me a break, Colonel!" Dariah loudly chastised, still livid after her latest, disconcerting exchange with Prosecutor General Horn. "I don't need *you* to tell me that! These guys aren't kidding around. I need to move on these praying fools, and you can't give me anything better than this vague bunch of garbage?" she went on. "I want to know *who* we need to take out to make this whole thing disappear for good! Don't get back to me until you can give me names... I want names! Now go!"

"Yes, right away, Commander," nervously answered the cog officer, who saluted and then hurriedly exited the room. "Let's go... Move it!" he directed his troops.

Commander Dariah was determined to quell the American Resistance, and to do so especially to please her demanding superior, Adammus Horn, whose upcoming and long awaited official visit to the American Province was looming large. Privately, Dariah hoped Horn's brief scheduled stay would also be an opportunity for her to reconnect with him, an old acquaintance, on a more personal level. Although it had been years since their often tumultuous relationship had formally ended, Dariah somehow still longed to relive the relatively rare but sweet moments, when she wasn't the prestigious Marshall and Commander of the American Province, but simply Horn's "beautiful Misha," as he once liked to call her. Almost two decades ago, they had chanced upon each other, as university students in the Northeast, and soon began intermittently dating; she a bright undergraduate at MIT, and he a rising star at Harvard Law School.

In several other locations worldwide, police operations had turned quite incisive, as widespread and far-reaching intervention campaigns by teams of cogs systematically searched for and moved to forcibly deal with non-conformity to the Code by members of this countercultural, grassroots Resistance movement. In the Chinese, Korean, Polish, Slovak, Turkish, Ethiopian, and Brazilian Provinces, just to name a scattered few, there had been serious leadership losses as a result of concerted police action. Consequently, in these locations, as well as in other suspected Resistance strongholds, the movement was fast losing considerable ground.

But although the mood had been quickly turning somber for many movement members throughout the dominion, there were those, particularly in the American South, who had nonetheless remained strongly determined to stay committed to their anti-Allianz cause. In grateful awe, they credited their faith in **The Name**, and His sovereign hand of protection over them, for the remarkable success they had been enjoying, mobilizing so great a number of people, and especially youth.

The Dreamers of Allianz

Sometime in that same early spring of GDM-13, during a relatively small, week-night Brethren Gathering, as the Resistance's corporate services were commonly called, John "the Baptist" Waters, the young pastor of the Children of the Promise group in Tennessee, reported on a troubling communiqué from a trusted friend in the Resistance, which had been reliably circulating among various groups in the southern Community of Brethren. The feeling in the air was that things were about to change dramatically, but they could only guess as to exactly how.

Relaying the warning, John said, "The message goes as follows: *Sisters and brothers, loved and kept by The Name, stand ready to be opposed soon. Your stirrings in the South have been closely watched, and Dariah is presently planning to make a move. But it is yet unclear just when. Watch out for infiltrators. I will be much in prayer for you. Pray also for me, as I continue to move about in concealment.*" Then, Tanner Daniel Christensen, a leader in the southern Resistance and the one through whom the message was first brought to the group, added, "This comes to us from Dr. C. I received it two days ago. It's for real...and I can tell by its tone that he's quite concerned."

Worried, Shen-il Waters, the young pastor's wife, asked, "Tanner, can we really trust him?" Having met and married John during his recent ministry years in Southeast Asia, Shen-il, a gifted pianist, had only been with the group for about a year, as its worship leader. So new in the group, she didn't fully appreciate the extent of Christensen's previous and meaningful involvement with the "old man," as Christensen charmingly liked to refer to me, when I was not around.

"He can be trusted, Shen-il," Christensen affirmed. "I've known the old man for a long while; in fact, since my college days, at Faith&Knowledge U. He was my sociology professor and mentor in the faith. For many years, he was also my master in **Aikido**, a Japanese self-defense system that was pretty popular back then. You know, I bet he could still pivot-throw me clear off the Aikido mat," he contemplated.

"All right, so he's an old acquaintance. But where has he been all of these years since? What's he been doing?" Shen-il inquired, still unconvinced of the trustworthiness of the source of the message. Suspicion and incredulity came easily for Shen-il Waters. Having grown up in the midst of religious persecution in her province of origin, Indonesia, she had been taught to always question every stranger's intentions. Her survival instincts as a Believer had helped her escape impending doom on a number of prior occasions, back in her native Java Island. She was not willing to part with what she felt was a divinely given intuition, especially not now.

"Well, it's actually been a long time since I last saw him," Christensen admitted, "...probably since he left the university, after it was shut down, almost ten years ago. But I've been in touch with him off and on, as he's moved around the world, gathering intelligence and helping out the Resistance."

"I see," Shen-il replied. "Tanner, I don't mean to be a hopeless skeptic, but I've just seen too many people get hurt by those who they thought they could trust."

"I understand, Shen-il," Christensen said, "but you can trust me on this one."

At that point, John said, "Tanner, we've been aware of this persecution going on all over. We knew it would possibly just be a matter of time for us now. Still, we've been holding out some hope of being left alone. After all, our public gatherings are put on as cultural and social events. Technically, we've not been acting illegally."

"True, John," Christensen said, "but Dariah must somehow be on to us. And I'm pretty sure we're fair game for cog interventions, now. We just can't afford to discount Dr. C's warning."

John paused and then called out, "Let's gather around, everyone." Following in prayer, John softly offered a word of exhortation to the thirty or so individuals gathered there, saying, "Most High, we do stand ready, in expectant hope that Your strong hand will accomplish Your will. We trust in Your deliverance. Be with us and with the courageous souls that will soon come and risk it all to find out who You truly are. And we ask also that You continue to graciously protect our good friend, Dr. C. In Your Name, we pray." And all assembled there responded in unison, "Amen."

Police offensives of the sort being heard about were having the unintended effect of galvanizing sentiments of indignation among the members of this community of Believers in the South. For the Children of the Promise group, their resolve to accomplish their part in the mission of the Resistance only seemed to be getting stronger, as more news arrived of stepped up repression everywhere. They truly appeared to stand unmoved in their ultimate aim of reaching the spiritually lost, and educating them about the true objectives of the Federation. Their gatherings, indeed, were not unlawful. For a long time now, the Resistance had astutely taken advantage of a loophole in the Allianz Code, which narrowly allowed for freedom of assembly at openly cultural and social events, for which the Brethren Gatherings qualified, as long as no religious coercion was used in attracting or converting anyone. But that window of opportunity seemed now to be closing, and fast.

But what exactly constituted the Resistance's ideology? Why had such a relatively small worldwide community come to pose such a considerable threat to the entire Allianz Federation System? The answer to these questions might be surprising.

Two

The Birth and Focus of the Resistance

Although details were at first sketchy, Resistance intelligence had been slowly piecing together a somber picture of what they were up against. To them, it had become more and more evident, even via cursory observation of numerous societal trends and global developments, that the world's assimilation to the Allianz Code was seemingly gaining apocalyptic significance. Alarmed, at first, by consistent reports of widespread apostasy worldwide, which seemed to strongly correlate with the onset of the new Allianz System, a network of global members of the Community of Brethren was formed in the autumn of GDM-3. Their initial aim was to share knowledge, compare experiences, identify leaders, and ultimately to create an alliance to struggle against world domination by the Allianz Federation and the enforcement of the Allianz Code.

During their first global conference that same year, held in Antigua, Province of Guatemala, on the site of a centuries-old monastery that had been converted into a hotel and conference complex, the brethren there present gathered to discuss a number of pressing issues. Among them was the emergence and growing pseudo-religious dominance of a strange, new world metaphysical phenomenon, officially sanctioned by the Federation, known as the **Path of Transcienz**. They also debated the dangers of assimilation to the new world order, and especially the disturbing developments regarding the forehead implant, which was being aggressively promoted by the system, as a way of fostering a novel form of participation in society. To those who fully assimilated into the Allianz system, there were many obvious advantages, including the ability to mysteriously acquire the new world language. In addition, implanted individuals gained access to more advanced forms of technology, and benefited from the ongoing implementation of programs designed to revamp labor market and economic structures, all of which translated into great stability and security for all supporters of the Federation.

As one of the few existing sociologists strongly grounded in the faith and still exercising his prophetic calling, I was asked to come and speak at the plenary session, at the first meeting of the three-day long conference in the quaint, cobblestone-paved, and volcano-edging town of Antigua:

"Beloved, if our thinking on this is correct, and by all accounts it appears that it is, then I'm afraid that what we have recently been witnessing globally is the materialization of the system that will set the stage for the darkest days of earthly humanity's existence, though the eyes of many will be veiled, as they fall prey to Allianz's convincing deception."

In disbelief, the audience sat silent. I then proceeded with some hesitation, while striving to convey my sense of urgency, as a Believer, in the face of mounting pressures on our community and increasing persecution worldwide. As I concluded my opening address that evening, I got right to the point of the matter, the principal reason for my being there, in the first place:

"Brethren, even as we expectantly await the imminent return of our Lord, I urge you to engage collectively, beginning immediately, in the act of mobilizing all of our resources, all of our gifts, and all of our will, for the purpose of globally resisting what is to come. For, if the Lord should tarry, what all of this means for us, his body, is that we may be about to encounter the most concerted, devastating, and horrifying evil opposition to our faith and way of life that our community has ever directly experienced in the over two millennia of its existence, even as compared to the terrible persecution of the early Church. For decades now, our community of faith has been labeled as countercultural and reactionary. We have suffered great losses in our ability to freely live out and assert our own norms and values. As you well know, repression has come over us in many manifest and latent ways. But what is now upon us, I am afraid, is a kind of targeted hostility akin to broad, real, and sustained warfare against the people of The Name, all over the world."

The audience's subdued response, at first, suddenly gave way to gasps and whispered expressions of fright punctuated by reactions of, "No! It can't be..." and, "Is he serious?"

"What exactly are you saying, professor?" inquired a troubled member of the audience.

"I am saying...watch the signs: The furious rise of the Allianz might and the materialization of its one-world government, the broad and sweeping reforms everywhere, the widening chasm between the privileged, **implanted** population and the excluded, marginalized **non-implanted** groups, the mind-polluting counterfeit of Transcienz, the astonishing apostasy trends worldwide, the persistent threats to all other religious institutions and traditions, and the list goes on and on." I then told them, "Friends, the 'Imagine' propaganda and its billions of followers worldwide notwithstanding, a deep, dark shadow has been cast upon this world since GDM, and an age of unimaginable terror, under the reign of Allianz, is all but certain for the followers of The Name. The Federation will not tolerate any and all who do not follow the system of this world."

At that point, I elucidated, "I believe we have only two options now before us...to run or to fight. Assimilation via implantation is forbidden to us, who belong to The Name. For, according to our best, collective wisdom, we regard the Cognit Implant to be the outward and visible manifestation of the spiritual 'mark' we are to reject, and whose underlying demonic system we are to struggle against, at all costs."

"You mean, take up arms?" asked a distressed woman, voicing the question on the minds of many others, who listened with grave concern.

"Yes, but I've thought long and hard about this. And I stand before you convinced that our best weapons at this point are peaceful and of the spiritual kind," I replied. "I believe that the task before us is entirely noble and surprisingly simple, yet most exceedingly challenging." I then explained, "...It is to urgently mobilize and reach, while we still have time, as many non-implanted individuals as possible, locally and throughout the globe. We must also reach out to the already implanted children, before the age of willful assimilation into the Allianz Code. Our only hope for success is that they will be enabled by The Name to supernaturally discern the true and eternal cost of assimilation, and to choose instead to be spiritually sealed in The Name, and be baptized in Him and into the Community. I strongly believe that this is the only way one can truly become immune to the implant and its many troubling effects."

"But what are we to do, professor, if repression and persecution rain down on our communities?" another member of the audience asked in alarm. "What if our worldwide community of Believers is forcibly scattered? Or worse even, tortured and killed for such clear defiance to the Allianz Code?"

"We know His grace has been sufficient for countless saints over the centuries. I have to believe we will not be forsaken, when our time comes. Though many of us may be numbered among the martyred saints, The Name will not abandon His remnant on the earth. That is Scriptural, and we can be certain of it."

"Is that it?" responded that same man. "You propose that we simply play Russian-roulette and hope that we'll be spared and delivered, while we watch innumerable others among us being violently wiped out?"

"What I propose, my brother, is that we make immediate preparations for an eventual tactical withdrawal by the remaining Believers, if need be, as the day comes when darkness truly overtakes the world and we find ourselves still here. But I believe this withdrawal will only be for a time. The community of the faithful will not remain invisible forever."

"What do you mean, professor," someone else in the assembled crowd spoke out.

I then carefully unveiled my doomsday scenario strategy. As I shared it in some detail, we were to create, in as many provinces as possible where communities of Believers were found, a network of subterranean tunnels, linking various secret bunker locations to undisclosed underground sanctuaries, consisting of interconnected caverns. This was not an entirely novel idea, for since the earliest days of persecution against our faith, primitive Believers had sought the protective shelter of catacombs and caves to escape from the heinous attacks by the Roman Empire. The difference in this plan, however, was in its broad scale and apocalyptic purpose.

As I continued in my exposition of the daring proposal, I stated that, upon the implementation of this plan, later labeled as the **Global Exodus** plan, via an agreed upon and universally transmitted signal in the heavens, the worldwide group of mobilized Believers would quickly move underground. At first, these hideaway locations would be known only to their planners and builders. I then explained how, inside each network of caverns, there would be galleries and chambers fully outfitted with at least rudimentary communal living spaces. There, we would also store and preserve, in insulated warehouses, seven years worth of basic supplies and non-perishable provisions for up to a half-million Believers, depending on the potential size of the displaced population. Once inside the caverns, the subterranean passages leading to each sanctuary complex would be completely sealed off and camouflaged from the outside world. Finally, a cloaked communications system would also be developed and implemented in such locations, for use in inter-cavern information exchange, but also with adequate capacity for global inter-communication.

It was admittedly a bold, almost inconceivable plan, shrouded in mystery. Not even the community of faithful, wealthy donors, who were to ultimately fully fund the project, was to be privy to any of its development and implementation. But despite the initial shock and hesitant processing of the proposal by those who were gathered at the conference, by the conclusion of our meetings it would be received with almost unanimous approval for further development and, ultimately, full commission. Upon the closing of that fateful gathering in Antigua, the Community of Brethren Resistance Movement was officially formed, and the mission for the Brethren Gatherings crystallized. With the robust momentum behind it, the building of the infrastructure that would make the Global Exodus plan possible began in earnest by early GDM-4.

In order to comprehend what they were really up against, however, a closer look at the world under Allianz is required.

Three

World Language and the Cognit Implant Protocol

An old adage from the world's colonial past said, "If you control language, you control culture." If what had happened in the planet over the decade which preceded GDM-13 was any indication, this alleged truism certainly seemed to be part of the Federation's reigning ideology. Since GDM-4, there had been one officially declared world system language, called Allianzi. Although other tongues were tolerated, Allianzi had been implemented to predominate in mainstream culture. All official Federation business and inter-provincial commercial trade were conducted in Allianzi, not to mention that, since GDM-7, this language had become required by the Allianz Code as the *lingua franca* in all educational institutions across the globe, beginning with the middle-school grade levels. While bilingual programs were available in select and expensive private institutions, by GDM-13 they were becoming a real rarity.

Strangely, however, Allianzi was not any ordinary human language. In fact, for those who had not yet acquired it, this language exhibited no structure or pattern, and its logic, if any, was uncommonly indecipherable by the unaltered human brain. Allianzi could not be traced back to any known root language, such as Greek, Latin, Semitic, African Nilotic, Mongolic, Turkic, or any other source among the known base tongues. Furthermore, its audible qualities sounded utterly incoherent and indistinguishable to the human ear.

The Dreamers of Allianz

Sonic distortions in speech and oscillating vibrations were all one could in effect hear if one were not a speaker of Allianzi. Even in its written form, Allianzi looked almost completely unfamiliar to non-speakers. Except for a couple of vowels, "a" and "o," written Allianzi appeared as strings of foreign-looking symbols, including strange geometric shapes and unrecognizable punctuations. Odd language, indeed, that Allianzi was.

"What does that pretty sign up there say, Momma?" asked little Holly Christensen, the youngest of their children, as she and her mother drove past a large advertisement screen, located just outside the nearby shopping complex, a few years after Allianzi had been declared the official tongue.

"I really can't tell, sweetie," replied Claire Christensen, revealing a bit of frustration. "It makes no sense to me, either. I wish they would have kept signs in English, as well, and not just in Allianzi."

Such exchanges had become commonplace, as most non-speakers struggled to adapt to the new linguistic reality.

"What then was Allianzi?" you might ask. One cannot easily convey what it was, except to say that language acquisition in this case was possible only for those who possessed an activated Cognit Forehead Implant. In essence, one's brain, via the forehead implant, could immediately absorb and interpret this bizarre language, thus allowing such an individual to comprehend and communicate in spoken or written Allianzi with others of implanted status, as if they had mastered the language through the normal, years-long process of human social interaction. Implanted individuals, then, would begin to instantly share a common language, and it appeared that once implants became activated, these same individuals would start to experience a steadily growing preference for communicating in Allianzi with other speakers, even over speaking in their own original language with non-implanted acquaintances. An Allianzi-based subculture was thus quickly formed, spanning the entire globe and, almost overnight, coming to predominate as the majority subculture.

Just how all of this was possible, was a mystery that at least partially eluded even the brightest linguists within the Resistance. However, our ongoing intelligence correctly surmised that the implant worked through programmed, nano-technological pathogens, controlled via electromagnetic and other rather obscure energy impulses, to redirect cyclosis patterns in brain cell fluid. This appeared to stand behind the generation of a number of mind-related alterations that could help explain this new language phenomenon.

The subject of human implantation, and the **Cognit Implant Protocol** that provided its guidelines and operational applications, begs further development. That is because, as is probably already evident at this point, there was something quite intricate and peculiar – one might even say alien, if the term even applies – about the whole business of this implant.

First, despite the fact that since GDM-1 specialized implants were already being extraordinarily done on the society's elite, including Federation leadership cadres, system bureaucrats, and other government functionaries, a curious process was soon evidencing. That is, the programming and activation of the Cognit Implant, which allowed for language acquisition and other interesting benefits and manifestations – as we will see – was only feasible and workable upon one's use of rational choice. In other words, conscious and willful cognition became the necessary means by which the implant's activation was actually achieved, strange as that may sound. What this meant for the world's billions, was that only upon reaching the **Age of Reason** – precisely estimated by the Resistance to be at age 12 – could anyone, once a recipient of the implant, begin to experience its cognitive, physiological, and other peculiar effects. Children under 12, therefore, were essentially immune to the Cognit Implant, even though they might have already been implanted as infants. A sweeping **Birth Implant** trend in fact ensued and grew dramatically over the previous decade. This explained the Resistance's special focus on reaching children under 12, before they were able to rationally choose to assimilate into the Allianz Code.

Conveniently, **Cognit Implantation** was relatively inexpensive. In those days, someone could acquire the implant for a mere MzU$99 (ninety-nine **Medallianz Units of Exchange**, the new official world currency), equivalent to the cost of a good pair of shoes. Family discount plans and other government subsidies had also become commonplace, as had additional incentives toward mass system assimilation. These included the ability to enter the fast expanding government job market, now that one was able to speak Allianzi.

Another aspect of implantation was that the procedure was actually quite fast, painless, and the process was fully automated. Implantations were performed on an outpatient basis, at the ubiquitous **Cognit Implant Outlets**, which were now easily found in every district of every global province. The following scene had become commonplace:

"Now, sir, please hold still for just a sec..." instructed a trained specialist performing an implantation. "You will see a bright, green flash, and it will be all over before you know it... Ready? [flash]... There you are... You're all done," said the specialist, adding, "Please stay seated for a moment, to make sure you don't experience any dizziness... It's quite normal if you do," he explained. At first, the implant felt a bit cool on the gentleman's forehead. But the excitement of it all kept him from paying much attention to the strange sensation.

"How does it look, dear," the gentleman asked his wife.

"Perfect, honey," she remarked, looking at the opaque, greenish mark in the middle of his forehead. "Doesn't it look interesting, dear?" she asked, referring to the peculiar implant. "I never really realized it 'til now, but...it looks a bit like the..."

"...Like the 'A' in Hawthorne's *The Scarlet Letter*?" her husband interjected, while looking into a hand-held mirror.

"Well, yes, dear...that's about right. Except, this is emerald green and on your forehead, not a red 'A' on your chest," she ascertained."

"Thankfully."

"Thankfully, indeed, dear."

Curiously, that exchange appropriately revealed the true significance of the implant, as a symbol of the hopelessly misguided, adulterous love affair between most of humanity and harlequin Allianz. One that would prove scandalously fraught with disillusionment, if it were not for the way in which it so impaired the ability of the natural man's heart to unmask such urbane harlotry.

Once the forehead implant was in place, between and above one's eyebrows, trained specialists, or **Implant Technics**, could then perform the programming procedure and, if so desired and ably chosen by the client, their **Cognit Implant Program** could be activated. The whole process typically lasted no longer than 15 to 20 minutes, and was effectuated via up-links to the powerful and global **CyberSat Network,** which was served by a constellation of four main and gigantic satellites, in addition to dozens of secondary ones. These had been launched secretly into orbit in GDM-1, by the then fledgling Allianz Federation, from an undersea base located in the Red Sea. The top-secret project had been given the code name, **Project Red Dragon.**

There was one more peculiar, if absolutely haunting, aspect of the Cognit Forehead Implant. Upon willful activation, the implant would actually proceed to embed itself into the implanted individual's forehead. In a matter of minutes thereafter, the implant would begin to undergo an ossification process, such that it would ultimately become permanently fused with the frontal bone structure of the skull. Essentially, it could never again be removed, as it would become integrated with the person's forehead, and even if removed, it would leave an indelible imprint on one's skull.

The compulsion to acquire the implant obviously stemmed from one's pressing need to speak Allianzi, which one could manage to do literally seconds after implant activation. For without it, any individual would eventually find him or herself virtually excluded from many spheres of society, including the economic, educational, in addition to the political, social, cultural and other sectors. Even mainstream forms of media, artistic events, and news broadcasts were now being required to function in the official Allianzi language, and thus could no longer be properly accessed or understood without the activated implant. Therefore, one's access to and participation in the growing mainstream culture reaching all corners of the planet had become directly dependent on one's having the Cognit Forehead Implant. To understand how things had gotten this way, would take another entire volume – and perhaps I might at some later point attempt that for your benefit – but it had not been as difficult as one might imagine, troubling as this proposition may rightly sound.

Society and culture, as well as the mass consumption of goods and services and mass communication, had also moved steadily and at an increasing rate of speed toward the **Cognit Implant Platform** and the **CyberSat System**. This will be the focus of our next topic.

Four

Society, Culture, and the CyberSat System

Humans had always been avid consumers. In GDM-13, the human race was still at it, and fiercely so, but with a significant twist. A novelty, the **Cognit Bracelet,** was the new means through which people could shop in general. Directly up-linked to the CyberSat Network, it functioned as a commercial transaction device, as it would add or subtract Medallianz Units of Exchange. It was worn by an individual on the left wrist and extended toward the left hand, connecting to the individual via the **Cognit Implant Palm Extension**, located on the center of one's left-hand palm.

In theory, the bracelet could not be used by anyone else other than its rightful owner, making its theft basically useless to the common criminal. However, a gifted "techy" might have been able to temporarily hack it, programming it to function independent of its proper owner for a couple of transactions, if it were sprayed with an electrolyte solution, resembling human perspiration. After a few irregular transactions, CyberSat would detect the infraction and the system would proceed to automatically neutralize and terminate the stolen device.

Since GDM-2, most retail and other commercial nodes had begun converting their systems to one based on the Cognit Bracelet, a fact which made it increasingly difficult for those without the implant to shop anywhere that had undergone the conversion, from convenience stores and fueling stations, to grocery stores and apparel retailers.

"*I'm sorry. We no longer accept conventional credit cards as a method of payment,*" announced an electronic voice to an unsuspecting younger Claire Christensen at the checkout counter of a local convenience shop. "*Please scan your Cognit Bracelet for payment.*" A store clerk then approached and uttered in English, for she did not see the mark on Claire's forehead, "Something wrong, ma'am?"

"I'm sorry, I didn't know... I haven't got one," Claire replied in uneasy embarrassment.

"Hey, Harry, we got another one!" the clerk yelled in Allianzi across the aisle to her manager, who was stocking items on the shelves. "She ain't got a bracelet!"

"Please excuse us, ma'am," the store manager said in English, walking toward the busy row of checkout counters. "We've recently converted. Did you not see the sign?" he asked. But, to the dismay of the now beleaguered and confused young woman, the sign was in Allianzi, and Claire was a non-implant.

"Um... I won't be taking these, then. I'm sorry," Claire said.

"Fine, ma'am. Next!" yelled the clerk, impatiently.

Occasionally, a few stores would still accept the outmoded forms of payment, but that was becoming quite rare, as time went on. An implanted woman, say, could shop for her entire family because the system was **Cognit Linked** to her bracelet, and provided information about implanted family and dependents, whether or not they were activated yet. Such non-activated cases were now becoming quite uncommon, however, since entire families had been gravitating toward getting implanted jointly, taking advantage of the added incentive of a family plan discount. Finally, dependents with a non-activated implant, such as a young son or daughter, could wear their bracelets and make purchases, if permitted to draw from a parent's medallianz account.

A secondary market of yet traditional stores was still in existence in GDM-13, but these businesses were increasingly being pressured to assimilate. The shipments of regular food and other standard and specialty items they once routinely received, were quickly becoming unavailable to these stores. Their product orders were instead being replaced with shipments of older and inferior quality products and ration-like foods, such that anyone still using the old system was ultimately being left with substandard nutrition and commodities. Thus, pressure to assimilate was felt even in terms of one's ability – or lack thereof – to simply buy food.

By GDM-7, medical treatments had been readjusted to the new cell cyclosis patterns, and treatment drugs for activated implant patients had come to predominate in the pharmaceutical market. With the exception of a few, mainly pediatric drugs, other medications for non-implanted individuals had been disappearing from pharmacies and hospitals, due to gradual but persistent declines in production, as had been stipulated by the Federation since that year. Patients, therefore, were being faced with a pressing and difficult choice; namely to assimilate to the Cognit Implant Protocol, or risk imminent lack of treatment.

Advances in the newly developed medical field, associated with the new implant protocol, had produced adequate cures for most diseases that had plagued humans for millennia. Improvements in **Cognit Biotechnology** had especially benefited the handicap population, including the blind and deaf, the wheelchair-bound, and the neurologically sick, once Cognit Implants had been administered to them and activated. The activated implants also appeared to be effective in alleviating a whole range of mental disorders, from mild depression to schizophrenia. In order to facilitate the diagnosis of a wide range of health conditions, implanted patients could be health-scanned with the use of a platform on which they would lay their left hand, and which allowed all of their vital signs to be instantly displayed in the doctors office, for his or her convenient holographic viewing.

By late GDM-12, a new wave of still non-implant-dependent interactive **CogniToys** for children and youth had become the latest young teens' craze. Under this technology, these toys would generate holographic images of sports gear, which were worn and played with by kids. A soccer game, for instance, was interactive, and children in different locations would be able to play in a match together, as if they were assembled collectively. The physical feel and touch were realistic, and the holographic image, believable enough.

"Wow, Dad. Look!" said Zeke, the Christensen's teenage son, who was trying on the soccer program. "I can kick this ball right through that window, and it won't break! Man, that sparks!" he said, excitedly.

"We sure could use that, son. It would save us some money and aggravation in other folks' window replacements...and ours, too. Let's think about it," his father reasoned.

Fashions varied, but many implanted individuals were adopting creative head coverings and headbands, which would hide the barely apparent forehead protrusion resembling the shape of an "A." A non-implanted person could conceal their status by similarly wearing such fashions, and would only be found out upon going through **Cognit Detectors** in facilities directly under Federation jurisdiction, such as airports, government buildings, and schools. Allianz Federation Police cogs operated and secured these facilities, and commonly referred to those without implants as "**N.I.s.**," for non-implants.

The greatest innovation in transportation was the **FlightPak**, a personal transport device that could hover and transit up to 45 feet above the ground, but which worked not via propulsion, but rather by CyberSat-enabled levitation, which also required that its user have the activated implant. Too expensive except for the quite affluent, the FlightPak was nevertheless a common means of transportation for the police and other emergency services.

For a long time now, personal and public transports, powered by liquid hydrogen-filled **H-Packs,** had been directly up-linked to the CyberSat network, which controlled traffic flows globally, being able to identify the location of all transports. Also, in the general arena of transportation, a subterranean transportation network was already highly developed, and was now interlinking most of the main cities of the world by super speed **WormRail**, which provided the best option for mass local and regional travel.

Commercial air transportation was still the fastest way to travel long distances, and super-sized, high-altitude aircraft were the main carriers now being used, since they provided the greatest stability and protection against the violent electrical storms in the mezzo-atmosphere. Over time, these storms had become severe, having greatly increased in their intensity over the previous decade. Incidentally, the entire transportation industry was Federation-owned and controlled.

The media was now being completely censored by the central government, and had largely ceased to be a carrier of independent – and some would say, genuine – information about world news, and instead transmitted a mixture of relaxing signals, government messages and commercial adds, and various otherwise approved films, news programs and sporting events for general entertainment. Since GDM-4, all broadcasting was being done in Allianzi.

Finally, a new information and telecommunications system, based on CyberSat pathways and post-digital-age **Cognit Links** to its **Data-Realm**, had been introduced since GDM-2, a necessary development following the Great Digital Meltdown. The new system worked via holographic images projected by an individual's **PSS**, or **Personal Sat Spec**. The PSS, typically worn on either the right or left ear, but equally functional as a handheld or desktop device, had literally replaced all previous forms of information management systems. The PSS gadgets also served as personal telecommunication devices, utilizing **Visual Coordinates,** or simply **"Visuals,"** and thus taking the place of older generation, wireless digital communication devices. The expression, "What's your Visual?" now corresponded to the old, "What's your phone number," and was a common slogan in CyberSat Network Ads. Whenever a PSS visualization was made, users would view each other's virtual and often more flattering image as the default setting. If so desired, however, users could opt for their actual image to be projected, which would require that one stand in front of one's PSS during the connection. The PSS did not at first require a Cognit Implant. However, the frequent upgrades were fast becoming incompatible with one's non-implant status.

The once dominant, digital-based Worldwide Web and Internet were now relics of the past, having been all but completely pulverized by the Minotaur Virus, which resulted in the Great Digital Meltdown. Over time, however, there had been numerous efforts by anti-Allianz groups to revive parts of the now obsolete digital gridiron. Therefore, CyberSat was constantly on the lookout for any clandestine attempts to reactivate the old network, and upon detection of any residual digital signals, CyberSat quickly moved to disrupt, interrupt and scramble intercepted communications. With minimal success, the Community of Brethren Resistance had actually managed to resurrect a fragment of the old digital network. In fact, with competent manipulation and operation during the off hours of the night, when CyberSat's energy cycle would be functioning in low-mode, limited use of the little that remained of the old wireless and fiber-optic cable-based technological platforms was still viable, and the Resistance managed to take full advantage of this weakness in the system. In a few cases, when the communication was brief – 3 minutes or less – CyberSat surveillance was still inadequate to detect it, and with the use of a modified digital descrambler, one could communicate briefly, day or night. This was especially important for short intercontinental Resistance communications, between individuals located in different day and night time zones.

Tanner Christensen, the Resistance's logistics man in the American South, was a gifted "techy," and was able to develop an alternate, descrambling communications program that fed off of this largely discontinued and disabled digital wireless system. Late at night, therefore, when CyberSat's energy cycle was functioning in low-mode, Resistance communications were still being transmitted largely outside the detection of the network's surveillance operations, at least for the time being.

"CyberSat energy?" you might inquire. Yes, for even colossal and multidimensional platforms, hovering some 400 miles above the earth needed to consume energy in order to support its multifarious functions. CyberSat in effect provided the very sustenance for the entire Allianz Federation's global strategic operations, and thus the continued existence and maintenance of the new system. And perhaps this represented the most ingenious, if not terribly deceitful and sinister element of the new world order. This very matter lies at the crux of this next portion of our intricate story, and has much to do with a particularly significant group of dreamers, the **Transcienz Dreamers**.

Five

The Metaphysical Path of Transcienz

"What about religion, in GDM-13?" you might wonder. First, let me simply say that, by that time, the whole institution of religion as humanity had come to know and experience it was on the verge of utter extinction. For, since the autumn of GDM-2, the Federation had declared one official world metaphysical path, known as the Path of Transcienz. This new spiritual path doctrinally integrated ancient Eastern philosophies that emphasized the cultivation of ancestral ties, with high teachings involving mind development and brainwave activity, through dream-like trances, called **Transcienz Dream States**.

Traditional mainstream religion had been denounced by the Federation as a perverse cluster of deceitful and exploitative spiritual teachings that fueled hatred and incited violence. By official decree, any and all overtly religious teaching and ritual practices had been forbidden and ultimately forcibly discontinued. Consequently, beginning in GDM-4, religious institutions were shut down, in accordance with the application of Provision 6 of the Allianz Code. This drastic move by the Federation had come in the wake of years of acute setbacks in religious freedom across the globe.

In addition, over the following decade after the world's religions had been outlawed, most of humanity witnessed what many in the Resistance called an alarming and generalized drop in the global population's interest in virtually all forms of spirituality, with the marked exception of Transcienz which, on the contrary, soared in popularity. After years of observing troubling correlates to this trend, the Resistance speculated that Cognit Implants were somehow responsible for this bizarre phenomenon. To the utter dismay of many observers of religion, their suspicions were not unfounded, for upon receiving and activating the implant, one's entire consciousness of The Name and any other believed in deities, semi-gods, and demi-gods, was suppressed. Implant recipients would soon begin to experience a loss of interest in matters concerning the sacred, as existent in previously conventional and mainstream religious modalities.

    The world's sacred texts, once fully digitized, had been destroyed in the Great Digital Meltdown, and a concerted Federation effort had been made to eradicate any trace of knowledge about and records of the **Word of the Spirit**, as well as other writings considered to be sacrosanct by a plurality of faiths. Old paper scrolls and books everywhere were no longer around, having been destroyed beginning in GDM-5, when all older and unsealed, low-grade, cellulose-based products quickly disintegrated in the same CyberSat-related event believed by the Resistance to have also caused the cancerous skin plague. From that point on, all paper products were treated with a costly, special chemical coating, very tightly controlled by the Federation, which ensured their preservation. By that time, however, no new printings of religious texts were allowed, and all texts backed up via digital, as well as the older, magnetic-tape storage systems, had also been lost to the Minotaur Virus.

    The world under Allianz, as it stood in GDM-13, had thus become almost devoid of The Name and of the literature and teachings of once widespread religious doctrines based on the knowledge of Him. All that remained from the Word of the Spirit rested largely in the minds of the members of the Community of Brethren; that is to say, any fragmented scriptural knowledge committed to memory or to lyrics sung and otherwise transmitted within the community. Although some clandestine rewriting of religious texts had been attempted in defiance of the Allianz Code, these works were incomplete. At best, they represented only a reconstructed shadow of the once well-established Holy Scriptures.

    Influential religious leaders had been publicly silenced and tried in court if they persisted in their subversive activities. Many among the worldwide Community of Brethren had suffered arrests in Federation Police blitzes, and were feared dead, given that they never resurfaced or were ever heard from again. Thus, the voice of religion in the public arena had by GDM-13 become virtually non-existent. Furthermore, religious education had been outlawed, and religious-based curricula in schools were prohibited. Homeschooling, which typically contained elements of religious education, was no longer recognized as a legitimate form of pedagogy. Denominational seminaries, colleges, and universities had been institutionally extinct since GDM-4 and were being reconfigured as Federation-controlled higher education campuses.

Due to their convenient locations in various communities, many of the largest formerly religious facilities were being disgraced, and re-outfitted as **Transcienz Halls**, while new structures were being built to comport the phenomenal growth, over the preceding ten years, in the world's population's interest in the Path of Transcienz. Human civilization's famous cathedrals, such as the magnificent St. Peter's Basilica, in the Vatican, as well as the great mosques and ancient religious museums of the Middle East, such as the Blue Mosque and Hagia Sophia, in Istanbul, had been undergoing a thorough process of redesign. And the now deserted, sprawling buildings that once had housed mega-churches, which had reached their heyday prior to GDM, were now being gutted, as they were being targeted for complete reform.

Tomazo DiPaoli, a globetrotting free-lance photojournalist in his mid thirties, was one of the Resistance's most valuable assets. A good friend of Christensen's, he possessed rich cross-cultural ethnographic experience, and a keen eye – literally his one good right eye, for the left one was covered by a black patch – for capturing significant events through his photo lens. A theologian and former priest as well, DiPaoli had been paying close attention to world developments in religion. Over the years, he had provided tremendous amounts of evidence for the southern Community of Brethren in America, and the Resistance in general, about the changes that had been taking place due to the emergence of the Path of Transcienz. He was now briefly stationed in Istanbul, and reporting from there on the amazing things he was witnessing.

Leaning against the terrace wall of a rooftop restaurant near Istanbul's Grand Bazaar, and with a clear view toward the Bosporus Strait, DiPaoli held his telescopic camera and watched in amazement. "*Incredibile!*" he said to himself in between shots, in his native Italian. "That's incredible! What are they thinking, demolishing and desecrating these historic, religious treasures? And where in the world is the public outcry? Wake up, people!" Then he thought to himself, *What is really going on, here? Why are people so interested in this pseudo-religioscientific mumbo jumbo? What's really behind the Federation's push for this?*

For DiPaoli and the Resistance, there were still many more questions than answers about this whole Transcienz phenomenon. He would remain in Istanbul for one more day. From there, he would catch a flight to Paris, to continue to document what had been taking place in the Federation's capital district.

In Paris' *Jardin du Luxembourg*, the tall Allianz Federation Palace overlooked to the northeast the **Grand Hall of Transcienz**, which housed the **Transcienz Sages** and the Path's **High Sage Andrus**. A notable mystic and consummate guru, Andrus was a trusted friend of Prosecutor General Horn and an influential counselor to the Allianz Federation Council of Regents. These headquarters had been built on the former site of the historic Notre Dame cathedral, which had seemingly vanished from its renowned site on the Seine River's famed Ile de la Cité. But this Grand Hall was built only as a precursor to the permanent headquarters, under construction in the "City on Seven Hills," Rome. Greatly anticipated by the billions of followers of the Path of Transcienz, the new Grand Hall was expected to be unfathomably large in scale, capable of serving a million visitors each day.

Elsewhere, in the Province of Brazil's Rio de Janeiro district, for instance, one traditional point of religious interest, the famous *Corcovado* mountaintop statue, with arms outstretched, overlooking the magnificent Guanabara Bay, had actually been removed, making room for a new Transcienz Hall, which was now being constructed on that lofty and world famous location. Many other such places of religious significance, in addition to churches, temples, synagogues, and mosques, were continually being turned into mere cultural spots and tourist traps, while they awaited their turn at Transcienz-style refurbishment.

Six

Transcienz Dream States

Increasingly, implanted individuals had been experiencing a growing desire for **Transcienz Dream States**. These could be entered into upon one's being **Dream Connected** at the Halls, which provided these services. These Halls, built with antiseptic-looking, crystalline walls, were shaped in multi-layered pyramidal patterns, and contained towering white pillars within. These classical Grecian-style pillars were uniformly scattered throughout the structure's cavernous interior, which would usually be filled with the white haze and the pungent smell of burned incense. At the center of the spacious interior sat an amphitheater, circling around a triangular, emerald-green pool, whose gently moving waters produced a reflection that glimmered and moved against the translucent, angling walls of the stunning edifices. At the amphitheater, frequenters would gather to listen to ongoing seminars on the doctrines of the Path of Transcienz, taught by the Transcienz Sages. On rare occasions, dedicated followers would be honored by the unparalleled opportunity to sit under the teaching of His Transcendence, High Sage Andrus, who regularly traveled to many of the global provinces, and taught at local Transcienz Halls.

In the Province of New Babylon – formerly, Iraq – Andrus attended the groundbreaking ceremony of the new Hall in Baghdad, and took the opportunity to give an inauguration seminar. Speaking in Allianzi, and in his usual flamboyant style, Andrus began his Transcienz lecture with the familiar, "My peace-loving children in

The Dreamers of Allianz

the luminous Path... For long I have waited for this opportunity to join minds with you in this, our pursuit of optimal realization, via the timeless Path of Transcienz." He then went on, "Now, let us open our minds and prepare to receive the ancient wisdom of our great and sapient spiritual ancestors, who must pass on all of their knowledge, and once having accomplished it, will at last find peaceful and perpetual rest." Gasping, the large crowd hung on to his every word. "Come, my children. Offer them your minds as hospitable hosts of that wisdom from of old. Create your own excellent dream connection with the ancients, and assume *your* place in the great, mystical succession of Transcienz light receivers and givers."

Implanted individuals who came into the Transcienz Halls to access Transcienz Dream States, would assemble around any of the tall, round pillars, and would proceed to lie down on comfortably-cushioned white platforms, having their heads pointing toward the particular pillar around which they gathered together. Collectively they formed a star-like arrangement. Assisted by the attentive staff, they would then be connected to the pillar via electrodes that were placed on their forehead. When "dreaming," their implants would glow in an emerald-green tone, turning opaque again when they exited the Transcienz Dream State. They would then awaken, feeling refreshed from their deep metaphysical sleep, which typically lasted close to one hour for those who were still relatively new dreamers.

"How did you like your dream connection, miss?" asked a Transcienz attendant to a young new dreamer.

"I feel so alive and tingly all over!" marveled the recent convert, having just come out of her first Dream State experience. "All my senses somehow seem heightened, and I'm feeling more in touch with my inner self than ever. This is wonderful and peaceful."

"We do hope you'll come see us again soon," the attendant said, as she promptly disconnected the young novice from the dreaming apparatus.

By all accounts the sensation was indeed invigorating. But as its sensual effects slowly subsided, over the course of the next twenty-four to forty-eight hours, it would lead to an unquenchable desire for a new fix, from another, slightly lengthier Dream State. In fact, it was long speculated by the Resistance that Transcienz Dreaming worked to significantly increase endorphin levels in the body of the dreamer, allegedly producing a sort of addiction to the experience; hence the ongoing craving for further dream connectedness.

"But how," you might ask, "did CyberSat's need for energy come into this picture?" That was, no doubt, the most disturbing aspect of the Path of Transcienz. At increasing risk to themselves, Resistance cadres were beginning to uncover a diabolical scheme that implicated the Allianz Federation and the Path of Transcienz. Their theories about a possible causal connection between Transcienz Dream States, multiplied by billions worldwide, and the harnessing of power for CyberSat, was a scenario that greatly troubled and mystified the Community of Brethren. For now, suffice it to say that CyberSat seemed to be getting smarter and more powerful, very possibly at the expense of billions of implanted and dream connecting human beings. With the marked exception of top Federation officials, whose modified implants did not cause them to crave Transcienz Dream States, all other dreamers were believed by the Resistance to actually be losing some of their own faculties of judicious cognition in the process of feasting on Dream States. That is, they appeared to become more prone to groupthink and less willing to maintain independent, critical reasoning, to the clear advantage of the Federation.

Yet again, it seemed that the questionable use of religion, albeit an unconventional form thereof, for gaining political power and exercising perverse domination, was evidencing in the world. To say, therefore, that the Resistance posed a threat to the system was a major understatement, for in reality the Community of Brethren's mobilizations were the only major factor that could seriously interfere with the Federation's master plan for complete system control. Their weapon, again, was simple and non-violent, even if limited in truly opposing the enemy in any systematic way. For even success in mobilizing the non-implanted few and the many implanted children, for acceptance of The Name and for Spirit-sealing, could not in the end actually change the course of history. The members of the Community of Brethren considered themselves agents in an apocalyptic process that they knew would have to run its full course.

Seven

Population and Environmental Pressures

In most global provinces, there had been fast-to-immediate assimilation. Especially in the poorest provinces, with huge metropolitan areas and dwindling rural populations, the fear of worsening social and economic conditions for non-implants had more readily led to mass assimilation. In richer provinces, the transition was at first slower, but subsequently achieved considerable momentum, as most had found it preferable to subscribe to the Cognit Implant Protocol, for its obvious practical advantages. Many were flocking to assimilate to the Allianz Code, over concerns that not doing so would create for them real economic complications, and possibly lead to unwanted friction with law enforcement.

Environmental problems still persisted in GDM-13. On the **Allianz Broadcasting Network**, or **ABN**, much attention was being given to climate and environmental issues affecting the world's population. A daily, 24-hour newscast informed in the Allianzi language:

"...Time-lapsed CyberSat images have revealed what many have been fearing for some time..." a female newscaster reported. *"Desertification between the two tropics continues to advance significantly, and the acceleration of the environmental degradation has been having its most*

severe impact on the already dwindling indigenous populations of the 4th world. Reports of a dramatic increase in out migration by populations living in large portions of this central geographical band around the globe, have increased Federation concerns over a wave of overpopulation problems in our largest northern and southern cities, where the desertification effects have been much less severe... In Sports, the Brazilian Provincial Soccer Squad continues to dominate the qualifying rounds, as the world prepares for the GDM-14 Soccer World Cup, to be held in the Province of Chile..."

Because of the desertification effects, most natives of these regions had been driven off their lands and given up their traditional ways of life. The majority of them had little choice but to settle into the world's large metropolitan areas, making their assimilation to the system increasingly more accessible, as they sought to better integrate into the larger society.

Demand for raw materials continued to intensify, and with no relief in sight. On a more positive note, however, world hunger had been almost fully eradicated, ever since the Federation's takeover of farm operations, and their subsequent appropriation by Federation-owned commercial enterprises, which had been completed by GDM-7. This had resulted in the state control of virtually all agricultural property, production, and distribution, as well as greater official oversight of food supplies and shipments. Highly restrictive government measures against non-commercial hunting and fishing activities were also put into effect. This was implemented as a way of appeasing wildlife advocates and environmental activists, both of which had intensified their extremist campaigns against unregulated practices that were deemed by these groups to be dangerous to fauna and flora worldwide.

Government-controlled industry jobs now predominated in the labor market, and had been attracting massive numbers of laborers. Official gender and ethnic non-discrimination policies translated into narrow differences in salary scales within the new system. This significantly helped to form a more homogenous social class system with great appeal globally.

The Dreamers of Allianz

With the unification of political control, the world was now enjoying significant, lasting peace among the provinces. In fact, since GDM-2, when the Federation gained its permanent mandate, the world's stockpiles of weapons of mass destruction, including nuclear arsenals, had been drastically reduced, to great worldwide public acclaim. Global provinces had signed weapons non-proliferation agreements with one another and, other than the Resistance and a number of diehard environmental movements, only small-scale struggles still occurred against the Allianz Code. Among these were the last-ditch efforts of an all-but-defunct Al-Qaeda, which were yielding little effect and attracting only negligible public attention anymore. Crime in GDM-13 was at an all time low, as poverty and social class distinctions had drastically been reduced. Also, by then, as the world's population gravitated in droves toward the Transcienz Dream States, demand for illicit drugs had all but disappeared across the globe.

Aided by CyberSat, police surveillance capabilities had advanced to such an extent that it had made it possible for the Federation and its local police branches to closely scrutinize almost all aspects of everyday life for nearly all of the world's population. Cognit Forehead Implants could be tracked by CyberSat global positioning. Even people's personal garbage was routinely being **Trash Scanned,** for signs of nonconformity, as enormous roving robotic vehicles would pick up the trash. The scanned information would then be fed into the central monitoring system connected to the CyberSat's DataRealm. Allianz Code challengers were increasingly being criminalized, and were frequently being targeted for harsh repression and imprisonment by Federation cogs.

For many members of the Community of Brethren, their interactions with implanted neighbors and others in their communities had grown reticent, at best.

"You may think we're dreamers," some of the folks in the majority group would sarcastically comment, "but we hope you'll join us one day," they would say, repeating the words from popular CyberSat ads, "and the world can live as one…a brotherhood of man."

Indeed, with the exception of a few weather-related inconveniences to which most had grown accustomed, for those who had been assimilating to the Allianz Code, namely the implanted population, the world had never seemed quite so wonderful, overall. In fact, one could say they loved the world under Allianz, and increasingly, the name and face of Adammus Horn were being equated with the Allianz system itself. The intrepid Prosecutor General of the Federation was fast ascending to the status of brilliant political genius and idolized popular hero.

As our story then continues, we find that the reality of the new world order under Allianz was beginning to seriously take its toll on the Resistance. And a different kind of dreaming was about to manifest itself in a peculiar way. These dreams would ultimately come to transform the entire world, and influence the fate of all of humanity...

Part II

The Dreamers And The Struggle

Eight

Growing Angst

The frantic pursuit had been intense. There was no sign of Claire and the girls, who had been left behind in hiding and hoping against hope that help would come their way. Escaping westward into the desert after two long days of driving, Christensen and his son, Zeke, had managed to elude their captors, at least temporarily. Yet, they found themselves alone and dismayed, with no clear sense of direction. Out of fuel, and now out of any prospects for its replenishment, they were forced to walk out into the desolate and sweltering expanse. But they had to press on.

The unrelenting sun burned their unprotected faces as they walked, and the taxing, dry heat sapped what little energy they had left. They were in desperate need of help, and if none were found imminently they might soon weaken to the point of collapse.

"Zeke!" Christensen cried, "C'mon, son, we've got to keep going. Focus, and don't give up," he urged his son, who was helplessly lagging behind.

"I can't, Dad," Zeke said, fast growing too feeble to sustain his own weight. "Dad…Dad, I'm…" he attempted to say, before he finally collapsed, limp and face down, spilling on the thirsty white sand the little that was left of their only source of refreshment, and life. Dashing back toward him, Christensen grabbed his son's spent body by the shoulders, turning it up, and revealing Zeke's sand-plastered face, now glaring under the cruel brightness of the daystar.

"Zeke! No!" Christensen cried out. "Son, come back!"

"Mom...Momma..." Zeke dimly groaned, as he briefly regained consciousness, just before fading away and completely passing out.

"Please, Zeke!" Christensen pleaded. "Oh, Lord, help us... Don't let us die out here in the desert! Please, save my son!" he clamored.

Christensen began to frantically dig a hole in the sand; some form of shelter in which to hide from the incessant rays and the scorching heat. But the brilliant grains of sand felt just as hot in the midday sun, and burned his hands. Tragically, the very shelter he so desperately tried to excavate for themselves could very possibly become their own arid gravesite. Yet, the more he tried to dig, the more the fine sand shifted and fluidly rearranged itself, stubbornly reinvading and resettling into its original place, to Christensen's utter exasperation. Overcome with anguish, and feeling his eyes burn from the unavoidable salty mixture of sand and sweat, Christensen prayed out loud, as his curved and blistering fingers still anxiously dug into the fine, bright sand.

Save us, oh Lord. Save my family, he repeated in mental supplication. And as he struggled to try to remove handfuls of sand, scattering the grains to either side of him, he began to utter continually, "He who dwells in the shelter of the Most High, will rest in the shadow of the Almighty... He who dwells in the shelter of the Most High..." Repeating the familiar opening words to Psalm 91 was all he could do not to succumb to his crippling exhaustion and despair, his son now lying unconscious in the punishing heat of the immense and barren desert floor.

All of a sudden, from the corner of his right eye, he saw a darkened cloud. It appeared as if it were moving swiftly in his direction. As he strained to look up into the intense glare of the sun, that nebulous and amorphous shadow grew larger, revealing itself as perhaps thousands of black birds in flight, preparing to dive down toward the unprotected pair. They were ravens. *Where have they come from?* He wondered.

Acting on a protective impulse, Christensen moved to shield his son's body with his own from the apparent menace; he guessed the birds might be searching for food along that desert wasteland. But as the dark band flew even closer and appeared to be preparing to attack them, Christensen noticed something rather strange about it. In their beaks many ravens were carrying pieces of cactus, filled with what looked like clear and glistening fresh water, some of which was spilling out and producing an unexpected, refreshing mist in the dry air. Christensen sensed some relief. As the ravens drew nearer still, he saw that some carried what looked like jagged chunks of flat bread, while others, some type of dry, brown meat. Christensen had never witnessed anything like it. Could this be a sign from heaven, or a miraculous display, just when all hope seemed to have left him?

As the ravens swooped down toward the still perplexed man and his son, they would drop off all of these items to their side, and would fly away together again. Christensen then saw another band of ravens that transported in groups contorted wooden branches, followed by others clenching in their black talons a single, long and hanging strand of vine. A last group of birds carried a large, coarse white linen cloth, with one edge waiving freely in the wind. After dropping the items down near the father and his son, these birds departed, in the same way the others did. *What...what is this?* Christensen thought, utterly confused by the surreal scene. He sat there, in unabated amazement, struggling to reconcile what his eyes were seeing with what his yet incredulous mind was telling him.

Suddenly, Christensen heard the voice of a man coming from somewhere; perhaps from his own head. By now he might actually be hallucinating from complete exhaustion and acute dehydration. The voice said, "Use the vine, the branches, and the linen, and build your tabernacle here. You will be fed and given to drink each day. The provisions, though limited, will be sufficient to sustain you. But your son must be allowed to sleep... and dream. Do not awaken him." Then the voice offered reassurance and guidance, saying, "Your son and family will be safe. In three days, when you are strong again, abandon your shelter, take up your sleeping son, and carry him in your arms. Walk directly east toward the great dune-covered caverns. There you will find help and rest for a season."

"Who are You?" Christensen said. "Lord, is that You?"

"I Am Who I Am...Creator...Savior...Comforter," the voice answered, "and I will send a helper, the 'one who proclaims My Name'...Eternal...Personal...Relational. 'The One Sent' will be called out of an ancient land, and I will equip him to do My bidding, as true darkness rears its defiant horn against Me and My people..."

After three days in the feverish, lonely desert, watching over his son still asleep, Christensen did what he was instructed to do. He arose out of his tent and headed east, carrying Zeke asleep in his arms. Just as they were approaching the rising dunes, a towering pillar of smoke suddenly materialized above the sandy mounds and began to move toward them. Then, Christensen heard a thunderous sound coming from behind him. As he turned around to look, he saw a massive, dark sand storm violently form before his eyes, moving furiously in their direction. Christensen instantly began to run, with an unconscious Zeke still in his arms. With muscles weakening and cramping badly from the physical and emotional exertion, Christensen cried out, "No! We're almost there! No!" As the cloud of sand and dust quickly reached them, it completely enveloped them in a thick, dark, and gritty storm. Christensen closed his eyes and fell to his knees. Soon after, the smell of fiery smoke filled his nostrils. The awful storm left as suddenly as it had come. But Zeke had vanished with it, it seemed, leaving Christensen alone with his arms empty. "Zeke!" he screamed loudly. "Zeke! Where are you?"

"Tanner!" a familiar woman's voice was heard yelling.

Drenched by his own sweat, Christensen then awoke from his fearful dream, and to the worried calls from Claire, as she ran downstairs to find him in his home's basement bunker.

"Honey...what happened? I heard you screaming. Are you all right? You woke me up!" Claire said.

"Claire...it was so real! I was running...and holding Zeke..." Christensen tried to explain, the right words still eluding him.

"The nightmares, again?" she asked. Christensen nodded as he looked down at his desk, where his head lay just seconds ago. "Yeah. But this time, it was different."

"Tanner, what's happening? Look at your hair? It's graying so fast. And are you eating enough these days? You're looking so thin and..."

"I know...spent," he replied. He then explained, "It was a terrifying ordeal. How else could I be feeling?"

"Do you want to tell me about the dream?" she added.

"Yeah...It was so strange, Claire..." Christensen proceeded to try and describe the dream, his whole body still tense from the dreadful experience.

"Oh, honey... It's okay," she consoled him. She paused, and then added, "What do you think it means, Tan?"

"I don't know. I'm scared to think of it..." Christensen confessed. "But it just feels like our time is short...really short."

Claire sighed, and then, as if to delicately change the subject, she said, "Won't you come upstairs for a bit? I could maybe get you something to make you feel better. You look exhausted."

"Thanks, Claire," Christensen replied softly, "but I can't leave. I've got to stay down here. I'm expecting a communications signal at any moment now."

"All right, if that's what you think... I'll just check on the kids and go back to bed," she said. "But please, Tan, come get some sleep and some rest for those baby blues as soon as you can. It's really late, and you just can't risk being this tired at the tower."

"I know. I'll try. I should be fine," Christensen responded. "Besides, aircraft these days can basically operate on their own, via CyberSat..."

"Tanner!" she exclaimed, irritated by his misplaced antics.

"Don't worry, blondie. It's just a little air traffic controller humor. Sorry," he said. Claire then bent down to kiss Christensen on the forehead, saying, "Feeling better, huh?" She reached for his hand. It felt clammy and cold to her touch. Squeezing it, Claire turned to walk away.

"Claire, wait," Christensen said.

"Yeah?" she replied. Christensen got up, drawing Claire to him, and kissed her in return, gently and slowly, on the forehead. He paused for a second, as if to reassure himself that it was all just a bad dream. They embraced for a moment. His tall and slender frame somehow still fit perfectly and comfortably against her athletic, petite figure. If only the honesty of their love for each other in that instant were enough to make everything right again, even despite the endless interruptions by the cares of the times. But the Christensens had been forced to become realists in recent years, and it seemed better to them to just let go of the fantasy of a normal, safe life.

"I'm feeling scared, too," she said. "Don't take too long, okay?"

"Yeah. Kiss the kids for me," he requested, lightly tugging on her pony-tale, whose characteristic wag was an enduring reminder of more hopeful and energetic days with Claire, years ago.

"I will... Bye," she whispered. And as she slowly walked up the stairs, she uttered, "I'll be praying for you, Tan."

"Claire... Pray for *us*."

Christensen sat back down at his desk. The clock on his screen read 2:13 a.m., and he just remained there, tired and motionless, waiting for the long anticipated contact to be made at any moment. The nightly long hours in his middle-class, exurban home's basement bunker were beginning to take much more out of him than when the Resistance had first begun, in GDM-3. At the age of 41, he was somehow beginning to feel like an old man, and the youthfulness of his once striking Scandinavian look had all but faded. By world population parameters he was actually not so young, anymore. The cancerous skin plague had not yet taken its last victim, and the lasting effects had come close to devastating the entire population of his elders. But it was the mounting worries that were getting to him; worries over his family, the Community of Brethren, and deep concerns about their future in Allianz.

On his old, backlit digital systems screen, there was nothing but the usual distortions and the on-again-off-again screen-saving mode that harkened back to the time when digital reigned. Little dignity remained of the old wireless digital technology ever since the great systems meltdown, which fatefully marked the start of GDM. It was also rather unclear how long this barely revived digital set-up was going to remain viable for the Resistance. Communications of this sort had become trickier to maintain. CyberSat's scrambling capabilities had gotten smarter every year, since its launch and activation in GDM-1. The satellite network's frequent daytime interruptions of the old digital pathways left only a small window of opportunity for system use; usually during the off hours of late night, when CyberSat's proxy sub-satellite, hovering directly over that geographical quadrant, relented some, in order to conserve energy. But, for now, that antiquated instrument was the life-blood of the Resistance when it came to relaying urgent information. And Christensen's role in the worldwide movement, though precarious and increasingly more difficult to manage, depended on it.

Suddenly, the screen lit up, and a digital tone indicated the reception of voice communication from the Istanbul outpost.

"Come in, Tomazo. How are you, my brother?" Christensen greeted.

"Hello, Tanner, my friend! Rise and shine," DiPaoli said jokingly, in his thick Italian accent.

"Funny... It's after 2 a.m. here, pal," Christensen replied, sarcastically.

"Well, Christensen, it's a beautiful sunny day in western Turkish Province, and I just wanted to send some sunshine out your way. You know...just trying to look up."

"We all could use some optimism, I guess... So, what's the assessment?" Christensen asked.

"About the same as last week. Things are getting really tough. The cogs' activity here is intensifying by the day, and the Community of Brethren is being closely watched. You can cut the tension with a knife. These cog interventions are now coming completely unannounced and unexpected."

"I was afraid of that..."

"They showed up at the gathering yesterday evening and escorted Arkadaş and many others away. He was doing nothing illegal, but has neither been seen nor heard from by anyone here since. I tried to reach his PSS and his home today, but no one answered. He might be gone, I fear."

Sound distortions then disrupted DiPaoli's voice.

"Tomazo, I didn't copy that. Could you repeat that, please?" Christensen asked.

"Yes... I said I'm afraid Arkadaş might be gone for good," DiPaoli replied, with audible anguish in his voice.

"But he hasn't been in the Community for long. Why him?" Christensen questioned.

"He's been talking with others. He just couldn't hold back. His gift is too strong in him. Bless him," said DiPaoli.

"Watch out for yourself, Tomazo," said Christensen, then adding, "and don't be foolish. Make sure you look out for suspicious behavior. There are more and more rats out there. You know, it's hard to trust anyone, anymore."

"I won't be staying here long, Tanner," his friend explained. "I'm catching a flight to Paris, after I shoot some more tomorrow. You won't believe what they're doing to these ancient mosques on the Golden Horn," he said, referring to an area in central western Istanbul, near the 15th century Sultan's Topkapi Palace, on the European side.

"I know… It's been like that everywhere, it seems," said Christensen. Then he reminded DiPaoli, "Hey, time's up. Gotta keep it short, my friend. You know…CyberSat."

"Of course," he replied. "I'll talk to you again from Paris, the Lord willing."

"Bless you, brother…and goodbye," Christensen said, as he terminated the voice-over-system contact.

Christensen had actually only personally met DiPaoli once before, during the GDM-3 conference that officially gave shape to the Resistance. Since then, however, they had forged a strong friendship, both of them deeply committed to the aims of the Community of Brethren movement. They also had both come to share a vital bond with good ole Dr. C, as I maintained contact with each of them on an ongoing, though sporadic basis.

Tired, Christensen briefly closed his eyes. But his mind wanted to wander back to the disturbing dream. He resisted, opening his eyes again, his body still stunned by paralyzing fright. He got up. Leaving the bunker as it was, he walked up a few steps into the main basement area of his house, closing the secret bunker door behind him, and leaving the entrance to the bunker now fully camouflaged and blending with the Japanese motif, which decorated that particular basement wall. Stepping around a matted Aikido area on the floor, Christensen walked across the basement and went up another flight of stairs, then through a narrow hallway, finally reaching the kitchen, where Claire had left a counter light on.

As was customary, Christensen checked all locks and ascertained that the security alarm had been turned on. He then climbed up the living-room stairs to the second floor, walking past the girls' room, then Zeke's. He just had to make sure, so he carefully opened the door and walked into his son's bedroom. There lay Zeke, peaceful, apparently dreaming. Christensen backed out quietly and finally went to bed.

Nine

Morning Routine

Early the next morning, Claire was busy getting breakfast ready. The kids were slowly making their way down toward the kitchen. Bethany, the Christensen's 14-year old, was the first to show up downstairs.

"Morning, Mom," said the sleepy teenager.

"Good morning, sweetie. Sleep well?"

"Sure. But Mondays aren't my favorite.

"I know, honey," Claire said.

"What's for breakfast?" asked the girl.

"Well, I've got eggs and toast in the auto-cooker for your dad. Do you want some?"

"I don't know…maybe," Bethany answered with some hesitation.

"Okay… Why so enthused?" Claire asked facetiously.

"It's nothing," replied Bethany.

Unconvinced, Claire insisted, "Something wrong?"

"I don't know, Mom, it's just that the food is tasting so strange these days. It's like…it's not how it used to be. It just doesn't taste right."

"You mean it's not fresh?" Claire interjected.

"Something like that…"

"I know, sweetie. I'm so sorry. It's the best I can do, anymore," Claire explained. Then she added, "I'll be going grocery shopping later today. Maybe they've received a better shipment this week. Mr.

and Mrs. Sanchez have been very apologetic about this, but I don't think any of this is truly their fault. I believe they're doing what they can to keep their store going, and they've asked for prayers for themselves and for most of their customers who are Believers and non-implants, like them and us. We seem to be running out of options for where to find decent food, anymore... Why don't you just have some cereal for now."

"All right... I'll get it," said Bethany. Then she mentioned, speaking of the new neighbor girl whom she had befriended, "By the way, Mom, Alyssa wanted me to ask you if it would be all right for me to have dinner at her house again tonight."

"Well, Beth... I don't know," replied her mother. "It would be the third time in the past week. I understand that she's your newest friend, but..."

"Practically best friend now, Mom," said the 14-year old.

"Already? But, Beth, Alyssa and her mother have only been our neighbors for a few months," Claire uttered with concern, "and they're...you know..." she paused for a second, striving to find a delicate way of expressing her hesitancy.

"Implants? You mean they're implants, Mom?" Bethany said, showing slight contempt.

"Well, for one, yes...they are implants. And you know how some of the other neighbors have been acting so strangely toward us, lately... But for another, I really don't want Alyssa's mother to think that we, and especially you, are taking advantage of them. We don't know them all that well yet, and it's still somewhat awkward with them," Claire said.

"Mom, Alyssa is just being nice, inviting me like that. You know, she likes you, too. She likes *us*. And she's been asking a lot about what we believe. She's told me that she's enjoyed it when you've talked with her about our faith. I've also been sharing with her some, when she asks. She seems really interested, you know? I just want to be her friend," Bethany explained. Then she said, "Mom, she's told me she doesn't want her implant to get activated. She's not really interested in assimilating."

"Hmm... Have you told her about the gatherings, yet?" Claire inquired.

"I want to. But I haven't, yet. I want it to come naturally," her daughter said.

"Then, why don't you ask Alyssa over instead…tonight? She can join us for dinner here," her mother suggested. "Maybe we could mention something to her about the gatherings."

"Mom, no offense… You're a good cook, and all. But food at her house tastes so much better. Her mom shops with the bracelet, and they've got the best stuff at their house. It's delicious. I would be embarrassed to have her come eat here," Bethany candidly replied.

"I see…" Claire said, trying to hide her discouragement, "Well, I guess it would be fine for you to go, then. But Beth… please don't overdo it, okay? You don't want to wear out your welcome."

"No problem, Mom. Thanks."

Just then, Holly and Zeke came downstairs and walked into the kitchen, with Christensen filing in behind them.

"Hey kids. Hi honey," said Christensen to his kids and wife. They all acknowledged him back, "G'morning, Dad."

"I'm late," he said.

As they all gathered around the table and sat down to pray, Christensen noticed Zeke, their curly-haired 16-year old, being unusually quiet.

"Son, are you okay this morning?" Christensen asked.

"Um…not too hot, I guess. I don't think I slept all that well," Zeke answered.

"How come?" Claire said, voicing concern.

"I'm not sure. My sleep was…troubled," Zeke indicated.

"Troubled, how?" his mother asked.

"I think I had a lot of strange dreams. But I can't really remember any of them."

"I heard you talking in your sleep last night. You sure were loud," Holly teased. Zeke then responded with an annoyed look, "Oh, really?"

At nine years of age, Holly was precocious, and she self-consciously tried hard to compensate for the age difference between her and her siblings. Yet, more often than not, her attempts at maturity ended up irritating and annoying her brother and sister, even if on occasion she did captivate them with her cute looks and silly antics.

"I checked on you last night, before I went to bed. You seemed fine to me," Christensen commented.

"I'm sure it's nothing. I'll be fine," said the introspecting teen.

"Let's pray, everyone," Christensen invited. He blessed the food and voiced a special petition for Zeke. Then they went on with breakfast.

Zeke was not the type to complain much about anything. He was a responsible, if mild-mannered oldest child, but who also enjoyed being active. He was not one to simply feign illness. His countenance that morning gave his mom reason for some apprehension. But she didn't want to worry the boy, so she didn't press the issue.

"Well, gotta run," said Christensen. "I'll check in on you later, to see how you're all doing. Although," he let them know, "my PSS is still malfunctioning."

"Feel rested?" Claire asked her husband, knowing of his harrowing dreaming ordeal the night before and how little sleep he had gotten.

"I've felt better...you know. But I can sleep a little in the shuttle. It's probably just old age," he replied lightheartedly.

"Don't remind me," Claire remarked.

"Dad, why don't you just take a break from that bunker, and get more sleep at night?" Bethany asked.

"I know. I gotta go...okay?" he said, avoiding the question.

"Bye, Daddy. Don't forget your pass card again," said Holly.

"My WormRail pass card... Yep, got it," he said, checking the inside pocket of his light jacket. "Bye, cutie pie. Bye, everyone. Have a good school day. And don't frustrate your mom," Christensen warned, as they were getting ready to begin their homeschool routine. They all said goodbye to him, and Claire followed Christensen to the back door, located off of the kitchen area.

"Tanner," she confessed, "I don't know what to do. I'm feeling scared, and so overwhelmed and troubled by all that is happening. I can barely concentrate on their schoolwork, and I think they're beginning to notice something is really troubling me. I don't know how they couldn't. I just feel this huge weight pushing down on my shoulders. I feel weak, like I'm going to faint at any moment..."

"Oh, Claire... Are you getting sick, too? Why don't you take it a little easier, today?" Christensen said, trying to console her.

"I don't think I'm getting sick. Maybe this has more to do with thinking of my mother. Next week it'll be a year since she passed. You know, she fought so hard against the plague. We prayed so much while she was in treatment for the cancer, but..."

"I'm... I'm so sorry, Claire. I, too, miss her and her precious words of encouragement," he said, knowing little else to say.

"I don't know what to do when this starts to come over me," Claire continued, now with tears on her face.

"Hang in there, sweetheart," Christensen uttered, offering any encouragement he could muster. "Trust in The Name. We'll get through it. I'll be praying for you, okay?"

"Pray for *us*," Claire said.

Claire's words suddenly reminded him of his own words to her the night before. Christensen stared back for a moment. He then waived goodbye, as he turned and walked away toward the underground WormRail station, down the street a ways. From there he would catch a direct super-speed shuttle for his half-hour commute to the Memphis Inter-Provincial Airport.

Ten

Change In The Air

A few days later, as Christensen arrived home at night from a full day's work at the airport, Claire greeted him. But Christensen had a lot on his mind, again.

"Hey, Tan. Glad you're home," she shouted from inside the walk-in kitchen pantry.

"Hey," he said, struggling to hide his emotions.

"Why so quiet?" asked Claire with concern.

Christensen sat down on a stool and put his elbows on the counter. With his hands over his face, he said, "They're going to fully convert the Memphis airport, Claire. They announced it today. I'm going to lose my job." He sighed and then asked, "Are the kids here?"

"Yeah, they're all upstairs," she said, after a brief moment of silence. "Bethany's friend, Alyssa, is here, too," she added.

"The neighbor girl?"

"Right. It's Friday, and she told Beth earlier that she would really like to come over and have supper with us tonight… Even after our *sweet* daughter gave her fair warning about the food here," Claire remarked, attempting to humor her husband a bit. "I said it was okay, but I had no idea…" She then said, "I'm so sorry, Tan. I know you're hurting."

"This is my tenth year, Claire. I knew this was coming, eventually. But I sure wasn't ready for it to be so soon. The kids are still young, we've got expenses…the house…the car…braces…" Christensen went on.

"How soon will they convert?" she asked.

"Much sooner than I ever expected... in the next couple weeks," he clarified.

"Honey, let's not think about that right now. Let's just try and stay calm and share it with the group," Claire said, referring to their circle of closest friends in the Children of the Promise congregation. "I'm sure they can help us out, if we need it. Could we pray about it right now?" Claire suggested.

"You go ahead, Claire. I'm just... I really can't," said her despondent husband.

"That's all right..." she replied. She paused briefly, as if to gather her thoughts, and then voiced her short prayer.

The news had indeed come as a sudden shock to many, but especially to the non-implant minority working in the air traffic system, throughout the South. That Friday, it was announced by the airport authority that due to the imminent visit by a top delegation from the Allianz Federation, coming from Paris, the entire network of airports in the American Province would be required to finalize the system conversion, in order to become fully CyberSat-compliant. The only airports in the province that had yet to undergo the transition were the ones in the southern region. This meant that the new operations at all airports would now be completely done in the Allianzi language, and that they would necessarily have to be carried out by implanted controllers. Non-implants, who had been performing their duties in English, had been directing air traffic via a language converter, which simultaneously transmitted all flight vector instructions in Allianzi. Furthermore, CyberSat would now remotely take over most of these operations, and fewer controllers would be needed, even if already implanted.

"...In Your Name, we pray. Amen," she uttered, as she finished her prayer.

"I'm certain they're doing this because they want to make sure they look good to the Federation," Christensen remarked. "You know, Adammus Horn, the Prosecutor General, will be leading the official delegation. They say that Marshall Dariah is mandating all kinds of immediate reforms, and is personally traveling throughout the province, overseeing a number of Allianz Code compliance projects. She's on pins and needles. And I think I know a good reason why... The Horn-man, himself."

"That's fine, but...can they really do this to you, Tanner? Weren't you grandfathered in because you began there just before Allianzi was declared the official language, in GDM-4?" she asked in puzzlement.

"They're basically doing away with my whole department in the tower. A 'grandfather' clause doesn't protect me from discontinuation and area dissolution. I have no recourse. In simple terms, I'm out," he explained. Claire paused, and then asked, slightly shifting the focus of the conversation.

"Do you think she remembers you?"

"Who?"

"Dariah. Misha Dariah," Claire answered.

"Um... No. Surely she doesn't. It's been so long. And who remembers their teaching assistant from college, anyway? Although" Christensen paused, "I did give her a ride once and helped dig her car out of a snow bank one afternoon, after class."

"Well, *I* actually seem to remember a *really* cute TA in our Earth and Space Science class, at MIT..." Claire responded.

"I know. But we were already acquainted with one another, and we saw each other regularly at the student worship services. Misha Dariah was different," Christensen pondered. "She wasn't a Believer, from what I could tell, and she never really even needed my help in the class. She was one of those intense undergraduate students who would make any graduate TA feel nervous simply by her intelligence and by the way she talked. She was strikingly assertive, not to mention that she was very noticeable, too, if you know what I mean."

"Noticeable, was she, 'Mr. Observant' TA?" Claire exclaimed, lightly slapping his arm and betraying her jealousy.

"It wasn't like that, at all," Christensen sheepishly tried to explain. "Besides, all of her attention was definitely on Adammus Horn. And mine was on you," he uttered in his quick-witted defense.

"Good answer," Claire said.

"Don't worry, Adammus was *the man*." He continued, "But, oh honey, what wouldn't I give right now to just be able to stand face-to-face with both Horn and Dariah and really give them a piece of my mind!"

"Not literally, I hope. The CyberSat rumors, remember?"

"I know…brainwave energy."

Claire then mentioned, "I recall Dariah, but I don't remember Horn attending MIT, too."

"You're quite right. He was at Harvard Law School at the time, but looking back, I do recall several times when he would show up to meet Dariah outside our classroom. It seemed like everywhere he went, he was already making waves as a young lawyer-to-be," Christensen recollected. "I remember he would come on campus and would give impassioned speeches against the 'corrupting democratic principles of the industrialized nations of the West.' I briefly sat through one of them thinking to myself, *this guy really thinks highly of himself,* while I listened to his rhetoric, and that he was either a deranged lunatic, or some kind of warped genius."

"Good memory," Claire remarked. " So, what did you conclude about him?"

"I guess he was really both those things," Christensen said, "but I never could have predicted how much so, and how things would actually take shape…and so fast, it seems."

"True," Claire said. "…but much of it seems like ancient history, like a life time ago."

"I know. In many ways it *does* feel like long ago. Just before we were married, in fact. The world was still a different place then… seventeen years and an altogether different calendar system ago… Times were more hopeful, anyway," he said. "I used to imagine myself someday working for NASA, as an aerospace engineer. I would dream of one day even going up into space… I truly never thought I would descend this low, actually losing my job, and probably my career…for good."

"Oh, Tanner," Claire said, "why don't you visualize John. He's probably at home. I think he needs to know right away. And I think you need his support right now. Maybe this is a good excuse to finally have John and Shen-il over, later tonight, after the kids are all in bed."

"I guess that would be good. It's been too long since we've gotten together outside of the gatherings. But I guarantee you, they're super busy, finishing the preparations for the big gathering this Sunday. It may be enormous, one of the biggest ever, " Christensen noted. "They're probably feeling swamped."

"It's worth a try, Tan," Claire insisted.

"All right. I'll give it a shot. But, hey, could you let me use your PSS. Mine needs some recharging again, or something," he told her, "and uh...thanks for the prayer. I'm already feeling a little better," he added. "Now, where are the kids?"

"I think I hear them up in the playroom," she answered.

Christensen left the kitchen and climbed up the stairs to say hello to the kids. He missed them even more than usual, and he wished just to say hi and to briefly peer into their little world, before he got a hold of John, on Claire's Personal Sat Spec. The kids had always been a great mood boost for Christensen ever since they were tiny, and he greatly enjoyed just watching them do their thing.

Both girls, and Zeke as well, were in fact hanging out in the playroom upstairs, along with Alyssa, who was showing them her newest CogniToy acquisition.

"Now, Zeke, stand over there," instructed the 15-year old, "I'm going to shoot this bow-and-arrow right at you, but you won't feel thing. Watch this, girls. Ready?"

"Oooo! Zeke's getting an arrow shot through his heart..." Holly teased.

Zeke was a bit taken by the whole "Amazon Woman" routine, but he wasn't sure about being shot with an arrow, and it showed.

"It's holographic, Zeke, don't worry," Alyssa assured him.

"Fine, go ahead," he said, displaying a bit of bravado, so uncharacteristic of him, especially in the presence of a girl.

"Here I go... Pull back and...release!" Alyssa cried out.

"Wow!" they all jumped up with surprise. "That's awesome!" Bethany yelled out. "You shot him right in his heart! You're good, girl!"

"I've been practicing... Just aim right to the middle of the chest," Alyssa said, recalling the instructions from her archery coach, at the private, bi-lingual high school she attended.

"Cool beans!" Holly explained. "Can *I* shoot him, now?"

A bit stunned by the realistic image, Zeke protested, "Hey, wait a minute... I'm not gonna just keep getting shot all night." Then he muttered under his breath, "Crazy girls..."

At 16, Zeke was still too inexperienced when it came to girl's arrows being flung through his heart. But there was something about this he secretly fancied. He just didn't know how to process it, yet. To him, Alyssa was pretty; quite pretty, in fact. And in his private opinion, the implant only seemed to add to her charm. But Zeke wasn't really conscious of his emotions, nor was he aware of their potential impact on him. For now, he was much more interested in checking out the soccer features of her gadget, which he judged to be considerably more enticing to him at that very moment.

Fighting his shyness, he politely asked, "Alyssa, could you show me the soccer program on your CogniToy?"

"Why? Do you play?" she teased.

"I'd say so. I do all right... At least well enough to run circles around you," he boldly countered.

"Dream on," Alyssa replied.

"Hey, you two...why don't you settle it with a little *friendly* match?" Holly egged them on.

"You're on," Alyssa exclaimed, as she and Zeke looked at each other and smiled.

Just then, Christensen peaked in. "Hey kids. Hi Alyssa."

"Hi, Mr. Christensen," the neighbor girl greeted him.

"Hey, Dad," said his kids.

"Please, don't let me interrupt you. It looks like you were in the middle of something *very* important. I just wanted to say hello," he announced, and then turned around to go find Claire's PSS.

"What's that?" Alyssa asked, pointing to the wooden *samurai* sword, resting on its stand, up on a wall shelf.

"It's my *bokken*," Zeke replied.

"*Bok*-who?"

"*Bokken*. It's a wooden sword," he said.

"What's it for?" Alyssa asked.

"Well, it's a practice sword. I use it with my dad. We train together in Aikido. He's got a real one, with a live blade, up on the wall in the basement. It's really sharp," explained Zeke.

"Wow...Aikido? Is that a martial art, or something?" she asked.

"Yeah... It's Japanese, but it's different than most fighting arts. It's almost completely defensive," Zeke explained.

"Why the sword, then? It looks pretty offensive to me," Alyssa pried.

"Well, it's kind of hard to explain exactly. It's a traditional part of the training. But, also, by going through the moves with the sword, you develop skills and discipline that can actually be applied to empty-handed self-defense," he elucidated.

"Neat... Are you good at it?" she asked.

"I'm getting there. I actually just got my black-belt, but I feel like I'm just now becoming a serious student. Dad's great, though," Zeke said proudly. "He started before I was born. His Aikido master was a college professor of his, named Dr. C."

"What's the 'C' stand for?" Alyssa inquired.

"I actually can't remember," said Zeke. "There's a picture of him and Dad on the wall of the basement.

"Yeah, and they're both wearing *skirts*!" Holly teased.

"They're called *hakama*, and they're not skirts, you little twerp," Zeke corrected her. "They're baggy, black *samurai* pants."

"*Samurai* pants? Awesome! That really sparks! Hey, can you show me some Aikido sometime?" Alyssa requested.

"Um, I wouldn't want you to get hurt."

"Hey, I'm tough enough," she assured him.

"Maybe...maybe after dinner," Zeke said, feeling rather flattered by all the interest and unfamiliar attention. "But right now, how about we get into that sparking soccer mode in your CogniToy?"

"You got it," said Alyssa.

"Okay, y'all," said Bethany, "but first, how about a little Beatles music in the background, to liven things up?" A budding singing talent, Bethany was referring to her most recent musical discovery, thanks to Shen-il Waters, her voice trainer.

Holly then chimed in, "Yeah, those Bugs really spark!"

"Please, Holly... They're called the *Beatles*, not the Bugs. How rude!" chastised Bethany.

"Aren't they kinda like the Bee Gees?" asked Alyssa.

"Are you kidding me, girlfriend? No way!"

"Why not?" Holly challenged. "They're both named after bugs, right?"

"Right..." Bethany responded with a hint of sarcasm. "Hang on, Alyssa. Check *this* out..."

Before long, they were all singing along to the classic hit, *I Wanna Hold Your Hand.*

Eleven

Friends and Dreams

Later that night, the house was quiet, as the Christensens awaited the arrival of their friends. For Claire, that was a nice break from the usual routine. Even though this was a solemn occasion and not exactly her idea of kicking back with the Waters, she missed spending time with friends and had grown weary of Christensen's long nightly descents into the old bunker, leaving her in utter solitude. Loneliness had become her reliable late night companion. It showed up every night and at about the same time. Not that there weren't important reasons for it. The Resistance was paramount, and she was fully committed to doing her part in it. But, still, Claire couldn't pretend she didn't have longings, even in times of distress.

Some ten years back she and Christensen would have looked forward to a cozy night together. Things truly had changed. Romance used to be as simple and fun as turning off the lights, the kids still too young to notice or even to be awake past the early evening hours. But their life was different now; the polar opposite of how things used to be, in the early years of their marriage. And the unintelligible Allianzi programs on their crystalline **hyaline televisor** only served as a constant reminder to them that the life they once had was now distant and might as well have been just a lovely dream. But this night, they could almost remember how things used to be...

"Wow... It's just like old times," Claire reminisced. "The kids are in bed and friends are coming over... I'm even remembering what it was like to actually have a social life."

The Dreamers of Allianz

"I know. When was the last time we even had any friends over?" Christensen asked rhetorically, as he leaned back on the sofa cushions.

"It's been so long... Did it ever really happen?" she wondered out loud.

"Oh c'mon, Claire. It's not like we've been hibernating, right? I mean, we've been there for each other, haven't we?" he rationalized, feebly trying to put a more hopeful spin on their personal life together.

"I don't know about you, Tan, but I'm so ready to wake up from this so I can just breathe," Claire said, giving vent to the real agony she often times felt. "I want to wake up so I can begin to dream again... I used to dream about traveling the world with you. But the reality is, I haven't even once left the province. Everything's being taken away from me...from us."

"What are you saying?" he asked.

"I don't know. But I just don't think I can take much more of this change in our days. I can hardly recognize our lives anymore," Claire said, as she plopped down on the couch, next to him.

"Claire, I love you. How's that for constancy?" Christensen said. She didn't answer at first, her eyes looking down, tracing the tile patterns on the living-room floor.

"Hey, sweetie," he uttered, trying to find her eyes, "didn't you hear me? I love you. I do...with all my heart."

"I know. It's not that.... I love you, too," she said. "But, Tanner, can you tell me? I mean, *really* tell me that things will be all right? Can you?" she asked, afraid to hear the answer she already knew was coming.

"No. No, I can't," he confessed. "But, I can tell you this, and I mean it. It will *not* be like this forever, Claire. It's the only thing I do know for sure. Things *will* change. I know they will. And I believe we'll be there to see it with our own eyes," he replied, his hand touching her blond hair around her shoulders."

"This is crazy, but somehow I can still believe you when I hear you say that," she told him.

"I'm glad, Claire. Because I desperately need that from you." Then Christensen said, playfully insinuating romance, "You know, a part of me really wishes John and Shen-il weren't coming just now..."

"Oh, really? And what exactly did you have in mind?" she said, playing along.

Just then, the home alert system announced, *"Attention, please. A front door arrival has been detected."* The monotone but soothing female voice continued, *"Please advise."*

"Tanner Christensen, entrance authorized," Christensen replied.

"Entrance authorized by Tanner Christensen," acknowledged the voice-recognition system. The door was then opened and the two quickly got up from the couch and walked toward the foyer to greet their friends.

John and Shen-il Waters had been married about a year. John, however, was an old friend of the family. He used to be a regular guest at the Christensens' during his college days, at Faith&Knowledge U., until he graduated and moved to Southeast Asia, to live and minister there. Years before, Christensen had actually mentored John. Together, they used to have weekly meetings for spiritual mentorship down in the basement bunker, and John was a frequent, all-American moocher at the Christensen's place. That night might have been a sweet sort of reunion, if things were different. But the principal reason for their visit that evening was anything but jovial, and everyone knew that all too well.

As the couple entered the house, a flood of memories came rushing in along with them. "My goodness...when was the last time we were here?" John asked.

"I'm embarrassed to say it's been too long. A little over a year, maybe?" Claire commented.

"I think it must have been when you first brought Shen-il over here, for us to meet her, when you had just arrived back home from overseas," Christensen said.

"You know, I believe you're right," Shen-il remarked, in her slight, but always noticeable Indonesian accent.

"That's so odd. I used to practically live here, years ago," John remembered.

"Well, come in please, and sit down. It's a bit late, I know, so I've put on a pot of coffee for us. It's the good stuff, from our secret

The Dreamers of Allianz

Java stash," Claire revealed. "We know how the two of you love good coffee. In fact, if I'm not mistaken, it was you all who brought these coffee beans for us, direct from Java, last year."

This was a bittersweet moment for them. For, in reality, although they might see each other once or twice a week at the Brethren Gatherings, their work had become so focused on the mission at hand, namely proclaiming the message of freedom, the *Evangel*, and baptizing new Believers, that they had rarely had time to catch up with each other socially anymore. Outside of those mission-related occasions, their interactions had basically been limited to special debriefings about the status of the Resistance, about apparent danger warnings, and so on. More and more, they lacked the privilege of just being with each other, just as good friends. Indeed, the cost of their cause had largely been paid with their own private familial and social lives.

As Christensen shared with the Waters about his work situation and impending dismissal, tears began to flow, perhaps as a kind of collective release; a sort of spiritual and emotional catharsis. They remained in that mode, gathered around the dining room table for what seemed like hours; perhaps a much-needed time of mutual comforting and raw surrender before the Lord of all comfort.

Following that, John relayed a brief overview of the upcoming Sunday evening meeting of the Children of the Promise group. It was to be their biggest local Brethren Gathering in memory, and perhaps ever.

"Based on our estimates," John explained, "we're expecting anywhere between one and two thousand newcomers on Sunday evening. We've really got our work cut out for us, but by His grace, I think everything is just about all in place for it. We're counting on you, Claire, to lead the altar support team, as decisions are made by the people in the crowd." John was referring to those present at the gathering who would receive the message and believe unto Spirit-sealing and baptism.

He continued, "I'll introduce our new short play we entitled 'Follow Me,' and after that I'll be presenting a brief message and making the invitation. Shen-il, of course, will be leading the music worship. The band and the Gospel choir have been busy, fine tuning their sound. Tanner, I need you to run the sound check for us, as usual, and basically keep things functioning smoothly back at the sound platform. You'll again be our man for the announcements, towards the end of the service. I'll probably also need you to come up and help me with the baptism ceremony. I'm trusting The Name for many to be baptized Sunday evening. And finally, we've got many in our group who will help run security in and around the pavilion, but we'll all need to keep our eyes and ears open."

Having already put on several of these gatherings as a team over the past year, most of the planning for the upcoming event seemed rather routine. As was usual among this leadership group, there was fairly good unity in most areas of planning, and generally speaking, that night was no exception. However, the Christensens and Shen-il had not always shared the same outlook on certain musical aspects of the gatherings. Shen-il's ideas sometimes seemed too cutting-edge for them, and her notions of novelty often challenged their comfort zone. That evening, Shen-il again pitched a curveball that caught Christensen and Claire by surprise. This time, however, it struck too close to home.

"If I could share an idea I've been thinking about, I'm kind of wanting to try something new this time," Shen-il interjected, just as they were about to sign off on the plans for the gathering. "I really want to draw the youth into our program, and I would love it if Bethany could do a couple of solo pieces for us. I believe her singing will really connect with the audience."

"Bethany? You mean have her sing up there, on her own? And in this tension-filled climate?" Claire asked.

"Yes, Claire. I believe she's just what we need to really make an impact with the younger crowds there. Her lessons have truly been going well. I really feel she's ready," Shen-il answered. "She's got a beautiful voice, praise The Name, and I have to believe that He will make a way for her to pull through in safety."

"I don't know, Shen-il," Christensen stepped in. "Is this really the time for you to be innovating like that, again? I mean, I feel that so far things have gone pretty well with the gatherings, just as they've been. And besides, this is quite short notice."

"They *have* gone well, Tanner. But don't you see how this could really help capture the audience's attention? And especially the youth's? I think it's worth trying it," Shen-il argued back.

"I just don't feel right about using Bethany as a prop, for greater effect," Claire stated.

"I don't blame you for feeling protective, Claire," Shen-il replied. "But is it right to guard Bethany to such an extent, that we miss the opportunity to really allow her to be used of The Name for a greater end? Are you really unwilling to surrender her for His purpose?"

"I think that's an unfair question, Shen-il," Christensen responded, feeling rather irritated with her insistence. "We're not questioning Bethany's Name-given gifts. I, for one, am simply wondering about the wisdom of bringing this on at this particular time, with all that's at stake for that evening," he explained. "Perhaps that may be something we can consider for the future, but my sense is that we need to stick with what's already been tried and tested. What do you think, John?" Christensen asked.

"I was hoping you'd leave me out of this one," John replied. "But since you asked, I have to say I liked the idea when I heard it. I do agree that we shouldn't exploit Bethany just for effect, but I believe that what Shen-il is talking about is something different."

"How so?" asked Claire.

"The question for me, Claire, is this," John elaborated, "Do we really have the luxury of time? I mean, who knows how much longer we really have to reach these souls? I think Shen-il's heart's in the right place, and she's prayed a lot about bringing more of our kids into the program, and for Beth in particular. Perhaps The Name's been preparing her for exactly such a time as this."

"Guys, remember. This is not about us," Shen-il pointed out. "It's about getting the *Evangel* out and about the glory of The Name."

Sitting in silence for a moment, Christensen and Claire reflected on the difficult decision before them. Claire's concern was with tragically erring on the side of overexposing her daughter in the midst of those uncertain times. For Christensen, the question was more one of proper strategic planning, in light of such short notice. Breaking the awkward silence, John said, "I tell you what, guys. How about you take some time to pray about it tonight, and let us know what you think, tomorrow." Christensen then glanced at Claire, who appeared to already be lifting this up in private prayer. Finding Christensen's hand, Claire squeezed it gently. Suddenly, a feeling of peace came over Christensen. He then said, "No need to wait, John. I believe Claire and I agree."

"Wow, that was quick," remarked John. Christensen then added, "Like you said, there's little time. And we're going to have to trust The Name and Shen-il's instincts on this. Music really *is* Bethany's gift."

"Thanks, guys," Shen-il responded.

"You and Bethany do get along well together, and she really trusts you," Claire stated, looking at Shen-il and reaching for her hand across the dining-room table. "You're both so musical. And you know how Bethany's been so totally enthralled with all that music you've let her listen to, from your own collection." "You're sure, now?" John asked. "After all, out of all the music Shen-il let Beth sample, you weren't so sure at first about her newfound delight for the Beatles."

"That's true," Christensen replied, "but we've tried to deemphasize their whole countercultural, hippie stage, and focus on how John Lennon and the others sure could carry a cool tune." To which John briefly mused in response, "Well, at times a bit of counterculture goes a long way toward ridding society of its unexamined, stagnant, and even harmful routine. I mean, look at us these days…countercultural *par excellence*."

"Hmm… I guess Beth *has* been asking to join the worship team for quite some time, hasn't she?" Claire recalled.

"Why don't we bring this up with her tomorrow and make sure she's really up for singing to the audience this Sunday," Shen-il suggested. "I know she's already been working on a few songs, on her own. But I'll double-check, just in case."

"You know, guys?" Christensen commented, "I've learned, over the years, that having the gift of prophecy often makes one seem oppositional and very unpopular."

"Maybe so, friend," said John, "but I don't think you two were really being prophetic in this case. I think you were just being nervous parents. And that's perfectly all right."

Ultimately, the evening ended on an up note, as the Christensens recounted some memorable moments during John's college days with them, keeping Shen-il utterly amused, and repeatedly causing John to blush with embarrassment.

It was now past midnight. As the Waters were departing for the WormRail station down the block, Claire remembered to ask, "Shen-il, do you all have enough medallianz credits on your pass cards?"

"We're good to go, Claire, thanks. And thanks, too, for your faithfulness in providing these for us," said Shen-il.

"Hey, we take care of one another, right?" Claire commented.

"That's right. And who needs to drive at all in congestion like this, on a late Friday night? People are out in droves," Shen-il remarked.

"You're absolutely right," Claire agreed.

"Goodbye, you guys," said Christensen.

"Bye, you two. And kiss those great kids for us," John said, as he and Shen-il walked away.

"Will do," Claire replied.

"See you Sunday, the Lord willing," Christensen said.

A bit later, as Christensen and Claire prepared to go to bed, they heard Zeke talking in his sleep. It was well past 1 a.m., and the muttering startled them both. They entered his room and found their son restlessly moving around in his bed, having kicked all of his covers onto the floor. Zeke appeared to be mumbling what sounded much like portions of the Scriptures. It was nothing really coherent, but just clear enough that Claire could recognize some of it.

"Isaiah... It's Isaiah, Tanner," she whispered. "But why?"

"Have you been going over these as memory verses with him?" Christensen inquired of her.

"No, not at all."

"Should we wake him up?" he asked.

"No, I don't think so. Why don't I just lay here with him for a while, just to make sure he's okay," she suggested.

"All right, go ahead. I'll go on to bed, but call me if you need me," he said.

"I will… And, honey, I'm so sorry about…" Claire said.

"The job? I know. Me, too."

"Good night. I love you."

"I love you. G'night." After saying that, Christensen tiptoed out of Zeke's room and went to go sleep, resisting the slight but nagging temptation to sojourn in his bunker for a while, as was customary. "Nope. Tonight I'm getting some sleep," he convinced himself.

Twelve

Zeke at Risk?

Around 7:30 the next morning, Claire awoke to find herself still in Zeke's room. She left him sleeping, and went to find Christensen, who was already up, doing his morning devotions, downstairs in the den.

"Am I interrupting?" Claire asked, as she saw Christensen with his eyes closed.

"No, not at all. I'm finished," he answered. "So, any idea what's wrong with Zeke?"

"I haven't a clue. That was so strange last night. Zeke woke up briefly in the middle of the night, and I asked him if he was feeling okay," Claire recounted.

"What did he say?"

"He just said he was thirsty."

"Did you ask him about his dream, Claire?"

"Yeah. He said he didn't remember a thing. So, I brought him some water to drink and let him go back to sleep, and he basically slept well the rest of the night. But I stayed in there with him just in case," Claire explained.

"Do you think it's anxiety about what's been happening?" Christensen submitted.

"Could be," said Claire.

At that moment, Bethany walked into the den. Having overheard the conversation from the kitchen, she said, "Mom, I heard Zeke doing that the night before, too. But I just didn't think anything of it. I thought he was just talking in his sleep, again,"

"That's odd," Claire said. "Hey, it's Saturday, Beth. Why are you up so early?"

"I guess I had Zeke on my mind, too," she answered.

"Thanks, Beth, for letting us know. It's really nice of you to be so concerned about your brother, that way," Christensen commended her.

"You're welcome. He's a real pain sometimes, but I don't want anything bad to happen to poor Zeke," Bethany said. "Have you considered that it may just be love?" she added, jokingly.

"You mean, Alyssa?" Claire inquired.

"You didn't hear it from me, but you should have seen how friendly they were to each other last night. It's like they both drank from the passion fruit fountain, or something," Bethany kidded.

"I was wondering about that. I wish it were all it was. But this seems more serious to me than just puppy love," her mother commented.

"Maybe we should schedule an appointment for him with a psychologist. Someone with that kind of training might be able to pinpoint what's happening with him," suggested Christensen.

"Do you really think he needs a mental evaluation?" Claire challenged.

"I don't know. But it's evident to me that this is a recurring thing, and it can't be good for him if we just leave it unchecked," Christensen affirmed. "And, in the long run, who knows what effects this troubled sleep might have on him physically and psychologically at his age?"

"You're probably right. I'll make the appointment. There's that clinic on the 13th floor of the shopping complex, downtown. Maybe they can see him today," Claire wondered.

"Good enough. In the meantime, I'll work on a little Aikido with him later this morning. Maybe it will help him get his wiggles out," Christensen said.

Later that morning, father and son were down in the basement training on a matted area. As they were getting warmed up, Christensen took some time to ask Zeke about a few things.

"Zeke, I think we need to have a little man-to-man."

"You mean, right now, Dad?"

"Yes, right now. But let's just keep on practicing. How about it?" Christensen replied.

"Sure, but what do you want to talk about, Dad?" Zeke inquired.

"Well, I just wanted to know your thoughts about, you know, how things are going for you...and also for us. Just everything in general, you know?" Christensen attempted to clarify.

"Wow, Dad. That's pretty broad. Could you be a little more specific?" Zeke asked.

Feeling quite inarticulate all of a sudden, Christensen said, "Um...why don't we do a few warm up throws, first?"

As they practiced, going back and forth, first attacking and then throwing the other across the mats, Christensen put a few thoughts together.

"All right, son. Here we go."

"Okay, Dad, ask away. You're making me nervous with all the suspense," Zeke told him, still unsure of what exactly this was about.

"All right, son. How do you feel about what's been happening all around in the last couple of years?" Christensen asked, still focusing on the throws.

"Well, I know that things...have been changing...quite a bit... all around..." Zeke said, struggling to catch his breath after several break-falls on the mat."

"Yeah, but how do you feel about it?" Christensen then instructed, "Here, now you throw me a few times."

"Uhh..." Zeke uttered, trying to collect his thoughts, while his father grunted, taking break-falls of his own.

Christensen then quickly corrected Zeke on his Aikido form, saying, "Son, you're relying too much on your upper body muscles. Try to relax and throw from your center...your hips. And don't forget to breath as you throw me."

"Dad, wait. Let's stop for a minute," Zeke requested.

They paused their practice. Zeke then sat down on the mat and tried to elaborate, saying, "Dad, I know you've been having a tough time at your job, lately...and things don't really look good for you there. I also know that the way we believe has gotten us, and others, too, in some kind of trouble with the government, and you guys are worried about it. And I'm pretty sure something funky is going on with the food we've been buying in the last few weeks... Other than that, it's sort of like, life as usual. We do homeschool. We have worship gatherings. I hang out with Gustavo and other friends, and do stuff with them, like play soccer... Mom does her thing here around the house or she takes the girls out to the shopping complex. The girls get together with their friends or they have a friend over. And you spend a lot of time down in the bunker when you're not at work. So...life as usual."

"You're not too worried, then? Do you ever think about the world, or the implants, and all the changes going on?" Christensen asked.

"Sure I do, but I try to leave it alone. There's not much I can do about it, right?" Zeke said.

"Well, Zeke, I'd like to believe that we *can* do something. That's why we're working with John and the others, and why I spend so much time in the bunker. And you, too, play an important part in all of this," Christensen explained. "You've helped us a lot, actually, in reaching the youth and getting them to come to the gatherings."

"I enjoy doing that, Dad. That doesn't really worry me. I can understand why we're doing what we're doing," Zeke said. "By the way, our gatherings aren't illegal, are they?"

"Um...technically? No. They are generally considered to be social and cultural events. And as long as we're not coercing, that is, forcing anyone to do anything, we should legally be able to continue to have them," Christensen explained. "But a time may come, son, when things may be different. And we're seeing signs of it, already.

We may soon come to be personally persecuted for our faith and for our gatherings, no matter what..."

"Well, as John always preaches, our faith is free...but not cheap, right?" said the boy, with a tone of maturity beyond his years. "I guess I expected that."

"So, basically, in general, overall...you're doing fine?" Christensen awkwardly inquired.

"Well, Dad... Since you asked, I do have kind of a big question," Zeke mentioned. "Is it wrong for us to want to associate with other youth who happen to be implants?"

"You mean just as friends?" his father said.

"Um, more like close friends...or maybe even more," Zeke tried to qualify.

"Well, son, you know that Mom and I feel strongly that you shouldn't date, if that's what you're talking about. We believe in courting, as you know, and you're still a bit young for getting that serious with a girl. Having said that, it's quite clear to us that we cannot rightly be yoked together with a non-believer, someone outside of our faith, for many practical and spiritual reasons. But," Christensen continued, "if someone is an implant who has remained free from assimilation, we believe that such a person can be reached for the Name. And if that person receives the message and becomes Spirit-sealed, and then gets baptized, then to us that person is renewed. She's born again. She then belongs to The Name, and that makes her one of us. In that case, yes, she can become special to you in that way, when the right time comes for that."

"I see, Dad... Dad, please don't tell anyone about this, but I can't seem to stop thinking about Alyssa. And I've been unsure about how to deal with it, because she's an implant."

"Do you think that's why you've been having sleep troubles, Zeke?" Christensen asked.

"I don't really know what the problem is there, actually. But, if anything, I would think my dreams would be sweeter for it," Zeke asserted.

"Well, she *is* a nice girl...and a cute brunette, at that. I guess we'll keep trying to figure it out. And, by the way, we'll keep this just between the two of us."

"Thanks, Dad."

"Just in case there's more to this, though, your mom and I want to have you looked at by a doctor... I gather she's made an appointment for you this afternoon. We'll all go together, I think," Christensen told his son.

"That's fine, Dad," Zeke replied.

Following their conversation, the two continued their vigorous work out until just before lunch. For Christensen, there was little he enjoyed more than spending time like that with Zeke. In his heart, there was some sense of fulfilling his calling to mold his son. He enjoyed time with his two daughters, as well. But there was something about this connection with his son that touched Christensen deeper in his soul, and he had learned to be honest with himself about that.

Thirteen

Shopping?

At the shopping complex, later that Saturday afternoon, Christensen and Zeke made their way up to the doctor's office, while Claire and the girls remained down in the lower shopping levels, doing some showcase browsing. For a long time now, this aspect of life had lost almost all of its appeal for Claire, but she could still find pleasure in watching her daughters' delight in contemplating the latest styles in fashion and other innovative products in the retail world. Claire instantly noticed the rich variety of colorful head coverings, hats, and bands, as well as decorative and even sparkling bracelet shells, which were taking over the world of apparel accessories. This was truly a fast changing commercial reality, fervently geared toward the implanted consumer base.

Malls never did go out of style, as had once been predicted with the advent and spread of online-shopping, around the turn of the century. Yet, these magnets for vibrant economic and social energy had decidedly changed significantly since Claire used to tread this ever-popular cultural turf, as a young woman. For one thing, stores were now almost entirely geared at the teen and young-adult markets. And the novelty creators in the market-place were going at it full-force, taking complete advantage of the new possibilities that the Cognit Implant protocol provided, as well as the unbridled consumerism of the youth, equipped with Cognit Bracelets, fully programmed with their often considerable spending allowances. Furthermore, a casual perusal of the store varieties in the complex

The Dreamers of Allianz

revealed the omnipresence of trendy and chic Cognit Implant outlets, and a seemingly continuous streaming of entire families flowing in and out of them.

After a long half hour of aimlessly wandering around the mall, the increasingly monotonous window-shopping began to take its toll on the Christensen trio. The contagious initial excitement of their surroundings soon gave way to a sharp sense of alienation for the two girls and their mother. For Bethany especially, the whole experience was beginning to deeply disturb her, as she felt utterly disenfranchised as a non-implanted shopping mall wanderer.

Suddenly, Bethany stopped dead on her tracks and said, "Mom, what's the point?" she uttered, revealing her frustration and real sadness about the futile exercise. "Why even bother looking at all this stuff, when we can't even dream of buying any of it?"

"Well, uh..." Claire attempted to respond, unable to offer anything but a non-answer at first.

"Really, Mom. This is so pointless. Without the bracelet, there's absolutely nothing here we can get, even if we do have the money. The nicest fashions, the trendiest styles, the best of everything, and all we can do is wait months until it begins to show up at the dinky outlets we're stuck shopping at. How I wish I had an implant, sometimes."

At that, Holly reacted with great scornfulness, "Bethany Marie Christensen! How dare you say that? Take it back this instant."

"Holly, that's okay. Calm down, girls," Claire intervened. "It's all right. I understand your frustration, Beth. Believe me, I know how you feel. I really wish I could magically change things so that my girls could live more normal lives, like the other girls we see spending time and shopping at the mall. But I'm not able to do that. And I'm truly sorry."

"But Mom, didn't you hear her? She said she wishes she had an implant!" Holly indignantly pointed out. "And you, yourself, taught us that our bodies are temples of the Spirit of Truth."

"I know, sweetie. That's right. I did teach you that. But, you know what? These thoughts *will* come and go. And we must try and be patient with each other and with ourselves, whenever we're struggling with them," Claire replied. "You know, Beth, your mom was once into all the latest fashions, too. I, too, liked to look pretty and in style, especially for Dad. As things began to change, though, I was forced to slowly give these things up. But at the end of the day, I had to decide for myself what was most important to me. And the Lord helped me accept the fact that there's a real cost to following him, but it's the most important thing any of us can ever choose to do."

"I understand that, Mom. But it's just so incredibly hard, sometimes. And I do, at times, wonder how it would be to just live like they do," Bethany explained, pointing toward the cluster of youth, gathering a few yards down the storefront esplanade. "For once, I'd like to be able to do all the things they do and enjoy all the things they freely enjoy because of the implant."

"I know it's not at all easy, especially at your age, Beth. But I also know for certain that we're called not to love the world, or anything in it," Claire said, doing her best to recall some wisdom from Scripture, "because the world and its desires will pass away. They'll pass away, girls. But the ones who do the will of The Name will live forever."

"Mom... I know you're right... I'll be fine, one way or another, okay? Thanks for caring," Bethany said.

"Sweetie, I do care. I really do. And I totally feel for you. All three of you kids have been really brave, and I'm so proud of you all," Claire said, as they resumed walking together.

There was one aspect of this conversation, namely Believer implantation, that Claire chose to avoid, for the time being. Yet, what she didn't know was that this very serious issue would be thrust upon them concerning Zeke, and soon.

A couple of minutes later, with eyes drawn toward the approaching, large teen cluster convening in front of a series of restaurants and smaller food retailers, Claire thought she recognized a familiar face among the many implanted youth gathered there.

"Hey, girls. I think I see Alyssa over there," she said, as she discretely pointed in the direction of the crowd of teens.

Brightening, Holly yelled out, "I see her!" and she immediately took off toward her. Bethany, embarrassed by her sister's eager display, also moved in that direction, but lagged behind, a bit unsure of how she felt, being a non-implant and a non-Allianzi speaker in that social situation. With determined vigor, Holly cut through the crowd, pushing here and nudging there, "Excuse me! Sorry people! Coming through!" until she managed to arrive right in front of Alyssa. Looking up, Holly let out an excited, "Hi!"

Alyssa, having noticed a familiar, pig-tailed, big-eyed, strawberry-blond little girl moving forcefully right toward her, quickly realized who this was. "Holly, hi! What are you doing here?"

"I could ask you the same thing, you know. But isn't it obvious? I'm shopping." Holly answered with a confident smirk.

"Wow, did you come with your family?" Alyssa asked.

"Hi Alyssa," she heard Bethany say, as her friend walked toward her.

"Double wow!" Alyssa exclaimed. "Hi Bethany. You didn't tell me you were coming here today."

"Triple wow!" said Holly, pointing to her mom, who approached them but was still several yards away. "There's Momma!"

"That's awesome. Want to hang out?" Alyssa asked.

"I thought you'd never ask," Holly replied jubilantly.

"Holly!" Bethany reprimanded, "Alyssa's here with her friends." Then, turning to her friend, she said, "That's okay, Alyssa. We can hang out another day. I don't want to, you know, intrude on…"

"What? Nonsense. I *want* to be with you all," Alyssa assured Bethany.

"Of course you do," Holly exclaimed. "Bye-bye people. Later!"

"Holly!" Bethany again rebuked her little sister.

"That's okay, Beth, I don't mind. I was getting bored and feeling ignored anyway. I don't speak Allianzi and I always feel locked inside myself when my schoolmates converse in their strange language. Just give me a second." Alyssa then proceeded to say goodbye to her friends and make her exit from the group.

As the three began to walk over to Claire, Holly reached into her light coat pocket and pulled out a little hand-made, colored envelope. Handing it to Alyssa, she said, "Here, it's from my brother…to you."

"What?" Alyssa replied, a bit confused, as she accepted the odd item.

"Actually, she made it, herself," explained Bethany.

"Shhhhh!" said Holly. "Just open it, girl."

Going along, Alyssa opened the already slightly crinkly envelope, which revealed another improvised, colorful note. "Hmm...a Valentine. Thanks, that's so sweet," said Alyssa, looking at Holly. The note showed Zeke's and Alyssa's names inside a heart with an arrow through it.

"Don't thank me. I'm just the messenger," Holly insisted.

"What in the world? Don't mind her, Alyssa," said Bethany, feeling incensed with her sister's petulance.

"That's okay. I *don't* mind." Then she added, looking at Holly, "I think the messenger is weaving together something sneaky. Isn't she?"

"Crafty little one," said Claire, as she joined them.

"But it's true, Momma!" Holly yelled out.

"Never you mind!" her mother cautioned her.

"Come, you guys, let me buy you a treat," Alyssa said.

"Oh, honey, that's quite all right. We're fine," Claire replied.

"It's not a problem, Ms. Christensen. I've got plenty of medallianz on my Cognit Bracelet. Really...it would be my pleasure."

"Please, Mommy, pleeeease!" Holly begged.

"Oh, all right. Thank you. It's very kind of you, Alyssa. But just get some for the girls. I'll have a little taste from theirs," Claire said. They then moved back toward the food court, Holly running ahead, as was the usual thing, toward the ice-cream stand.

"Yippee, ice cream!" Holly cried out.

Fourteen

Psychology?

Meanwhile, on the 13th floor, Christensen and Zeke were finally being called in, after waiting for over an hour, to see the psychologist. Feeling somewhat apprehensive, they briefly prayed together, and then walked past the receptionist's desk, making their way toward the unoccupied consultation room. As they reached the room, they entered and sat down to wait for the doctor. The ambiance was pleasant enough; soothing soft lighting, well-appointed leather furniture, including the quintessential divan. There were a number of expensive-looking art pieces well placed throughout the room and up on the walls. One could also hardly miss the myriad of certificates and framed diplomas, perfectly arranged on the wall across from where they sat. A plaque on the large doctor's desk read, "Isaac J. Ibrahim, Ph.D."

As the doctor entered the room, both Christensen and Zeke started to get up.

"You're fine," the doctor said, gesturing for them to remain seated. "I'm Dr. Ibrahim." Then, Looking at the holographic chart via his PSS, the doctor uttered, "Let's see… Ezekiel Michael Christensen, male, age 15. I assume that's you, young man," he said, looking at Zeke.

"Yes, sir," Zeke answered nervously, as he noticed the implant on the doctor's forehead.

"There's no need to be nervous, Ezekiel," the doctor reassured him in a deep, calm voice.

"Actually, doctor," Christensen interjected, "he goes by Zeke."

"Thank you, Mr. Christensen. I'll make a note of that. But I think the boy's old enough to speak for himself."

The doctor then proceeded to ask a series of mainly family and medical background questions on Zeke, which Christensen was able to help answer. He also inquired as to the reasons why they were seeking psychological help for the boy.

Once satisfied with the gathering of preliminary client information, the doctor's next request caught Christensen rather off guard.

"Mr. Christensen, I will need to be alone with your son for a few minutes. I need to chat with him without his being too anxious to speak in front of you. This is absolutely essential for a proper assessment of his condition. You may return to the reception lobby, and I will have my staff call you back in again, when it is time."

Feeling a bit unsettled, Christensen replied, "Uhh, sure, that... that's fine. Zeke, I'll be right out there, in the waiting room. Don't worry, all right?"

"Okay, Dad," Zeke stammered, betraying his unease.

After fifteen or so minutes had passed, a staff member announced that Christensen could return to the consultation room. Anxious about the wait, he quickly got up and headed down the hallway, to rejoin his son.

"Please, sit down, Mr. Christensen," the doctor instructed.

"Hi, Dad," Zeke said, looking at his father with evident confusion in his eyes.

"Mr. Christensen, I've had a bit of a chat with your son, and I would like to recommend a referral to a psychiatrist colleague of mine," the doctor informed him. "He's a very good doctor, and will be able to take care of your son's condition."

"But, wait a minute. What's this? What's the matter?" Christensen questioned.

"Mr. Christensen, this is a complex issue, and I hesitate to fully disclose the details at this time. Your son needs a full psychiatric evaluation. The specialist will be able to more adequately discuss with you this young man's diagnosis and prognosis after treatment."

"I'm sorry, doctor, but I brought my son here to get some answers, and so far you've kept me completely in the dark. This is my son we're talking about," Christensen asserted.

"Mr. Christensen, I can see you are troubled and disturbed by this development, but I can assure you, this is common procedure. What I am recommending is the very best medically advised course of action for your son," the doctor replied.

"It may be common procedure to you, but you will have to forgive me, doctor, it surely is not common to us. I will ask you one more time. Exactly what is wrong with my son?" Christensen pressed him.

Removing his glasses from his face, the doctor looked at Christensen with obvious contempt and offered a distressing, if harsh, remark, seemingly ignoring Zeke's presence in the room.

"Sir, your son's condition is beyond psychological manipulation. He has clearly been suffering from delusion-induced sleep disorder, which, if left untreated by a high combination dose of new generation psychotropic and anti-psychotic medications, could deteriorate into a serious and irreversible mental disturbance. I have neither the time nor the inclination to discuss this any further with you. I will be submitting my report to the physician to whom I am referring you, and he can help you from there."

Feeling rather defensive by now, Christensen forcefully replied, "You have got to be kidding me! My son's a normal kid. He's just been having a little trouble in his sleep. I know my son, and I will not stand by and watch you subject him to this humiliating and unnecessary process." At that, Zeke began to beseech his father to refrain from arguing and just leave the premises with him.

"Mr. Christensen, let me be perfectly clear," the doctor said, attempting to diffuse some of the tension. "You are probably unaware of this. However, and most unfortunately, there seems to be a growing number of these cases worldwide, which show great similarity to what your son has been experiencing. They are happening with increasing frequency and, thus far, it appears that only non-implanted children are being affected." The doctor then added, "I will be honest with you. I would strongly suggest, and I am confident that my colleague will concur, that the only alternative to this intensive line of treatment, is to have the boy imminently implanted. Cognit implants have conclusively been shown to significantly reduce symptoms of mental illness, once activated. That is probably your best route at this time. And it would be most neglectful on your part, as the parent responsible for Zeke, to ignore his serious problem," warned the doctor.

"That is absurd! You have no idea, doctor, what you are condemning my son to," Christensen cried out.

Indeed, Christensen had every reason for alarm. For what he dreaded, and what Claire had earlier avoided addressing with her girls, was that Believer's implantation was not only forbidden on spiritual grounds, but he also feared that it would have critically damaging physical ramifications, as well. The Resistance rightly surmised that a true Believer's body – as opposed to those who evidenced their unbelief by apostatizing, or those who came to believe sometime after implantation – upon receiving an implant, would violently reject it, and would most assuredly undergo instant physical shut down. This meant that, Zeke, if implanted, would continue to exist, but in an indefinite and possibly permanent state of coma.

"We're leaving at once. This was a terrible idea," Christensen said, then exclaiming, "This is quackery of the worst kind!" Zeke and a very altered Christensen then stormed out of the office, and toward the elevators.

"Miss Mandy," Dr. Ibrahim said in Allianzi, contacting his office assistant, "Get me central law enforcement on my PSS… That's right…D.C. Command. And get me an appointment at the local Transcienz Hall for today, if at all possible. I am going to need it." When a connection was made, he proceeded to report in Allianzi, "This is Dr. Isaac J. Ibrahim, registration number 60916. I wish to file a report here in the South… Another peculiar non-implant 'dreamer' case… Yes… Ezekiel Michael Christensen… No, with an 'en'… Yes, I am submitting his history and profile… Yes… Goodbye."

As Zeke and his father looked for Claire and the girls at the shopping complex, in order to go home, Christensen said to his son, "Zeke, don't be worried, son. Forgive us for this horrendous mistake. We felt so rushed in getting you some help, and we messed up terribly. We'll take care of you, son. Trust me, we will."

"Dad, are all psychologists like that?" Zeke asked, reacting to the traumatic experience.

"Son, I've met some fine psychologists in my time. I even took some classes at the old Faith&Knowledge U. with some cool psychology professors. This one psychologist in particular, however, does not make the list. Let's just leave it at that," Christensen stated, trying to soothe his son.

Back at home, the Christensens sat down for a difficult and long delayed family conversation regarding the grave spiritual and bodily consequences of Believers implantation. Later, still struggling to process the incident at the psychologist's office, Christensen and Claire felt paralyzed with angst, and so they sought comfort from their Lord and each other, entirely unaware at that point that what was about to happen would shine a new light on their quandary.

That night, Zeke experienced another intense, restless dream. This time, however, the words were coming clearer and the episode's duration more extensive. Claire and Christensen watched their son in disbelief. Talking while dreaming, their son was seemingly uttering the words, almost in their entirety, to the long, and virtually lost canonical book of Isaiah, from its beginning to that point. At that moment, they knew… This was not a mental problem. Perhaps, this was a sign from The Name, they immediately inferred.

In complete amazement, Claire whispered to Christensen, "Tanner, I believe Zeke may be dreaming in the Spirit." Christensen remained speechless for a few seconds. Then, being reminded of the very words from his own strange dream, just days before, he said, "Don't awaken him, Claire. Let him dream."

"Zeke needs to know," Claire said in a sober, calm voice.

"Yes…he does. We'll sit down with him when he wakes up, tomorrow. We'll need to explain it to the girls, as well… I think the sooner we tell them, the better. Maybe before we leave for worship in the morning."

"What *can* we tell them, Tanner? We still don't know why this is happening to him," Claire remarked.

"I know. But they at least need to know that their brother is not just getting sick," Christensen replied. "If this is from The Name, then I know sooner or later He'll enable us to discern why Zeke is receiving His Word in dreams. I also need to tell John about it tomorrow."

"Tanner, this seems like a wonderful and awesome, supernatural gift. But it's also so frightening. I don't understand it all… I feel scared for Zeke and for us, but at the same time, so incredibly blessed," Claire confessed.

"Me, too. But we mustn't give into fear, neither for Zeke, nor for ourselves. I feel that somehow this is His amazing grace given to us, and perhaps a much-needed blessing, right now… Claire, think of it. Can we even grasp this? It's the Word of Truth entering the world again. What an encouragement this will certainly be for our entire community, especially at a time like this, when we desperately need encouragement and strength from Him. Pray with me right now, Claire," said Christensen.

Joining their hands together, Christensen prayed, "Lord, give us spiritual eyes to see the awesome way in which your Spirit is moving, through our son, for the edification of your people. And give us abiding grace to know how to minister to each other in these uncertain times. Watch over us and keep us safe. We ask, too, Lord, that as peril grows, your right hand of protection and peace be upon our community in a powerful way, especially at the gathering, tomorrow night. We pray this in the matchless name of your Son, the Anointed One. Amen."

Fifteen

Word of Vanishings

Feeling perplexed and unable to sleep in the early Sunday hours, Christensen returned to his bunker, only to realize an unusual flurry of communication activity being directed at him. As he tried to access the content of the encrypted messages, he realized that they were all from the same source in the Resistance. To his dismay, the messages had failed to fully transmit via the crumbling digital network, a fact that explained the multiple attempts. Despite the reprocessing of the content by the descrambling program, only certain portions of text had been successfully retrieved and displayed on the screen...

> "Tanne... serie... Brethre... famil... vanishi... glob... Provinc... possib... Federa... watch ou... dangero... Urgen... Daria... mov... sout... bless... C."

The messages appeared to Christensen to have been sent earlier in the day, but their ultimate delivery had probably been intentionally delayed until evening, likely due to the expected decrease in CyberSat's monitoring capabilities at night. In trying to piece it together, the broken up text appeared to Christensen to be another warning from me, his old mentor. It seemed to him to concern some sort of strange vanishings of entire families among the Community of Brethren in various parts of the world. My message to Christensen in fact urgently referred to some sort of looming operations in the southern region, led by the American Marshall. In some sense, the two pieces of information looked to be causally related. Perhaps the kidnappings were only the most recent tactic by the Federation, as police forces continued their offensive operations against the Resistance.

"Sensei, what is this you're trying to alert us to?" Christensen wondered, as he struggled to make sense of the forewarning.

In Washington D.C., an attentive Dariah and a room-full of members of her executive cabinet were being debriefed early on a series of disappearance cases being reported out of provinces in all populated continents, including North America. One of her chief intelligence deputies had been extensively profiling some of the occurrences.

"Commander, based on CyberSat's Data-Realm, which is being updated every hour on the hour, we're finding no apparent logic or explicatory pattern to these vanishings, except for the fact that they involve non-implanted families."

"Where?" she demanded to know.

"Just this week, we've received intelligence from the provinces of Canada, China, Singapore, India, several in Europe, including Romania, Slovakia, and Britain. Also the provinces of Senegal and Uganda, Brazil and Uruguay, and, most recently, Belize, not to mention our own American Province, just to name a few. As you can see, these are widespread, indeed."

"How many in all?" Dariah asked.

"We estimate, so far, around 58, with 55 confirmed," the deputy answered. He then went on to further report, "We have also been able to confirm with help from local law enforcement and Federation officials that, without exception, these disappearances involve the constituents of the Community of Brethren found in these provinces. The incidents have been increasing in their frequency, and we have managed to positively track them to as far back as two weeks ago. We believe that whoever's carrying out these disappearances is a rather recent player."

"You're telling me that this is rampant, but we know nothing about who's behind it. How can this be?" Marshall Dariah sternly reproached her officer. "How do we know these aren't our own secret operations in these provinces?"

"Commander, we find absolutely no logs tagging such operations," the deputy responded.

"Let's not be so naïve, deputy. The Federation has been running indirect surveillance and covert operations on this group for years, focusing on known Resistance movement hotbeds. Places like Israel and Lebanon, Brazil, Italy, Romania, and more recently Turkey, have been our continuous foci of activity for our stealth units for quite some time now."

"Sir," the deputy replied referring to Marshall Dariah, as she demanded to be addressed, rather than ma'am, "with all due respect, unless my clearance level, high as it is, precludes me from being privy to these cloaked C-OPS, I have compelling reasons to conclude that these are not Federation interventions."

"I see... And what reasons might these be, deputy?" Dariah probed.

"Sir, our office has been contacted by Paris," he informed.

"The Allianz Palace?" she exclaimed. "Does anyone else in this room have prior knowledge of this?" she said, confronting her cabinet members and officers present there. Their heads shaking timidly, one of them replied, "Negative, sir."

"Commander Dariah," the senior deputy continued.

"Speak!" she said impatiently.

"Recently, the Prosecutor General also has directly inquired with our intelligence apparatus regarding the vanishings in our own province. He will want to address these with you upon his official visit to D.C., in a few days. He, too, seems to have no reliable data on who's behind this. He also desires to address with you the bizarre reports alleging non-implant children having some sort of ancient scripture-related dreams."

"That's just great!" Dariah yelled out in repugnant response, as she stood up, fists pounding on the long conference table. In furious countenance, she looked up, speechless.

"Your orders, Commander," the deputy requested.

"Out! Everybody, out! Now!" Dariah bellowed explosively. Without hesitation, the mob quickly maneuvered all around the large room and collectively headed toward the double-door exits. "You, deputy, stay!"

"Yes, sir," he replied.

"I want to know every move that Horn and the delegation make from now until the time when they arrive here. Every move," Dariah ordered. "Am I making myself perfectly clear?"

"Yes, sir. Affirmative," the deputy answered.

"One more thing. At 16:00 hours, I want a meeting with the entire tactical operations division in charge of southern cog operations. I'm not taking any chances with these clowns down South. I want mounted attacks on the main Resistance mobilizations down there. Let's get these praying fools either arrested or sent permanently scrambling for cover. Their days are numbered, and you can stake my reputation on it. I *will* not accept failure. Not with Horn's visit now just days away... Or my name is not Misha Dariah."

"Yes, Commander. We'll be ready at 16:00 hours," said the senior deputy.

"Dismissed."

"Yes, sir." He then saluted Dariah and departed.

Sixteen

Zeke and Alyssa

Early that Sunday afternoon, following the morning worship service, a mixture of excitement and fretfulness filled the air at the Christensen's home. The Brethren Gathering was looming large, but so were the uncertainties stemming from the ominous message that Christensen had partially decoded earlier that morning. Christensen, himself, had stayed behind after the morning worship gathering, to meet with John and the Children of the Promise group, in preparation for the event. Claire and the kids had gone home, and she got busy, working through a considerable batch of Visuals, in an attempt to finalize the mobilization goals for that evening. While Holly played upstairs, Bethany, too, was making a final few strategic contacts, from home, with other youth with whom she had had prior communication regarding the gathering. Much to her disappointment, she had not yet been able to reach Alyssa. During intervals between Visual contacts, Bethany took time to practice her songs for later that night.

Zeke had been charged with passing out ribbons, which announced brief details about the big nocturnal event. That afternoon, after a short soccer practice with other teens from the Children of the Promise group, he was walking the halls of a local hospital, distributing the colorful reminders to anyone who showed interest in that sort of "cultural" soirée. Most serious takers were non-implants, although an occasional implanted youth would show interest and would take a ribbon. Implanted adults seldom would motion to receive an invite. Any vestige of a religious activity, any whiff of a spiritual happening other than Transcienz-related assemblies, even if veiled as a social event, aroused suspicions, and tended to repulse most implanted individuals of mature age. By now, Zeke, a veteran mobilizing agent, had gotten used to these dynamics and took rejection in stride.

As Zeke exited the hospital and headed toward the WormRail station to catch a ride home, he was followed. For roughly the last hour, in fact, his every move had been watched from a distance. As he approached the escalator leading down to the WormRail port, someone intercepted him.

"Stop! What are you doing?" As Zeke turned around to identify the person speaking, he was caught completely off guard.

"Alyssa!" Zeke exclaimed, rather surprised and a bit shaken. "Wow, you startled me."

"I can see that," she said. "I'm sorry. I didn't mean to scare you. I'm just curious about what it is that you're doing with those things."

"These? They're ribbons," Zeke inadequately explained.

"I can see that, too. But what are they for? Why are you handing them out, like that?"

"Been spying on me, have you?" Zeke countered.

"Well, let's just say I'm doing research," she replied. "I'm sort of intrigued by what you and your family do for your faith community."

"Here. Have one. You'll understand," he said, handing her a bright red ribbon.

"For me?" Alyssa said, taking the ribbon and then attempting a cursory reading of it.

"Yeah. It's for tonight. Will you be there?" Zeke asked.

"I don't know, I... Your sister mentioned it to me, and I'm still thinking about it. I really need to talk to my mom, first," she replied hesitantly.

"If you really want to know what we're all about, then you must see for yourself what we do when we come together with our community. I'm sure that if you come, you'll find it a moving experience. The play is so powerful, and John will really speak to your heart. It's not something I can easily convey in words," Zeke explained.

"Well, I've got some time. Why don't I come along with you now, and you tell me more about it. Are you headed back home?" Alyssa inquired.

"Yep, I am," Zeke told her. "Let's catch the shuttle first, and then we can talk some more. Just don't make us miss our stop," he teased her.

"Don't worry. I haven't messed up, yet," she assured him.

"Swear?" Zeke replied, getting back a serious stare.

The two then proceeded down the escalator and got ready to board a WormRail shuttle to go home, in the next exurban ring, a few stops away.

"Here, I can get this fast. I can use my bracelet," said Alyssa, referring to the automatic payment for the shuttle.

"That's all right, you don't have to. I've got my pass card. Thanks, anyway," Zeke replied.

"Okay," she said, signaling for him to go ahead. "Zeke, I think I'll stop by at your place a little later...to see Bethany," Alyssa remarked, insinuating a smile.

"To see Bethany... Sure," responded Zeke.

Getting off at the right stop, they exited the underground station and parted ways. In that moment, as Zeke watched Alyssa leave and head home, he began to feel something he had never experienced before. Fighting off every impulse to run after her, he felt a warming sensation that was exhilarating and sickening, at the same time. Managing to turn away and walk home, he realized Alyssa's perfume still lingered in the air, like an intoxicatingly sweet aroma. Closing his eyes, he stopped and dwelt in the moment, hoping that his brain would hang on to that fragrance long after his nose had forgotten it. Soon realizing how strangely he was acting, he opened his eyes and took off for home.

Sometime later, the Christensen girls were preparing for Alyssa's arrival. Holly announced, "I'm going to go wait for her outside."

"Wait, young lady," Claire admonished. "You'll have to put on your jacket, first. The temperature seems to be dropping quickly and it's starting to get really cold out, especially for this time of year. And bring your sister with you, will you please?"

"Yes, ma'am," Holly answered.

"Mom, can you believe Alyssa's coming tonight?" Bethany said, excitedly.

"I've been praying for her," Claire replied. "Her mother seemed to be pretty okay with it on the PSS, a while ago. Not the least bit worried or threatened by her coming along with us. She had a few questions about it, but then she politely conceded. I find her to be unusually cordial with us. So different from what we've gotten used to from implants in the neighborhood, lately."

"When do we leave for the gathering, tonight, Mom?" Bethany asked.

"Well, I'm still waiting to hear from your father," her mother informed her, "but I'm guessing around 6:30, right after supper."

"Great! That gives us plenty of time to plan for our slumber party," said Bethany.

"Excuse me, but when was *I* consulted on this?" her mom questioned her.

"Mom, you said I could, if I promised to clean up my room and keep it really neat for a whole week," Bethany reminded her. " I'm doing pretty good so far, and on Wednesday it will have been a week. So pleeease, Mom, can we?"

"I guess that's right. I do remember now. You can go ahead with your slumber party plans," her mother said.

"Thanks, Mom. Besides, Alyssa's mom's leaving town on Wednesday for one night, on a work trip or something, and it will work out great for her to have Alyssa come stay with us that night. I can't wait to tell her we're on for the slumber party, *and* to show her my latest Beatles acquisition from Shen-il this morning. I'm crazy about their sound. They really spark!" Bethany reveled.

"Slumber party?" shrieked Holly, "a most delightful idea, my dear sis..."

"Oh, no, you don't," Bethany said. "This is for big girls only."

"My thoughts, exactly. When shall I be there?" Holly responded, trying to sound grown up.

"Mom, please…" Bethany appealed, in light of Holly's insistence.

"Holly," Claire intervened, "you and I will make plans of our own for Wednesday night. How about popcorn and a movie?"

"Ooooh, goody! With coke and M&Ms, too, like old times?" Holly suggested, raising her heels and rubbing her hands together, in visible corporal inflexion.

"Sure, honey. Just let me make certain that we can get some."

"Oh, I hope, I hope, I hope…" Holly said, in buoyant cheer.

"C'mon, Holly, let's go outside to wait for Alyssa. She should be here real soon," prompted Bethany.

"Hey, does Zeke know yet that she's coming?" Holly said, amusing herself.

"I'm sure he does. He's been in the shower forever…" Bethany played along.

"Girls…" their mother reproved them, "you behave."

"All right. We will, Mom," the two girls agreed.

Seventeen

Dariah's Plan Conceived

At 4 p.m. sharp, in the White House's Situation Room, Marshall Dariah convened with her tactical operations division, which coordinated cog interventions in the southern region. More details were shared about the Resistance mobilizations, including the specific repertoire of "social" and "cultural" activities that were becoming widespread, and which presented the most direct threat to the Allianz Code, by virtue of their effectiveness in subverting the targeted populace. Dariah listened attentively to the entire briefing, while she mentally calculated the best plan for disrupting and, ultimately, defeating the Resistance.

"How well armed are they?" she queried.

"Commander," answered the Colonel who provided the strategic overview, "we have no evidence whatsoever of any significant weapons arsenals or arms stockpiles being used by these groups. In fact, gathered intelligence indicates that their usual security apparatus is very rudimentary, involving no more than a small contingent of roving volunteers, carrying walkie-talkies, flashlights, and occasionally some pepper-spray."

"How curious," Dariah facetiously commented. "Go on."

"Sir, they tend to be grouped two-by-two, and oftentimes they are father-son teams, casually walking around the perimeter of the gathering facilities. We believe, sir, there may possibly be a couple of small caliber, traditional firearms present among the members, but that is highly variable and mostly hearsay. To our knowledge, there has never been any violent attempt to oppose us, neither here, nor abroad. The Resistance has continued to maintain a peaceful, non-violent stance throughout their campaign."

"So, they are practically defenseless. Is that what you're telling me, Colonel?" Dariah mockingly pressed him on it.

"Yes, sir. It appears so."

"Does anyone else have anything to add to this? I am findings this a bit too easy." Dariah inquired.

"Yes, sir," said another officer, as she prepared to project for the assembled group a holographic dossier of specific items of interest. "We have prepared a brief profile on a number of possible targets of special import to us, as well as on leading Resistance agents operating in this region." As she scrolled down through the displayed items, she added, "As you can see, Commander, the list is sizeable, but by no means do these groups constitute in the aggregate a formidable opponent. Over here, we have the most active cells, and these names, in particular, come up as key coordinators of the so called, Brethren Gatherings."

"Are we prepared to step in and take them all out in one major offensive?" Dariah asked.

"Commander, I would advise a great deal of caution in this," said the ranking General at the meeting. "Although these are significant targets, we do not want to generate too much attention via a massive and widespread mobilization, at least until we can be certain that strong evidence of subversive activity can be amassed for justification." Then he recommended, "I favor well-studied and more incisive operations that have the potential of sending a strong message and shockwaves throughout the Resistance strongholds."

"What do you suggest, General?" she followed.

"Sergeant, project regional map, please..." he requested. "Sir, this being Sunday, their holy day, we have been alerted about three or so major events this evening, mobilizing a few thousand people, each. One of them is to take place right here," he pointed, "in this exurban region of the larger mega-metropolitan district of Memphis, Tennessee, called Midville... Another one right here, just outside of the Atlanta mega-region... And one more, over here, located in the central district of Charlotte, North Carolina. There are a number of smaller events going on throughout the region, but these are expected to attract at least a thousand or more newcomers, each."

"I see. Thank you, General," Dariah said.

As the American Marshall sat for a moment, staring at the large display, the room fell into a haunting silence. The only sound evidencing was the gentle humming of the holographic projector, and the occasional nervous clearing of one's throat. Suddenly, Dariah broke out into an eerie laughter, but stopped herself abruptly, utterly puzzling all who were present there. As she proceeded to give out detailed instructions, the ranking General positioned himself to accurately capture her words, in precise dictation.

"I want three cog units," she instructed. "Only about two hundred cogs each, separately targeting these locations you've identified here. I want them lightly armed and able to move swiftly, but pre-warned to call for backup, when the arresting process begins. Have these units arrive several minutes into their programs, but well before the expected high point of the events. I want our troops to position themselves so as to create a hermetic seal around the premises. No one is to come in or out from that point on, until we move in. If their security puts up any resistance, I want them subdued and apprehended. If they offer armed opposition, take them out quickly, any way you have to. I don't want to fool around with a drawn out exchange of fire. Then, have all power cut off immediately, and all communications to and from these locations completely interrupted. At that point, the commanding officers will announce the maneuver to the crowd, and warn against any false moves by the Resistance. Do you follow, General," Dariah confirmed. She then continued with her master plan, "At that point, the cogs will move in, to meticulously process the crowd. First, separate implants from non-implants. And then, carefully produce evidence of *any* religious content you can find in their programs. Collect and secure any evidence of infraction against the Allianz Code. We know it will be there. That will serve as undeniable justification for the arrests. Then have their leaders identified. If they cowardly refuse to pronounce themselves, just round up any and all non-implanted adults, and apprehend them for interrogation at the local police precinct by a team of special cog agents."

"Commander, what about their facilities?" asked the General.

"Burn them down. I want them gone. And then," she added, "I want the real-time images on our province-wide media, with CyberSat feed to our subsidiaries abroad. It will send a clear message to any other group planning to pull similar religious stunts."

"Yes, Commander. We'll run some model simulations and study them on-screen. We'll then dispatch and coordinate all maneuvers from our central operations room, here in D.C.," replied the General.

"Make darn sure you time this correctly. I want no mistakes. Is that absolutely clear, General?" Dariah yelled out, as she left the Situation Room and headed straight to the Oval Office.

"Affirmative, Commander," he answered, as he followed behind her.

"In the meantime, I'm going to study this Resistance data more carefully. I want to gain intimate knowledge about these key names among the Resistance cadres, and be able to debrief the Prosecutor General on them, when he and the Allianz delegation arrive, on Wednesday."

"Yes, sir. May we have your permission to put this plan into effect immediately?" asked the General.

The Marshall offered no immediate answer. Entering her office, Dariah walked toward one of the windows, behind her Oval Office desk. Gazing upward through the window, and with her back toward the General, she sternly said, "I *will* be looking forward to your report this evening. Now, go and execute my orders… And don't you and your cogs dare disappoint me, General."

Eighteen

A Foreboding Message

As the time to depart for the gathering that evening was fast approaching, there was still no sign of Christensen. Worried, Claire attempted to contact him once more via her PSS. "Rats! Tanner's PSS must need recharging, again," she figured, after being unable to reach him for the third or fourth time that afternoon.

Minutes later, Christensen at long last arrived home, but quite more tardily than expected. He and many others had indeed had a long day of preparation for the big gathering that evening.

"Hi, honey. Sorry, I know I'm terribly late," Christensen apologized.

"Well, there must be a good reason for it," Claire rationalized.

"Yeah," he said, "There was a lot we had to work on with the sound and other technical concerns. I also had to help John, who got hung up with all of the arrangements for busing, and car-pooling, and other transportation needs, especially for those needing a ride out to the land from the WormRail station. It was a nightmare. Plus, the temperature seems to be dropping a lot this evening. And now, on top of it all, it looks like we might even get snow, if you can believe it."

"Snow? Are you sure about that?" Claire replied, surprised.

"I'm not sure of anything, at this point."

"Oh, that's all right, honey. Don't worry too much about it. I did try to visualize you a number of times earlier on, but I figured your PSS was in need of a recharge, or something," Claire said.

"You're right. My charge was too low and so I turned my PSS off. But I think what it really needs is some upgrading. Unfortunately, this is the last PSS model before they switched to the implant protocol. I really need to look at it sometime soon, and maybe see what I can do to it, myself. Perhaps, later tonight," Christensen said. "I know it's late, but I really have to run downstairs to the bunker and check whether any recent communication has come through. I'm feeling really unsettled about tonight."

"I thought you might be feeling that way. I'm feeling uneasy about it, too. When I talked with Shen-il this morning, she told me she had sent word out about the need for everyone to bring extra candles tonight, in case of a forced blackout or other power disruption," Claire reported.

"Great. It makes good sense to try and stay ahead of the curve, especially since the latest rash of Federation-forced power failures at Resistance gatherings elsewhere." Christensen replied.

"I know, just last week, out East, remember?" Claire recalled. Then she commented, "Honey, I'm really not trying to make you feel even more rushed, but do you think you'll still be able to get ready on time for all of us to leave together? The kids and I already ate."

"Sure. I've just got to run downstairs quick, and then I'll go get cleaned up in a hurry, and before you know it, I'll be ready to go," he affirmed. "But if you would, could you fix me just a small bite to eat?" Christensen requested.

"Peanut-butter and jelly sandwich, okay? Or else, I could quick heat up some leftovers," Claire checked with him.

"Uhh...I'll just take the sandwich, thanks," Christensen replied, as he hastened to head down to the basement.

Upon arriving at his bunker, Christensen noticed his screen indicating some recent system activity. As he accessed the incoming messages, it was evident to him that they mainly consisted of a series of graphic files, sent from abroad, by DiPaoli.

"What's this?" he wondered, as he read the decrypted text.

"Tanner, things are definitely taking a dark turn here in the French Province. I fear I've stumbled upon something truly diabolical, that I am sure wasn't for me to know. They may very possibly

be implanting Believers, too, against their will. I overheard something about coma chambers in large catacombs, but I cannot be sure what all of it is about. I think they may be coming after me, now. I'm copying you on these files. Please guard them, for they may someday help explain all of this. Be well, my brother. Tomazo."

As Christensen glanced at the first snapshots, he was horrified. The distressing images appeared to depict a recent cog intervention at a Brethren Gathering DiPaoli had evidently attended, very possibly in the capital district of Paris. The subject of a number of them was clearly focused on a man sitting on a folding chair, bound and gagged. Other images portrayed another male individual being questioned by a uniformed man and possibly being tortured by cogs. A few other pictures seemed unrelated to the first several and captured the ongoing construction or re-outfitting of a number of Transcienz Halls in numerous locations worldwide.

Suddenly, the screen alerted: *"Message Transmission Interrupted."*

"Tomazo… What's happened?" Christensen said to himself.

Extremely concerned, he uttered a prayer on behalf of his friend. He then copied the data onto a disk. As he walked across the bunker from where his desk was located, toward the hidden safe deposit, he could feel tremors spreading throughout his body. The short distance he had habitually covered countless times before, appeared to him elongated. As he tunneled toward the opposite wall, Christensen's awareness of time changed, as he felt things slowing down.

Even as he placed the recorded evidence inside the wall vault, covered by a large, wooden sliding bookshelf, he sensed fear paralyzing him. Images of a possible cog intervention that very evening flashed through his mind. The terrified faces of his wife and children, and thoughts of violence, generalized chaos, and ultimately the real chance of arrests being made that night, played before his fixed eyes over and over again, as if his conscious mind were being besieged by an enemy aerial assault.

Like a breaking tidal wave, Christensen realized, DiPaoli's message brought over him a deeply disconcerting crash of reality to now long held fears he had desperately been trying to resist and avoid, not only for the sake of his own sanity, but also for that of the already fragile tranquility of his wife and kids. But to forsake his loved ones now, by surrendering to fright, would be most damaging to their tenuous security and wellbeing. He had to somehow search for inner strength. He needed to choose to stay calm and trust in the reliable promises his own faith offered him. As he reluctantly closed his eyes, he experienced his thoughts shifting to the comforting ancient words from the Apostle Paul to young Timothy, "For The Name has not given us a spirit of fear, but of power and of love and of a sound mind." Once again, he was reminded of the supernatural resources and power available to him. His whole body then began to relax. Like a stream of fresh air blowing against the familiar stuffiness and musty odor of his bunker, yet another well-known Scripture verse he had memorized long ago, from the book of Joshua, came rushing in, "Have I not commanded you? Be strong and of good courage; do not be afraid, nor be dismayed, for The Name, your Lord, will be with you wherever you go."

As Christensen briefly meditated on these words, there was once again peace. Though momentary, it was enough to enable him to regain his strength, take a deep breath, and go forward. Watching the mechanical movement of his feet, one in front of the other, he climbed up the stairs to ready himself for the momentous Children of the Promise gathering. "Help us, Lord," he pleaded out loud.

Nineteen

The *Evangel*

While Christensen was getting ready, the others began convening downstairs, until they were all gathered around the always-busy eat-in kitchen table. Their thoughts were mainly on Alyssa, and for entirely different reasons. Holly wanted to be sure she would be able to sit next to Alyssa during the event. Bethany felt a bit nervous, hoping against her friend's possible discomfort, or perhaps even disgust, with the whole experience, no doubt so strange and new to her in so many different ways. Claire's concern was for Alyssa's peace of mind, knowing that in all likelihood many important questions of deep spiritual significance were still left unanswered. Zeke struggled quietly, feeling a mixture of embarrassment and a growing but still awkward desire to just be near her. But at that moment, it was Claire who was to reach out to the implanted young lady.

As soon as Alyssa arrived, Claire approached her and cautiously probed, "Alyssa, sweetie, is there anything you'd like to ask regarding tonight?"

"No, ma'am, not really," she replied. "I'm fine. But I did bring something I wanted to give to you…" Alyssa said, grabbing a plastic bag filled with groceries she had sitting by her feet, under the table. "Here, I hope you don't mind." Realizing what that gesture signified, Claire asked, with evident emotional trembling in her voice, "What, what's this, honey?"

"It's nothing, Mrs. Christensen. My mom and I just wanted to help out a little," Alyssa said. "I do hope you'll be fine with it. Think of it as just a thank you gift for…for everything."

With tears welling up, Claire took the bag and gently sat it on the table. Slowly wiping a tear off her face and struggling not to disclose the range of sorrowful emotions she was all at once experiencing at that moment, Claire took a deep breath. Her eyes then momentarily glanced down at the items inside the bag. Then she exhaled, unable to fully hide her lament in a mixture of brief sobbing and nervous smile.

"I…I don't know what to say," Claire responded, in a whisper, "but, thank you, dear. Thank you so very much…and may The Name bless you and your mother. Please be sure to thank her for me."

"You're very welcome. And don't worry, I'll let Mom know how you appreciated the gifts."

"Mom, don't cry. Your make-up's gonna run," Bethany said.

"Yes, what little I have on…" Claire agreed, trying hard to present a smile.

"Look, Momma, there's M&Ms and some coke in here! Awesome!" cheered Holly, as she explored all of the precious contents found inside the bag. "Wow! Graham crackers and marshmallows…and look, chocolate bars!"

"I thought you might like some s'mores!" Alyssa mentioned.

"Like them? I live for them!" the thrilled nine-year old answered. "Thank *you*!"

As Claire then began to put the food items away, Alyssa uttered, "Mrs. Christensen, if you don't mind, I guess I do have kind of a big question…"

"Yes?"

"Well… Other than the fact that I'm a single child of a single mom, you all seem so much like us, in most every way. I mean, you seem like normal, sensible people. Not…you know…fanatics," Alyssa went on.

"Why, thank you, dear," Claire said, in light self-amusement.

"What I mean is, we live in the same nice neighborhood," Alyssa said, "You and Mr. Christensen are well educated. He's had a nice job and both of you seem to believe in working hard, but also having fun. And you all seem like you care about similar things as us, like your children, their education, their well-being. You believe in doing good to others, as we do." She then continued, "You do have different beliefs than us, which I'm learning about, and so far find quite virtuous and respectable, but..." Alyssa paused, struggling to find the right words.

"Uhuh..." Claire answered after a few seconds of awkward silence, and as she listened intently to Alyssa's heart.

"Well... You don't... That is, you've rejected the implant. Isn't that right?"

"Um...yes, that's correct."

"But...why?" Alyssa asked, "I mean, I just want to understand why you're choosing to go through so much hardship for things as basic as getting good food, and proper medical care, and other necessities, like work, because you refuse to be implanted."

"Well, that's a very good question, Alyssa. A big question, indeed. I...I'm afraid a proper answer would take longer than we have time for, right now. But, um...I'll make an attempt," Claire said, as her kids paid close attention to the exchange.

"Great," Alyssa replied.

"This is quite unexpected. But it's fine. It's really fine, dear... Let's see, now. Where do I begin?" Claire said. "All right. Here we go. The Word of Truth teaches..."

"Word of Truth? What's that, again?" Alyssa interrupted.

"Oh, right. Um... When The Name gave us His Word..." Claire continued.

"Uh, wait one second, please. Can you back up a bit, and tell me what exactly you mean by, The Name?" Alyssa inquired.

"Wow. This is harder than I thought. I'm not really making a lot of sense to you, am I? I guess we really never got into a whole lot of detail about all of this, have we?" Claire asked.

"No, I guess not," the girl answered, still feeling quite confused.

"Okay. I'll really try to make this simple, then. You see, Alyssa, we believe that a long time ago, The Name, or our living spiritual Father...that is, the Creator of all there is, chose to reach down to us, stepping into history to redeem *us*, His greatest creation, from our lost condition and in-born rebellion against His perfect moral character. He knew we stood separated from His glory and would perish in our own darkness, without His intervention," Claire explained.

"That's when the Anointed One came as a poor baby, as Bethany told me, right?"

"That's right. The Name loved us so much, that He gave His only Son, who was one with Him and His Spirit, so that he would come show us that love, in a human way…a way which we could grasp."

"Uhum…" Alyssa followed. Claire, then, continued, "When the Anointed One came into the world, he grew up and modeled for us a life of perfection. That means he was pure in every way, as each of us was intended to be, but failed. He came, first, so that we would come to know more about his Father, and his Father's Kingdom, a place called heaven, which had finally come near to us because of him. But, at that time, there were many important people who felt threatened by him and his message of redemption, which challenged their longstanding religious traditions. Because of it, he was put to death by the Roman government."

"On the cross, right?" Alyssa responded.

"That's correct. He was crucified and died. He was then buried in a borrowed tomb. But on the third day, the Anointed One came to life again by the power of his Father. That's the Day of Resurrection, or Easter, which we still celebrate, today.

"But why do you have to remember such a difficult time?" Alyssa asked.

"Well, when we realize that The Name requires that same perfect life from us, we become aware of our own inability to meet that high standard. It's like each of us should receive that very same punishment for our rebellion, that is, our sin. But the greatest news of all is that we can claim that perfection for ourselves, by believing in the death and new life of this Son, who took our punishment for us at the cross, in *our* place." Claire then said, "That's why we have reason to celebrate. Everyone who trusts in this sacrifice and comes to confess that the Anointed One came from the Father and was like the Father, can also supernaturally inherit that same new life, forever and ever, just like His Son, the Anointed One. You see, we continue to struggle, but we can be forgiven for all of our offenses, past, present, and future, against that perfect moral character, which is demanded by The Name, if we are to come into His holy presence, one day."

"I think I understand that, sort of. But what does that have to do with the implant?" Alyssa gently pressed.

"Well, if we believe in what I've just told you, then we belong to The Name. We are His children. The Anointed One called it, being born again. But not of flesh and blood, which is impossible, but reborn from above, that is...spiritually. We can then enjoy a relationship with Him, as we continue to try our best to live by His holy code, which is expected of us, as His children, just as your mother has expectations of you, in your important earthly relationship with her. But here's the thing... The implant, we believe, once activated, makes it impossible, for some strange reason, for a non-believing person to ever desire to know The Name, to fellowship with Him, and to belong to Him. This means, as far as we know, that such a person cannot be saved from their condition of separation from Him," Claire highlighted. "And His wrath is reserved for that person. That would be horrific, indeed."

"So, what would happen to such persons?" Alyssa asked.

"Well, upon dying, anyone in that condition would remain eternally separated from The Name. That means that they would never be allowed to enter heaven and experience that new life, in communion with all that is love and all that is good. They would be judged on the basis of their chosen rebellion and separation, and would be banished from the presence of The Name. That place of total separation is called hell, where no love exists, but only judgment and infinite torment. It's really not a place made for humans, but for demons, or angelic beings that rebelled against The Name. Nowhere on this earth, has anyone ever experienced that, because even those who do not belong to The Name while living, can still enjoy the presence of His love and goodness generally present in this world, no matter what their life is really like, here. The grace of The Name is all around, and all of us can experience it some in this life." Claire told the implanted young lady.

"I see..." Alyssa replied.

"But the reason we, as those who belong to The Name, cannot accept the Cognit Implant, is that we are convinced, Alyssa, that it is a mark which ultimately separates those who belong to The Name from those who do not. In fact, it is quite evident that those whose implants are activated, quickly lose all of their consciousness of The Name and are unable to desire to know and trust in Him. We believe that this implant system is somehow a part of a plan conceived by the one we call, the Enemy. This evil one is not only opposed to The Name, but is opposed to us, as well, who belong to The Name. The Enemy is also known as the Accuser, and the Deceiver of all of humanity."

"But, Mrs. Christensen, what does all of this mean, exactly, for me…and for my family, and my friends?" Alyssa asked in obvious deep concern.

"Alyssa, only The Name knows for sure. What we do know, however, is that in His Word, revealed to us long ago, He says He desires for *all* to come to Him, and that *anyone* who calls on The Name, *will* be Spirit-sealed. I believe the Spirit of Truth has been stirring in you, and I would never lose all hope for your family. The Name can do miracles, still. And as for you, as long as you do not willfully activate your implant, you can still hear and receive the message, and *believe* in that liberating knowledge. You can then enter into the waters of baptism, which is your profession of faith before the community and The Name, symbolizing your eternal connection to Him by His work of grace in your heart. That means your implant will never, *ever* activate. Essentially, you'll become immune to it, and you will be just like us. Do you understand, Alyssa, what I am telling you?" Claire asked.

"I believe I do. But it feels so scary, Mrs. Christensen."

"I know. But we will continue to pray for you, dear. That is about all we really can do for you, right now," Claire said. "We cannot force you to do it, nor choose it for you. It is a personal decision, and it's between *you* and The Name, whose grace you may find irresistible."

"I understand… Thanks, Mrs. Christensen. I guess I have a lot to think about," Alyssa replied.

"You do. And, sweetheart, if at any time tonight you feel you have any more questions, please don't hesitate to ask. We just want to be helpful."

"Thank you. I believe that you do."

By now, Alyssa's chest was feeling tight. Her young heart sensed the difficult battle between her concern for herself and her own mother, her family and friends, and her growing and sharpened awareness that this was a time for an eternal decision to be made. Her concern was also for her estranged father, even though she greatly resented him for having left her mother. Alyssa also felt extremely uncomfortable with the whole idea of a heavenly father figure in whom she was supposed to trust. This time, however, and perhaps for the first time in her life, the valuable advice from her mother and even peers, on which she had come to rely fully at just about every important step in her life, somehow seemed inappropriate. After all, how could they truly understand the difficult choice before her? Most of them believed they had every good reason to choose to assimilate into the Allianz Code? Her own worldview, up until recently, had matched theirs in virtually every way. For them, the pragmatic thing to do had always been to choose the path of least resistance, psychologically, socially, economically, religiously, and also politically. She had slowly come to realize that this was different, and from what she was enabled by the Spirit of Truth to understand, she was faced with having to decide on a course for her own everlasting destiny. And she understood she literally had to make that choice all on her own. She felt like she was drifting, alone and unsure.

As she considered the Christensens, here was a family that seemed passionate about something much greater than themselves, their circumstances, and their very lives. How she yearned, deep inside herself, to have that kind of passion for something. At that point, surrounded by that family and their contagious warmth, people who in different ways grew more endearing to her each day, there was so much that appealed to her. But the object of her passion, the motive behind any decision she would make, could not be merely the Christensens. No, that was not what was being offered to her. Her decision would either have to be for or against something she barely even knew; an acceptance of a deity that felt so foreign to her, a relationship with a savior that she had never actually met, a faith she had only known vicariously, and usually through others she had known for a relatively short time. Faced with that internal struggle, all she managed to decide at that point was not to decide. That crucial decision would need to wait, even if she were not at all yet sure of what would need to happen for that struggle to finally be resolved inside of her.

"Look, you guys! It's starting to snow!" Holly yelled out, as she peaked through the kitchen window.

"Sparks!" Zeke said.

"What?" said Claire, "That's really strange. It's spring already, and we haven't really seen any snow for, like, five years."

"I told you, didn't I?" Christensen said to Claire, as he came into the kitchen, all ready to leave for the evening. "They said the white stuff could come tonight… Now, where's my sandwich? I'll have to eat it on the way."

"Right here, 'Mr. Weather-man,' sir," Claire joked.

"Let's head out, gang," he told them.

Alyssa and the Christensens then squeezed in their family vehicle and left on their 50-minute ride to the place of the gathering, remotely located in a rural property, outside Midville.

"Please drive carefully, Tanner," Claire pleaded. "The roads could be slick."

"I'll be careful. But I think we'd better go ahead and replace our H-Pak at the station, just in case we get stuck in the snow, somewhere, and need the reserve fuel," said Christensen.

"Good idea," Claire concurred.

Twenty

On to the Brethren Gathering

Sunday evening traffic was relatively light, as the Christensens and their guest approached the nearest refueling station in their residential neighborhood; one of the remaining few they knew still accepted payment under the old system. A new notice, however, placed on the H-Pak replacement module they pulled up, to alerted them in English:

> *Attention, customers. Our establishment was fully converted to the Cognit Implant Protocol as of March 21st, GDM-13. Please note that this station no longer accepts any form of payment outside of the Cognit Bracelet system. Please be advised – Sincerely, Management.*

"Look, Claire. Another sign of the times…" Christensen said.

"What are we supposed to do?" She rhetorically asked, in frustration.

"They sure keep on making things interesting for us, don't they?" said Christensen.

"It makes me sick, Tanner," Claire responded, as the kids listened.

Alyssa then mentioned, "Maybe I can talk to my father about it, Mr. Christensen. He's in city management. I think he may be able to help, although it may take a few days." As a minor, Alyssa's bracelet was not programmed for fuel purchases. Even as an implant, she found herself unable to assist the Christensens in that instance.

"Thanks, Alyssa. You can try, but I've got a feeling it's no use in he long run."

"We can still ride on the WormRail. Right, Dad?" asked Bethany.

"For now, we can. But it'll be tricky getting to our worship gatherings. The land is some ten miles from the outermost station," Christensen reminded them.

"We'll bike there!" Holly replied.

"That's the spirit, Holly," said Christensen.

"What? And have to get up with the sun? No thanks. Not me, uh-uh..." Zeke chimed in, in a rather negative tone.

"Zeke! That's enough, thank you," Claire warned.

In haste, they left the fueling station. With the snow getting steadily heavier, however, driving was slow, and they began to wonder if they would get to the gathering in time for the start of the event. "Pray we won't get stuck anywhere, especially running low in reserve fuel," Christensen said.

The buses operated by the Children of the Promise group had been going back and forth, to and from the farthest WormRail stop out on the way to the property where the gathering would take place. They were also running behind schedule. Having passed a number of such buses on their way, the Christensens finally arrived at the site of their gathering, with apparently enough fuel left for their trip home. Christensen quickly identified a likely parking spot, and as they exited their vehicle, they all ran inside the building, several minutes later than John had expected them to get there.

It was now 7:25 p.m., and Christensen and Claire walked into the large sanctuary, ultimately ending up backstage with just enough time to gather with the others for a short time of prayer.

"Welcome, guys. Glad you've made it," said John "the Baptist" Waters. "We'll need to delay by a few minutes because of the snow. I think we'll still have a good turnout, though."

"They're coming. We saw a number of buses slowly headed this way, just a while ago," Claire said.

"Good," said John.

"John... Brother, I've got some news from Tomazo I need to share with you before we all pray. Is that okay?"

"Sure. Is everything all right? How's our Italian brother doing?" asked the young pastor. Christensen then proceeded to briefly relay the somber details he had learned earlier on from DiPaoli's troubling message and pictures files. As the close-knit group of leaders, supporters, and musicians gathered backstage, they prayed for DiPaoli, and also for the Spirit of Truth to come powerfully onto the gathering that night, and to provide protection against any mishaps or incidents for them and for all who would take part in Resistance mobilizations around the region that evening.

The Christensen party of kids at first walked around inside the spacious, but windowless oblong building, eventually entering the sanctuary, a great room inside the large structure, which was filled with many rows of seats, neatly arranged semi-circularly around the front stage. They then moved to try and find some seats, toward the front of the sanctuary, where seating had been especially reserved for the younger crowd.

Bethany introduced Alyssa to some of her friends, who were already there, saying, "Hey, y'all. This is my friend, Alyssa Lorentz. It's her first time here."

"Hi, Alyssa. Welcome, we're so glad you're here," a number of the youth said to her.

As Bethany and Alyssa found their seats, Holly ran up and sat down on a chair immediately to Alyssa's left.

"Doesn't this spark?" Holly said, unable to contain her excitement. "Stick with me, girl, and I'll give you all the scoop."

Zeke positioned himself in the next row, just behind Bethany, who sat to the right of their guest. Zeke's best friend, Gustavo Santiago, sat beside him.

"Hey, man. Who's the knockout brunette implant?" his friend indiscreetly asked.

"Be quiet!" Zeke whispered forcefully. "She's a friend. Don't embarrass yourself." Then he added, "You may know a lot about soccer, but this is beyond your expertise, *amigo...*"

"Oooo! What's this? Do I sense a little jealousy, *hermano?*" said Gustavo.

"Stavo, I mean it..." Zeke cautioned.

Over the next few minutes, as more member families and large groups of newcomers began to arrive in cars, vans, and buses, the sizeable, remodeled old pavilion began to fill up. Christensen walked quickly past the kids and waived as he headed toward the soundboard station, located on an elevated platform in the back, near the entrance doors to the sanctuary. While singers and musicians were taking to the stage in front of them and began doing brief warm-ups and sound checks, Bethany took the opportunity to go over some preliminary basics with Alyssa.

"Alyssa, since it's your first time here, let me tell you what's going to happen."

"Hey! *I* was going to be her tour guide," Holly protested.

"That's okay, Holly," Alyssa said, "Why don't we let Bethany do this now, and you show me around some more, later on."

"It's a deal," Holly agreed.

"Check, check one, two..." said Shen-il, speaking into a vintage microphone from her place at the piano. "All systems are go," she heard Christensen say through her earpiece.

Shen-il was a sound-master in her own right, having spent years touring as a semi-professional musician with her band of Believers in many parts of Southeast Asia, before leaving for the American Province as John's wife. In fact, it had been during one of her concert tours to the district of Shanghai, that she first met John, who was not only immediately taken by her piano and singing virtuosity, but was also powerfully captivated by her unusual professionalism about all things technical. To her, achieving a great and pure sound, to back up her theologically rich lyrics, was as powerful a tool for evangelism as a well-prepared sermon. Together, Shen-il and John truly made a dynamic duo up on stage, and they had been joining forces almost ever since their introductory meeting overseas.

As the praise band started playing, and the multicultural gospel choir broke out into their opening chorus, many in the congregation began standing up to follow in worship. Bethany took the opportunity to briefly go over the program with Alyssa. Looking up toward the big screen hanging above the stage, Bethany pointed out, "See, right there, just before the presentation of the short play? That's when I go up to sing."

"Wow! I can't wait," her friend said. "Are you nervous?"

"I guess so, a little. But Shen-il told me that if I can focus on my singing, and not on the audience, I'll be just fine."

With music and voices now soaring throughout the place, and having to speak a lot louder, Bethany exclaimed, "Don't be embarrassed. Just join in, if you feel like it!"

"I like it. It's a sparking sound!" her friend yelled back, as she felt a warm little hand hold on to hers, on her left.

Just then, they noticed Claire coming back out to take her place up front with them. As the musicians continued, John came out on stage, but stood to the side, clapping along and watching Shen-il, his amazing pianist wife, and the band perform, along with the jubilant choir. Down lower, Claire was looking back to try and locate Christensen, but could hardly see him all the way in the rear of the auditorium, through the already considerable crowd. The place was finally filling up, and more were still coming in, many still sprinkled with the white dusting of fresh-fallen snowflakes.

"Hey, Beth," Alyssa called out, "I was meaning to ask. Why is there a little pool, over there to the side of the stage?" she wondered, noticing the baptistery.

"Remember earlier, when Mom was telling you about entering into the waters of baptism? Well, that's where it happens. You'll probably see it, tonight," Bethany explained, secretly hoping her friend would experience the "sweet plunge" for herself.

Seeing her sister point to the rectangular tank, Holly presumptuously added, "Yeah, girl. You'll get to go in wearing a white robe. And it gets all wet.

"Uhh...I'm not sure about that, yet," said Alyssa.

"Don't worry. It's fun...and they've got plenty of towels," Holly tried to reassure her.

While many in the audience clapped to the praise music, John took a moment to look around the now brimming and softly lit place, from his loftier vantage point. At last, the greatly awaited moment had come for him and his team, gathered there. Implants and non-implants of diverse cultural and racial backgrounds, men and women, young and old, all together, none fully knowing what to expect, but nearly all searching for some kind of personal answer, some clearer insight, for why they were there, converging in community, in that remote setting, on that very unusually snowy evening.

True to his calling as a shepherd of that flock, John marveled at the Lord's grace, as he felt any and all trace of fear about the unknown leave him. At that very instant, as he beheld that glorious sight, his heart began to be filled up with unspeakable gratitude to The Name, for John knew, assured by the promises in the Word of Truth, that it would not return void, if obediently and faithfully ministered that night. Something in him wished he could freeze that moment in time, for to him it could very well be the closest thing to heaven he would ever truly know in this world; those who were seekers, gathered around the altar, with their eyes drawn up, in expectation of awesome things to take place and His glory and majesty to shine in and all around them.

The celestial wonder of that moment, at the Children of the Promise gathering, however, stood in stark contrast to sinister happenings tragically taking place elsewhere, as the Allianz Federation, under Marshall Misha Dariah's command in the American Province, took the Brethren Gatherings in the southeast region by fiery storm.

Twenty-One

Allianz Repression

Out East, it was already 9:00 p.m., and the cog operations were in full swing, as Dariah targeted the two other large gatherings that night. Communities of Brethren in Charlotte and outside of Atlanta were just then receiving a devastating blow, and footage of the interventions were starting to be simultaneously televised all over the province.

"*Little is really known about these subversive religious communities*," reported an Allianz Broadcast Network correspondent, speaking in Allianzi, "*but legal searches have turned up evidence that these were much more than social or cultural gatherings. In fact, our sources confirm that these groups, among many other smaller cells currently in operation throughout the province and around the globe, have been engaged in covert, ritualistic religious mobilizations, aiming at enticing implanted and non-implanted individuals, but especially and most disturbingly, youth and children, to stand against the Federation and the Allianz Code. Officials claim, we have learned, that these are pseudo-religious cults that actually have a political agenda to resist and sabotage the Allianz system, while also reeking havoc on the lives of these youngsters and their families. Reporting live, from downtown Charlotte, this is Cornelius Voit-Moss, for ABN News.*" The news anchor then added, "*Thank you, Cornelius. A most disturbing revelation, indeed. We hope you'll stay tuned for further updates, as this and other similar situations develop, possibly late into the night, tonight... And now, for our weather report, here's our weather-lady, Vanessa Do-Gong, who's going to tell us about this surprising cold front, causing all of the unusual and record-breaking snowfall, this late in the season, for much of the South and Southeast..."*

At this point, anyone watching their televisor had certainly learned about Dariah's maneuvers against the Resistance. News media coverage was incessant for the better part of that evening, just as Dariah had instructed. Dariah's aim was becoming clear to the Resistance, as its members in the targeted cells, as well as others following the developments via the telecast, stood shell shocked. She was determined to discredit the Community of Brethren by portraying these faith-based groups as being part of a wider criminal insurgency that threatened the very social fabric and equilibrium of average American communities, and ultimately the future of Allianz as a system. And by many accounts, the astute Marshall appeared to be succeeding at it.

"They're getting what they deserve," a man commented to his wife, as they closely followed the news coverage from their home. "These people can't continue to deceive, manipulate, and lead our young people and others astray. They should pay for what they've done to our Nick," he said, as he looked over to his son, who sat in silent grief, elsewhere in their televisor room. Their 12-year old boy had come to believe the *Evangel*, during a Brethren Gathering earlier that year. Unable to accept or understand, his parents shunned his newfound passion for The Name, and forbade him to have anything further to do with the Community of Brethren in their southern town.

Meanwhile, in the Province of Italy, Mr. Adammus Horn was making a very early morning, and previously unscheduled ABN News appearance, via CyberSat link, at a network subsidiary in the district of Rome. In another one of his impassioned speeches highlighting his zealous protectiveness of the Federation, Horn praised the news coming from the American Province, declaring:

"As the Allianz Federation's Prosecutor General, I have been in close contact with our American Province Marshall, over the last few hours. I cannot fully express my deep satisfaction with the way

Marshall Misha Dariah has handled these recent operations in the territory under her jurisdiction. These interventions stand in long worldwide succession, along with an increasing number of strategic crackdowns and ongoing investigations regarding many now defunct branches of the Resistance. As a Federation, we cannot, and will not tolerate any law-breaking activities against the Allianz Code, and we will apprehend and prosecute, to the fullest extent of the law, any and all operatives of this subversive global movement. We will not allow yet another hate-filled group of religious fundamentalists, no matter what their ideological roots, to terrorize our unified society and inflict fear upon our citizens." Horn then stated, *" I give you my word that I will act decisively and effectively, as the Council of Regents and the Allianz General Parliament give me greater powers, to arrest, bring to justice, and thus eradicate these last strongholds of religious deception and political corruption from the face of the planet. And with the help of dedicated and capable allies, such as Marshall Dariah, we will establish a strong and incorruptible front to defeat these criminals, once and for all. Thank you very much. Vigor to Allianz,"* Horn said, as he concluded his statement.

"Mr. Prosecutor General, do you or do you not categorize this group as a terrorist organization?" one reporter in the background was heard asking Horn.

"The Resistance has clearly been growing in its radicalism, as it has acted to oppose us politically. That is a non-debatable fact. If we stand by and simply watch these events unfold, we may indeed be confronted with horrific acts of terror and violence. That is how these movements have typically evolved in the recent past," Horn purported. *" Just look to the track record of groups like Al-Qaeda and other radicalized religious fronts, such as the insurgent movement in the former Iraq, as well as in the Province of China, and more recently in the Sri Lankan Province, among other provinces with long histories of religious-based struggle against the established order. We can no longer afford to wait for the same thing to happen in this case. We must and will act preemptively wherever the conditions dictate that we do so. Therefore, yes, I do in fact categorize the Community of Brethren Resistance as an imminent terrorist*

threat, and consequently our actions here are fully justified, legally. Thank you. Vigor to Allianz."

With this proclamation, a new era of high-profile government-sponsored opposition to the Resistance had begun. Horn's announcement to the entire world raised the stakes for both sides, and the vilification of the Community of Brethren would now become part of the official rhetoric and would occupy news headlines for the next few days following these Federation operations.

At the Children of the Promise gathering, however, things continued to proceed well, at least for the time being. No one yet had any awareness of the terribly troubling goings-on elsewhere in the province. As the band, along with the Gospel choir, concluded the opening songs, John "the Baptist" Waters welcomed everyone, and officially opened the evening with a word of prayer.

"It is truly a joy to have you with us here tonight, and I want to warmly receive each and everyone of you to our very special time together. I'd especially like to extend a heart-felt welcome to our new guests. My name is John Waters, and I am the director of the Children of the Promise group," he said, intentionally avoiding the potentially compromising title, lead pastor. "Those who know me around here, call me John 'the Baptist' Waters. That's because I have a reputation for causing folks to want to get splashed in our little pool, as our gatherings come to a close... I'm sort of kidding, but surely you'll find out tonight what exactly I do mean." Then he continued, "No doubt, you have for some time been hearing a lot about our event tonight, as our members have gone out and made many contacts over the past few weeks. I, therefore, want to thank you for being willing to come and join us in our program this evening. This is a moment we've greatly anticipated, and I do hope that you will enjoy it and find it personally meaningful." John then went on to outline the evening's events, "In our program, tonight, we have a special musical program by our own great musicians and by a talented young lady, who's part of our community here. I'll then present our new mini-play, entitled 'Follow Me.' After the play, I will follow with a short oration and invitation, toward the end of our time together. We'll finish with a few announcements, mainly directed at our members. So please stand with me now, as I lead in a brief word of invocation, after which time our band will continue to perform and uplift The Name, who's our creative inspiration for putting on these gatherings. The words to the music will be projected on that screen up there." John then offered the opening prayer, and the music resumed.

As the night advanced, Dariah followed the developments on the cog interventions from the operations room, below the White House. Thoroughly pleased with how things were evolving up until that point, she allowed herself to repeatedly savor Adammus Horn's words earlier that evening, as she played and replayed the recorded CyberSat media feed.

"That's music to my ears, Lieutenant," she carried on in revelry.

"Yes, Commander, things seem to be progressing very well."

"What's the status on the Tennessee location?" Dariah inquired.

"The operation is already underway, sir. The southern Federation forces have dispatched a police convoy that is en route at this very minute, transporting one hundred fifty lightly armed cogs, as per your exact orders. They should arrive there within the next half hour. Local authorities have reported roads there to be a bit treacherous, due to some heavy and slick snow accumulating on the ground. However, we do not expect any significant problems as a result of that."

No sooner had the Lieutenant uttered those words, than an urgent adverse update arrived from the southern Federation operation, telling of an incident involving one of the transports in the convoy headed to the Children of the Promise gathering. A large vehicle carrying some forty troops had overturned, injuring a couple dozen cogs, some of them seriously, and the vehicle now lay stuck sideways in a snow-filled roadside ditch. Ambulances and backup troops were rapidly being mobilized by air to tend immediately to the situation.

"Commander, this will cause a delay, but will not deter the operation, neither will it affect the outcome. The convoy will continue on its current trajectory, as soon as backup arrives," the Lieutenant assured Dariah.

"Very well, Lieutenant. I do hope you are correct in your evaluation, and that this is not some kind of omen for us," she replied, revealing some degree of superstition.

"Sir, I have no doubt that this intervention will succeed, as have the other two, already. Tomorrow, America will wake up to news of a shaken Resistance, whose days are indeed numbered. You can count on it, sir," he predicted.

"Indeed," Dariah replied. "Lieutenant, have the dossier on this particular group down-linked to my PSS, immediately," Dariah requested. "I especially want to review the leadership profiles in more careful detail, while we prepare to execute the intervention on this third meeting of worshiping clowns."

"Right away, sir."

Twenty-Two

Danger

Back at the Brethren Gathering, there was no word on the Federation attacks out East. A bit nervous, Bethany watched her pastor for her cue and prepared herself to walk up to the stage and to sing her two songs, as indicated on the program. Her mother, sitting behind her, touched her gently on her left shoulder and said, "Beth, I know you'll do well. Sing to Him. Lift Him up, and He will draw everyone to Himself."

John then announced, "I am delighted, tonight, to introduce to you a talented young lady, who will grace us with her voice. Bethany Christensen, please come on up."

As Bethany stood up, Alyssa got up with her and gave her an embrace before sitting down again, next to Holly.

"I'm proud of you, Beth," Alyssa told her friend.

"Thanks," Bethany said.

She then proceeded toward the aisle, her mother waiving emotionally and struggling against tears of pride and joy, and trying to let her daughter go, despite her anxiety over her overexposure and safety.

Acting boldly on an impulse, Zeke skipped up a row and sat next to Alyssa, while his sister left her place.

"Hi," he greeted the young lady.

"Hey…what a nice surprise," she said, indicating her approval. "Are you looking forward to Beth's singing?"

"I have to confess. That girl can really sing," he said in compliment to his sister. This impressed Alyssa, as she caught a glimpse of Zeke's endearing character.

"You know? It's really nice to hear the love you have for your sister. That says a lot to me about you, Zeke," Alyssa remarked.

"Really? Well, that little one next to you is very, very great, too," he said, referring to Holly.

"Now you're just trying to impress me…" Alyssa joked.

"Well…" Zeke replied, in embarrassment.

"Excuse me. But I happen to agree with him, Alyssa," Holly interjected.

"I actually do, too, little friend," Alyssa replied.

"Well, good," Holly added, in all the self-praise the prodigious little nine-year old could suggest.

The light murmuring of the audience soon gave way to astonished silence, as Bethany started singing. The 14-year old sang so demurely, drawing little undue attention to herself, as she looked upwards and smiled gently for most of the time she was at center-stage. Alyssa, as well as most of the audience, were captivated by the message, delivered in such dazzling singing and from such a young and gifted performer.

While she sang so beautifully, Bethany managed to elevate the thoughts of many present there to a place near the throne of The Name, Himself. It was as if His Spirit of Truth was softly prodding the hearts of several among those whose eyes and ears were fixed on Bethany, who was giving testimony to the eternal truth being brought forth from the mouth of a babe. As the Spirit of Truth began to move in and around the congregation, the minds and hearts of seekers were being carefully prepared for the powerful message to be delivered that night, by the mini-play and by John "the Baptist" Waters, himself.

Meanwhile, a few miles away from the gathering, the cog convoy was liberated from the traffic incident and started again to move with determination toward its destination that evening, cutting a path through a layer of fresh-fallen snow, now almost 4-inches thick. As they came within one mile from the location, being accurately directed via a CyberSat global positioning signal, the convoy diminished its lights, now activating their night-vision capabilities. With all vehicles slowing to a crawl, just before entering the property, the officer in charge ordered the smallest transport, carrying only a handful of cogs, to move up ahead of the long line of cog vehicles and to precisely confirm Visual contact with their intended target.

A small detachment of two FlightPak-equipped cogs then levitated toward the large pavilion where the gathering was being held, now within sight. As they flew closer to the structure, they noticed a group of two men standing in front of the closed outside doors and running security checks. Drawing virtually no attention to themselves, due to the very muffled and low-frequency humming sound coming from their Flight-Paks, the cog duo hovered several feet above ground, fully cloaked by the lack of lighting in the night and by their inconspicuous, black attire, which by design neither produced nor reflected any luminosity.

As they circled around the building, they captured images with the use of a camera device built into their helmets. The footage and photographs were then transmitted via CyberSat link to the coordinating centers, both local and at the D.C. headquarters. Upon their surveillance, the two cogs detected the presence of other pairs of security personnel, roving and guarding the perimeter of the pavilion.

"Did you hear something?" one of the men running security asked his partner.

"No…just the music inside."

"I'm sure I heard something out there. Just keep a keen eye out for anything strange," he instructed his mate.

Satisfied with their tactical survey of the situation, the silently hovering cogs returned to the convoy location, which was now stationed just inside the unguarded main gateway to the property.

From there, the commanding officer awaited further instructions from the southern operations center and prepared to lay siege on the Brethren Gathering.

Twenty-Three

Preparation

Back again in D.C., Dariah's PSS was being fed detailed intelligence information about the leadership and workings of that specific Children of the Promise group in the South. As she reviewed the records, she browsed through the alphabetical register listing the names and the preliminary biographical sketches on each leading cadre in that particular ensemble, within the broader organizational structure of the Resistance. Her attention was first drawn to the obvious leader, whose name appeared highlighted in the system, for clear identification. In Allianzi, the information read:

File ID APTN-RC034-00001-G

As Dariah accessed this Resistance file, being Federation coded for "American Province; Tennessee; Resistance Cell Number 34; Agent 1; G (seventh agent in that leading role up to this point)," she opened the file, which revealed an initial but precise biographical profile for John:

Name John Walton Waters; Resistance cell leader.
Alias John "the Baptist" Waters.
Status Non-implant.
Bio White male; Age 32.
D.O.B. March 16, GDM-Minus-19.

Origin Born in Savannah, Georgia, former United States of America.

Personal Married to Shen-il Miang Waters; no children; Residence: 100 Woodland Lane, Midville, TN, since February, GDM-12.

Affiliation American Province Resistance; Community of Brethren.

Cell Status Active; Children of the Promise (current membership, over 2,000); significant growth potential based on mobilization record.

Primary Role Lead pastor; Spiritual mentor.

Strategic Function Heads local congregation; Top recruiter and indoctrinating agent.

Prior Trajectory Undergraduate degree in pastoral ministry and sociology from Faith&Knowledge University, GDM-3, Midville, TN; MDiv (Interrupted) at Applegate Seminary, GDM-4, Strawberry Grove, CA; Youth minister (active cell) Vallejo, CA; 3-year overseas field ministry experience in Southeast Asia.

As Dariah studied John's profile, she noticed his short time in his present role. "What's this?" she thought. "This is a new lead cadre for this group. Waters has only been there about a year," she ascertained. This fact raised her suspicions that, because of his novice status in this Resistance cell, John was most likely functioning under the tutelage of other leading figures. She therefore proceeded to undertake a careful search of the additional profiles, looking for details on more established operatives within the Children of the Promise group.

As her eyes returned to the top of the alphabetical list of names and prepared to scroll down the list, she noticed a familiar name. *What's this? Could it be? No...certainly not*, she thought. *But how many Tanner Daniel Christensens can there be?* she reasoned, as she recognized the name and vaguely remembered her old teaching assistant, at MIT.

"Commander," a young cog Sergeant interrupted her during her intelligence data browsing.

"Yes," Dariah answered, as she looked up and deactivated the holographic screen produced by her PSS. "What is it, Sergeant?"

"Sir, the Lieutenant sent me to inform you that our forces have reached their destination in the South. They are awaiting further orders from central command," relayed the young cog.

"I want the place surrounded and the power cut off, first thing," she instructed. "Then I want a minute-by-minute update on the developments as they unfold from that point on."

"Commander, our forces will soon be ready to move in. Do they have clearance to do so?" the Sergeant asked.

"Negative," Dariah replied. "My orders to the Lieutenant are to have our troops simply report and standby for further orders from me. Once the facility has been surrounded and the power interrupted, no one is to make a move, nor fire a shot, without my permission. Is that clear?"

"Affirmative, Commander," answered the young cog, as he saluted and quickly departed.

Unable to resist her curiosity about her latest find, Dariah reactivated her PSS database and refocused on that familiar name. As she opened the dossier, she began to scan for confirming evidence that this was indeed the same Tanner Daniel Christensen she once knew, almost twenty years ago.

The time had come for the "Follow Me" play to be presented at the Brethren Gathering. As Bethany left the stage and made her way back to her seat, she noticed Zeke occupying her seat. Before his sister said anything, Zeke signaled to Alyssa he was leaving. He then got up, and as he and Bethany edged past each other between the rows of seats, he gently squeezed her arm and said, "You did good, sis."

"Thanks, Zeke," she answered back. She then sat down next to her friend.

Looking at his friend, Gustavo, Zeke indicated he was headed out to the lobby. Gustavo then got up to follow him out of the sanctuary.

"Where are you going?" Claire asked Zeke in a whisper. "The play's about to begin."

"Bathroom," Zeke replied. He and Gustavo then walked past the sound system platform and waived at Christensen, who noticed them and waived back.

Out in the lobby, as they walked toward the men's restroom, Gustavo expressed his amazement at Zeke's boldness toward Alyssa. "Wow, man. You must really have a thing for her."

"Yeah. I like her. But we're not going out or anything. It's purely platonic."

"Platonic-*shmatonic*, *amigo*," Gustavo responded.

"I'm serious," Zeke said. "It's not right, yet. She's an implant and I can't even think about courting her before she makes a choice for The Name. But I have my hopes that she will, and soon..."

"Maybe she'll do it tonight, huh? Then you'll be home free," Gustavo commented.

"There's no guarantee, Stavo. I know this sounds cheesy, but I might not be able to hold back if she does," Zeke remarked.

"Oh, man, you've got it *bad*," said his friend, "*really* bad."

Twenty-Four

The Play and the Siege

Meanwhile, John announced the theatrical number. "Dear friends," he began. "The short play you'll now watch is an artistic interpretation, based on the words of a book that is no longer really around, as a book. Oh, how I wish that this great book were still with us and intact from beginning to end. And how we took it for granted that we would always have access to copies of it. But now, without it, life for many of us who belong to this place has felt incomplete. Yet, in some providential way, the words once found in that book somehow still remain in and around us, in precious bits and pieces. These are the very words that give life to those who hear it. But while our minds cannot recall all of the original words, as they were once given to us, our hardworking drama and artistic team, along with many others of us, laboring intensively together, have made every effort to guard the truth found in that book and to transmit to you the very essence and core of the message contained in it, even though we cannot reproduce them in their exactness. Again, this one-act play is a creative piece, based on many aspects of that word of life, which we feel faithfully conveys the key message of importance in that writing. We hope you will hear and appreciate the meaning of it and contemplate in your hearts what it is saying to you."

The play then began with total darkness. Dramatic, but somber music played. Lights dimly faded in, revealing the shadow of two men lying on separate sides of a holding prison cell floor. Just then,

The Dreamers of Allianz

the audience heard the loud sound of footsteps. It was a group of four men, who were dressed as Roman soldiers. As they entered the stage from the left, they dragged a beaten and badly bruised and bloodied man, enshrouded in a purple cloak and wearing a dark crown of thorns. The soldiers then opened the cell door and threw the man in the center of the floor, inside the cell. Gasping and choking, this man just lay there, barely moving.

"Son of man!... Man of miracles!... All hail the *great king*!" yelled one of the prisoners, scoffing at this man, who lay on the floor, in silence.

"Leave him alone!" the prisoner to the right of this man said, struggling to move toward him, despite the heavy chains and shackles around both ankles, wrists, and neck. As the chains stretched and pulled back on his neck, this prisoner stopped short of the man on the floor. "I want to help you. But I can't come any closer," he said. At this, the man on the floor let out a grunt of pain and strained to slowly lift his blood-covered head, to be able to see this kind prisoner.

"Drrrnn..." the disfigured man said.

"What did you say? Drink? You want a drink?" the prisoner asked. "Wait, I've got a clay pot with some water still in it. You can have some."

"What for?" arrogantly exclaimed the angry prisoner on the left. "We'll all be dead in a few hours, anyway... Unless this holy man of miracles can set us free," and he cackled in scornful disdain.

"That's okay," whispered the prisoner to the right of the injured man, who was still bleeding from his long and recent flogging and scourging, in the hands of the Roman soldiers. "I'll help you sit up and have some to drink. Just try to move a little closer."

As the play continued, the audience grew more focused on the dramatic scene being presented before them. Most of the new guests that night had never witnessed anything quite like it.

As the snow continued to fall outside, just a short distance from the gathered crowd, the lineup of police vehicles slowly advanced toward the large pavilion and prepared to form an almost complete ellipse around the oblong building. Right behind the pavilion, thick woods prevented the convoy from forming a full enclosure. Their formation, however, would provide almost no chance for anyone to escape their grip. By now, a group of men standing by the large front doors noticed the fearful sight, as the police vehicles came within some forty yards, around almost the entire building.

"Oh, my gosh... Oh, this is not good," said one of the men guarding the door.

"What is going on? Are we being attacked?" another man said, as he struggled to see clearly in the night, through the evergreen shrubs, pine trees, and the dark shadows on the snow-blanketed ground.

"Quick, one of you run inside and alert John and Tanner immediately. Hurry!" said another one of the men standing there. He then radioed the other security teams, alerting them about the incoming police vehicles.

First reaching Christensen, the messenger relayed the menacing situation into his ear. Hearing in disbelief, Christensen did not know just what to do. A part of him wanted to run outside and see things for himself. A part of him urgently needed to reach John, up on stage. But a greater part of him just wanted to pretend it was just a nightmare and continue to enjoy the gathering, which seemed to be going so well, up until that point.

"Are you absolutely sure?" Christensen said, trying hard to present a calm countenance and not stir up unnecessary fear among the almost four thousand people gathered there that night. In his mind, however, he was beginning to imagine the worst. "Wait here. Help the others guard the doors."

Just then, Zeke and Gustavo were making their way back from the restroom and toward the sanctuary. Passing through the lobby, they noticed something was terribly wrong. Security personnel scurried inside, with a look of alarm and fear on their faces.

"What's going on?" Zeke asked.

"Boys, get inside the sanctuary...now!" one of the security men commanded the two young men.

"Why? What's the matter?" Gustavo yelled out, now feeling extremely worried.

As Zeke ran toward one of the front doors still left open as the security teams rushed into the lobby area, he was able to see the cause of the alarm.

"The police... The police are here. Lots of them," Zeke said, looking back at Gustavo.

"Get out of there, Zeke. Come inside," Gustavo pleaded. Zeke obliged, just as a member of the security team grabbed a hold of the front doors and securely locked them from the inside. "All the other doors stay locked at all times. I hope this will hold them back for a while, until we can figure out what to do next."

While part of the security team gathered dismayed inside the entrance foyer, Zeke ran in toward the sanctuary, looking for his father, whom he saw hurriedly walking around and to the right of the seating section of the sanctuary, in the direction of the closed access door to the backstage area.

"Dad," Zeke called, without making too much noise, and trying not to draw too much unwanted attention. Getting no response from Christensen, Zeke quickly followed his father backstage.

"John...John," Christensen said, calling to his pastor friend, who stood just behind the right-hand stage curtains, unsuspectingly watching the unfolding of the play. John looked back, to see a distressed Christensen. John then walked toward his friend to see what was the matter.

"John, the police are here," Christensen told him.

"Where? In the sanctuary?" John asked, very surprised and apprehensive about the news.

"No. Outside."

"They're surrounding us right now," Zeke added, standing just behind Christensen.

"The security team alerted me. I told them to remain waiting in the lobby," Christensen explained.

The Dreamers of Allianz

"Why us?" John asked, struggling to understand the reasons for such action against them. "We're not doing anything illegal. They have no right to be here," he stated in righteous indignation.

"John, remember Dr. C's warning message to the southern Community of Brethren? He said we, in the South, would be opposed soon. And just earlier today...the message from Tomazo?" Christensen reminded John.

"I know. It seems to be going down everywhere, Tanner," replied John.

"Dad, what are we going to do?" Zeke asked his father.

"Zeke, go get your mom, Shen-il, and the other members of the band. They're all seated in or near the first row on this side of the sanctuary. Tell them they need to come back here right now, but don't tell them why, yet," Christensen instructed his son. "Son, please, don't be obvious. The last thing we need is a panicked crowd getting out of control for fear of what might be happening. When they get here, we're all going to pray...hard."

"Okay, Dad."

"Yes, Zeke. Please be discrete," John urged him. "If we have chaos because of this, many people could get hurt."

"Got it," Zeke said. He then walked out into the sanctuary, to go make contact with the group, but headed first toward his mother.

"John, the old televisor in the office. Is it still broken?" Christensen asked, thinking that perhaps they might get some clues as to what was taking place via ABN images.

"I tried to turn it on earlier to see if I might catch a glimpse of the weather reports, but it was not working. It's too old," John replied.

"Shoot. I can't believe this is happening..." Christensen said.

While all of this commotion was secretly happening, the one-act play was proceeding uninterrupted and appeared to entrance most spectators in the audience. The scene displayed the prisoner on the right tending to and attempting to talk some with the new captive.

"Why have they done this to you?" the prisoner asked the badly hurt man, who was now sitting up and slowly taking sips from the cup being gently brought to his lips.

"The Anointed One has come… The sacrificial lamb… has been provided, to take away… the sins of the world," said the man in a barely audible tone. The prisoner at first didn't understand what he meant. But the man continued, now in a slightly stronger voice, "If you follow me, your sins will be forgiven."

"If we follow you?" yelled the prisoner on the left. "If we follow you where? You're going to the same place of death as us… to be crucified, upon that cursed skull hill."

"Don't listen to him. He's paying for what he has done. And so am I," the prisoner on the right said. "But what crime have you committed? Why are you here with us, convicted criminals?"

"He, though he knew no sin, was made to be sin… and he was numbered with the transgressors. He was bruised for all iniquities… And the chastisement for peace was upon him," the man answered.

"Is that you? Are you that man?" asked the prisoner on his right.

"I…Am…" the man answered. At that moment, the audience heard the loud clap of thunder coming from the stage, which shook the foundations of the prison cell. While many in the audience marveled at that, those who were aware of present danger lurking just outside, were feeling great anxiety, which grew even worse with the thunderous noise.

"Oh, Lord," responded the prisoner on the right. "I feel my heart burning within me. What must I do?"

"Believe in The Name, Who sent me… Believe on His Son, who came to save the world. I and the Father are one," answered the man.

"Ask him if he'll free us. Ask him, you stupid man. Ask this reject, who can't even hold his own cup of water. If he can do it, then believe him. Otherwise, you're just wasting your last hours on this forsaken earth as a fool," cried out the prisoner on the left.

"Lord…tell us. Can you give us freedom? Can you take away our punishment?" the prisoner on the right asked.

"I have come to give life abundant, by laying down my own life. I am the Good Shepherd, who gives his life for his sheep. No one takes it from me, but I lay it down of my own accord, and will take it up again, and be raised up..." Then he said, "If you try to save your life, you will lose it. But if you lose your life for my sake, you will gain life eternal," said the man, still agonizing from his injuries.

"He's a farce," accused the prisoner on the left. "I saw him violate the Sabbath. He's a delusional impostor... a fraud. Don't trust him."

Ignoring the voice of slander, the prisoner on the right said, "Lord, I will follow you up the hill. I will lose my life for you. This world has given me much sorrow, and I have committed a crime that took someone's life," confessed the prisoner. "But I want to taste that life eternal that you offer me, when you have risen again. Take away my sorrow and my sin, oh Lord."

"Come," said the wounded man, "draw near, and kneel down before me." The prisoner then got up from where he sat and knelt before the purple-cloaked man, as he had instructed. The man then strained to reach down for the cup from which he had drunk, still partly full and now sitting on the floor. Holding the cup with both hands, the man slowly lifted it up, high above them, and said, "Father, I thank you... My heart is glad and my tongue rejoices... For in this way, the Son of Man is glorified." He then moved his right hand, still covered in blood, and placed it on the prisoner's bowed head, and said, "I now baptize you, my brother, in The Name, in the Son, and in the Spirit of Truth." With the other hand trembling in physical weakness, he poured the water onto the prisoner, first wetting his head. Water from the cup, blood from the wounded man's hand, and tears from the prisoner flowed mingled down the prisoner's face, then shoulders, then his curved torso. It then dripped on the prisoner's legs and formed a puddle beneath him. "Rejoice, my brother, for this day you have seen the light. You have known the truth, and it has set you free."

"I believe, Lord. I *will* take up my cross and follow you," he said, looking up.

Just then, the soldiers were heard returning. They opened the prison cell door and removed the first two, who sat closest to the door. The last prisoner, the man on the left, would not move. Haunted by what he had just witnessed, he sat, overtaken by fear and paralyzed.

"You, prisoner…" yelled an angered Roman soldier. "Follow me!" Rage then immediately came over the prisoner, and he screamed, "No! No!" At that moment, soldiers stormed in and took the prisoner, forcibly leading him away.

The men then exited the scene, on the left side. The play had ended. The audience sat silent, many still grappling with the message, and others trying to take it all in.

At that very instant, the lights went out. The power had been cut off. The audience soon noticed something was not right, as two emergency floodlights quickly engaged, shining a light path toward the sanctuary's two main exit doors, while most of the large auditorium remained in almost total darkness.

Twenty-Five

Dariah's Discovery

Glancing at the profile displayed before her in Allianzi, Marshall Misha Dariah perused the dossier on her new suspect:

Name Tanner Daniel Christensen; Founding member.
Alias Christensen.
Status Non-implant.
Bio White male; Age 41.
D.O.B. October 7, GDM-Minus-28.
Origin Born in Victoria, Minnesota; former United States of America.
Personal Married to Claire Jeanette Christensen; 3 children (Ezekiel, Bethany, Holly); Residence: 75 Juniper Drive, Midville, TN, since June, GDM-3.
Affiliation American Province Resistance; Community of Brethren.
Cell Status Active; Children of the Promise (current membership, over 2,000); significant growth potential based on mobilization record.
Primary Role IT/sound support; Spiritual mentor.
Strategic Function A leading member of local congregation; Avid recruiter and indoctrinating agent.
Prior Trajectory Undergraduate degree in electrical engineering (sociology minor) from Faith&Knowledge University, GDM-Minus-4, Midville, TN; Masters in aerospace engi-

neering from MIT, GDM-Minus-1; Worked at NASA for 2 years; Pilot and air traffic control training completed GDM-3; Air traffic controller at Memphis Inter-Provincial Airport, since GDM-3.

Recent Data Input On Christensen's son, Ezekiel: "Dr. Isaac J. Ibrahim, registration number 60916. I wish to file a report here in the South... Another peculiar non-implant 'dreamer' case... Yes... Ezekiel Michael Christensen."

Upon reviewing Christensen's dossier, there was no question left in Dariah's mind. This was the man she had suspected him to be, her TA from the old days at MIT. *Wow. Long time no...nothing, Mr. Christensen... This is amazing coincidence*, she thought, as she soon recalled how Christensen had once come to her aid on a frigid afternoon, following class. She remembered him giving her a ride back to where she had left her car, completely stuck in a snow pile, or something like that, and then working for over an hour to dig it out for her, still in time for her rendezvous with Adammus Horn, later on. Feeling rather confident, at that point, about being in good favor with Horn, particularly after his public praise of her work for the Federation, Dariah thought to herself, *Oh, I have got to contact Adammus about this.*

As the police forces in the South maintained their position, almost entirely surrounding the place where the Children of the Promise group gathered, and as they awaited further orders, Dariah visualized Horn, on his direct PSS coordinates, to inform him of her intriguing discovery. Upon hearing about the interesting news, Horn was thoroughly amused, at first, and found himself enjoying the time spent reminiscing about his days in Law School, when he and Dariah were mutually involved romantically. As he sensed weakness in Dariah, however, and as she suddenly appeared to show uncharacteristic hesitation in following through with the intervention in the South, Horn grew more irritated and impatient.

"Are you asking me to adjudicate, Marshall Dariah? Do you really want my professional opinion?" he inquired of her.

"I just need to settle this in my own mind. You know, unbeknownst to him, I respected this man, Horn," she said, adding, "From what I can remember, he wasn't arrogant and full of bull, like the other ignoble TAs I had. He was nice to me and knew what he was talking about. I liked him…as a TA, that is."

"Look, Misha," Horn responded in clear annoyance, "this guy is with the Resistance. He's the enemy, and sooner or later, his group *will* be extinguished, just like the rest of them. You can delay this, if you feel you owe this guy something. But don't go getting sentimental on me for too long, or I'll be sick," he irascibly commented.

"Wait just a minute, here…"

"This is serious, Misha," Horn interrupted her, "and because of your obvious weakness and failure to act sooner, this cell is becoming one of the hottest things the southern Resistance has going for itself. *And*, they are in your jurisdiction, which only makes *you* look bad. Do I have to remind you of that, Marshall?" Horn lectured her.

"Look…I…" she said, struggling miserably to find able words, as she almost always did whenever arguing with Horn in the past.

"No. You look. Cut them too much slack, and I'll be on your tail like a ravenous rottweiller. I am not going to lose this war over your reluctant leadership. That's all I'm going to say about it," Horn sneered.

Dariah sat in angry silence for a brief moment, feeling furious at Horn and disgusted with herself for naively inviting his scorn.

"Thank you, Mr. Prosecutor General… I know what I need to do, now," Dariah replied in a serious tone.

"Misha," Horn added. "Are you that weak, or can I still trust you?" Horn asked point blank, implying a serious warning.

"You can trust me," Dariah said slowly and with sternness in her voice. And with white across her knuckles, she ended the visualization.

Dariah realized that visualizing Horn had been a huge mistake. At that moment, the American Marshall fumed with anger, as she was once again reminded of all the reasons why her former and tumultuous relationship with Horn had ended, as it did. Even after all those years, he was still insufferable and impossibly obstinate. She had come to know all too well, over the years, that if anything or anyone ever got in his way, he would mercilessly steamroll over them. And she couldn't forgive herself for allowing him to do it to her, yet again. *How stupid of me*, she thought. "But…this is not finished yet, Horn," she promised herself.

Backstage, the group of believers was still gathered in ardent prayer. John pulled himself away to go up on stage, as he noticed the gasps from the audience, due to the sudden and lasting darkness, which resulted from the power outage. Striving to speak more loudly due to the lack of electronic amplification for his voice, he tried to still the anxious audience, saying:

"Dear friends, please remain calm. It is a beautiful, snowy night outside. We've got plenty of candles for just such an occasion, and we will be lighting them up and bringing them out shortly. Soon we'll have some light again."

John, in response to his highest calling, was determined to complete his task that evening, whatever may come. He knew the outside doors could burst open at any moment, but he was going to carry the message forward and deliver an invitation to the audience, if it were the last thing he did. Not because he was uncaring or unfeeling toward their need to know about what was going on, but because of a worthy and more eternal purpose. To him, following through with the message was the most loving and lasting thing he could offer to them. He just had to try.

Meanwhile, the men and women gathered in the back were concluding their unplanned time in intercessory prayer. They prayed not just for themselves, but also and especially so for those who had come as guests that night, and for John to be able to accomplish his part of their mission that evening. Just then, Bethany, Holly, and Alyssa showed up backstage, after watching the play, still completely unaware of the goings-on outside, but concerned about the lengthy power outage.

At that point, while still gathered backstage, the women quickly transitioned from praying to fetching and lighting all of the candles they had brought along with them.

"Bethany, Holly, Alyssa, help us pass these out to the audience," Claire directed them. "Come back for more, as you give these out."

"Sure, Mom... But, what's going on?" asked Bethany.

"No time to explain. Just do it, please," Shen-il appealed to them.

While the girls moved to quickly attend to the urgent request, Zeke went out to the sanctuary to find Gustavo. Christensen walked out with him and headed toward the entrance lobby.

"Stavo, come with me," Zeke said. They both moved toward a back exit door, which opened up to the woods behind the pavilion. "Don't let it shut behind you. It'll lock us out," Zeke warned his friend.

"Got it," Gustavo replied, as he flipped down the doorstop, so as to leave the door ever so slightly ajar behind them.

They quietly exited the building, keeping their heads low. Through the narrow space between two snow-covered dumpsters, which sat behind the building, they could see some of the cog vehicles arranged in a somewhat staggered formation. Together, these vehicles faced the building, as if in ready-attack position. However, it appeared to the teens that no troops had yet been deployed, with the exception of some cogs, sporting FlightPaks and hovering just above the police vehicles.

"Why are they are just sitting there? I wonder what they're waiting for?" asked Gustavo, trying to keep his voice low. "Are they just trying to psych us out?"

"I don't know. But I sure wish I could throw something at those cogs," Zeke replied quietly.

"Zeke...we *can*," his friend said. "Remember the big sling we use for throwing water balloons at the enemy teams, during field day competitions here?"

"Yeah...let's do it," Zeke replied, excitedly. "But, we'll throw gigantic snowballs at them, instead."

"Let's go for it," Gustavo softly cheered.

Running back inside, they entered the equipment room, not too far down the hallway, which was now illuminated by a single battery-run emergency floodlight near the exit door. Once inside the

The Dreamers of Allianz

equipment room, they immediately located the red-white-and-blue sling, rolled up and hanging from a wall peg, just to their left.

"We're gonna need some help," Gustavo realized right away.

"You're right, Stavo," Zeke agreed. "Let's get moving!"

Twenty-Six

Resisting and Spirit-Sealing

By now, the sanctuary was intensely aglow with nearly a thousand flickering lights. As the crowd seemed once again to settle down and focus their attention toward the front stage, John prepared to deliver what could be the last message of his relatively short career as a pastor.

"If only you could feel what I'm feeling right now, as I look at you from up here... Folks, how fitting it seems that these countless points of light so luminously pierce the darkness in and around this place..."

As John continued addressing the crowd, Zeke and Gustavo searched for Bethany and a handful of other youth, to help them with their scheme. While the mobilized youth began to almost inconspicuously slide out into the aisles and move to the side of the sanctuary, Bethany briefly exhorted Alyssa to stay put and really listen carefully to the pastor's words. Alyssa, guessing that perhaps the youth were just getting ready for an upcoming musical number, did not think much about the slight commotion. Besides, Holly was still sitting next to her, holding on tight to her hand, and Alyssa somehow felt unable to even consider disengaging and parting from Holly's tender company.

As the young people walked out of the sanctuary and clustered by the back exit door, Zeke and Gustavo tactically filled them in on what was happening.

"You're, like, kidding, right?" asked a friend in disbelief.

"You don't have to take our word for it," Gustavo said. "All you have to do is take a peek outside."

Slowly, the back exit door was opened, and the handful of incredulous youth, agreeing to play along, slid out the door, soon to discover that this was no hoax. The police really were there, though still maintaining their position.

"My *word*!" exclaimed one of the handful of teens now ducking behind the dumpsters. "Y'all aren't kidding!"

"I told you," said Gustavo.

"Now what?"

"Get busy making snowballs… Make them the size of a snowman's head," Zeke instructed.

"Yeah, but whatever you do, be quiet…and keep your heads down," Gustavo added, as he and Zeke unrolled the large sling and favorably positioned themselves for a good launch.

"I can't believe we're doing this," said Bethany. "This is crazy, and we can get in big trouble."

"It's time we stand up and be counted," Zeke replied. "But not literally! Stay low," he whispered.

When a half-dozen snowballs had been made, Zeke and a friend took the ends of the sling, while Gustavo, capitalizing on his stockier build, pulled it back as far as he could.

"Place it on here," he said to Bethany and the others, who carefully lifted a basketball-sized projectile onto the harness at the end of the long, outstretched sling.   Zeke, holding on to his end, looked at Gustavo, who was about to release. As his friend looked back at him, Zeke began to softly hum an old action tune they all knew well, from the wildly popular, long series of *Mission Impossible* flicks. Soon, the others joined him, forming a quiet chorus of exhilarated teens.

"Ready? Aim…and launch!" Zeke quietly commanded.

The large snowball was then violently propelled upward, on a semi-elliptical trajectory, steadily angling downward and landing in a completely unexpected splat, right on top of a police vehicle, causing quite a ruffled reaction by those who sat inside it.

"What the heck was that!" exclaimed a startled cog. "Are we being attacked?" Then, a second impact was felt by another group of cogs inside a nearby vehicle; then another, and yet again, another.

As the officers in charge were assessing the bizarre situation, they too received an incoming blow.

"Snowballs!" one of them exclaimed. "Massive snowballs... Find out where exactly they're coming from!" ordered the ranking officer to a cog Sergeant.

Immediately, a triad of cogs wearing FlightPaks was mobilized and told to go investigate. But as this group levitated in tight formation and sped toward the back of the building from where the shots seemed to originate, one of them received a hard blow, which caused him to spin upside down and collide with great force against the other two following just behind him. This sent all three cogs spiraling downward and crashing hard on the ground.

"This is absurd!" cried out a cog Major. "We've got to take immediate control of this situation."

As the commanding officers then established contact with the command center, word was rapidly relayed to the D.C. headquarters.

Meanwhile, the intrepid teens continued their offensive campaign.

"This is awesome! Don't stop now. They're not responding. Keep on making those snowballs!" Zeke instructed.

Inside the pavilion, the audience was listening to John, as he began to conclude his short but compelling oratory:

"And so, my friends, your response to our message tonight is not about signing up for a religious program or committing to an organization. Know that the human institution of religion, no matter how formally organized or how loosely structured, can never adequately substitute for a personal choice for a real relationship with the Savior. That is what I hope you will understand tonight. That kind prisoner had no time for religion. He was headed to a death on the cross. He did, however, personally respond to the truth of the *Evangel* and, in return, was granted a freedom that no chains can negate. At the moment he believed on the Son, he was made new, and his eventual birth into eternity led to life everlasting in the glorious presence of The Name, who washed him pure...whiter than the snow falling outside tonight." John then asked the audience, "Will you consider, tonight, your eternal destiny, my dear friends? If you died tonight, where would you spend your eternity?"

As the question lingered in the candle-lit auditorium, John invited the audience to bow their heads and join him as he led them in prayer, saying, "Heavenly Father, I stand separated from you and judged already because I have not perfectly kept your moral law. I ask that you grant me forgiveness for my sin, as I put my faith and trust on the sacrifice of the Anointed One on that Roman cross, in *my* place. As he rose again, I too desire to rise out of my darkness and into an eternal communion with you. I give myself to you this day. Come into my heart and lead me beside quiet waters. I want a life of obedience to you. This I ask in your Son's name. Amen."

John then said to the audience, "If you prayed this with me tonight and believe in your heart what you've professed, then you have entered His rest and are no longer lost in this world... Would you be willing to publicly signal your commitment, tonight, by raising your hand right now?" Slowly hands began to be raised. More and more among them indicated that they had entered a new covenant and given their lives to The Name that very evening. Hundreds of hands were ultimately raised. John marveled and praised The Name for His wonderful work in the lives of so many.

At that moment, Holly looked at Alyssa and noticed the tears rolling down her cheeks. Alyssa knew in her heart that her time to decide had come. As Claire moved up and sat in Bethany's seat, next to Alyssa, she gave her a motherly embrace, saying in a pleasant tone, "You don't have to say it out loud. Say it in your heart, for now. The Name can hear it loud and clear."

Just then, Alyssa raised her hand. Holly, Claire, and Alyssa held each other, knowing they had at last come together as spiritual sisters.

Back in D.C., Dariah was being made aware of the stupefying situation in the South, as the police forces were being snowballed into abject, helpless humiliation, while they held to their passive position. In response, she promptly requested a Visual-feed from the cog surveillance system. As the images began to come in, it was evident to the cog establishment watching the embarrassing moment from afar that the situation called for extreme measures. Unable to contain herself, however, Dariah exploded in uproarious laughter, as she found the whole display quite unexplainably and unexpectedly refreshing and more than a little amusing to her. Forcing herself to control her comical reaction, Dariah turned to her Lieutenant, asking, "Colonel, what is your impression of this?"

"Sir, we've got a few options at our disposal for quickly snuffing out our adversary. We can fire a warning flare shot, followed by a loudspeaker announcement. We've also got rubberized ammunition. Or, gas-bombing them is an option as well." Then he added, "But, sir, if you don't mind my speaking candidly on my personal inclination at this point, I say send in the troops to teach these bozos a real lesson... Your orders, Commander?"

"Very well, Colonel..." Dariah prompted him, as she prepared to dictate her command, while the contingent of cogs in the room seemed to salivate in anticipation of her orders. "...Pull out!"

"Sir?" asked the confused and surprised officer.

"Pull back, disengage, abort the operation," Dariah repeated.

"But, sir?"

"Did you not hear me, Colonel? I want an immediate retreat!" she yelled.

"Uh...sir... Yes, sir," the astonished Colonel replied.

"Commander, what about the news media? They've been covering our operations tonight," another cog officer reminded her.

"No media. Not this time. But we'll keep a close eye on this group."

Dariah surprised even herself. Somehow, her conversation with Horn had spurred her on to a kind of independent action that she hadn't really contemplated in years. But was she risking too much? Could this sort of spontaneous attempt to somehow resist against Horn personally prove detrimental to her professionally? Could her daring decision stem from an unwise intermixing of personal and political interests, where her conflicted sentiments would end up jeopardizing and undermining her standing with the Allianz Federation, as well as her authority vis-à-vis her subordinates? Time would surely tell. But it was too late now to go back on her orders. She preferred to face the consequences later, rather than to appear even weaker by changing her mind on her hitherto unprecedented decision to retreat.

Twenty-Seven

Liberation?

Almost running out of good snow in large enough quantities to produce more projectiles, the teens began packing smaller snowballs between their hands. The stickiness of the frozen precipitation was still just right, and each youth began trying to hurl their compacted spheres past enemy lines. A few attempts would hit their intended target, but most were simply falling short of the cog vehicle barricades, positioned several yards away.

All of a sudden, something changed. The cog transports' headlights, which had been turned off during their surprise approach, were turned on almost simultaneously. The unexpected brightness brought real terror to the hearts of the defiant youth, who froze in their tracks.

"Uh-oh," one of them said, voicing the concern that was now in all of their minds.

As they heard the rumbling sound of moving vehicles shifting the snow beneath their wide cross-terrain tires and slowly breaking the enclosure they had formed, Zeke told them, "Guys…time's up. We've really got to get inside…now!"

Without skipping a beat, the group moved quickly toward the back exit door. But suddenly, something went terribly wrong.

"It's locked!" Bethany said, in sheer horror.

"Oh, no!" said Gustavo. "The doorstop must have gotten flipped up when we got out here."

"Oh-my-gosh!" said another girl, in desperation. "If we don't die out here, our parents are going to kill us!"

"Too late to worry about that now," Bethany replied.

"We've got to get inside," Gustavo said, "Let's bang on the door and get someone's attention."

"Oh, Lord. Please forgive our stupidity and help us to get out of this with our lives," a repentant young man cried out.

In their frenzied attempt to get someone to open the door, the frantic group of youth began to panic, not resisting the urge to cast blame on someone.

"Who's crazy idea was this, anyway?" one of them asked.

"Don't look at me," said Gustavo, as he pointed his gaze toward Zeke, "I was recruited, too."

"Y'all, shush! There's no time for this," Zeke scolded them.

Inside the building, a nervous group of performers heard the loud pounding on the back exit door. Certain of their impending doom, they moved out into the sanctuary, creating quite a stir and interrupting the deeply spiritual moment many in the audience were experiencing. Noting the commotion, Christensen ran up to find out what was wrong. By now, the audience again began to demonstrate palpable restlessness.

"Tanner, there's loud banging coming from the back door," Shen-il told him with urgency and fear in her voice.

"Please, everyone, try and stay calm. I'll go check it out," he replied.

Just when it looked like things could not get any worse for the group of teens gathered outside in the back, Zeke beheld an amazing sight.

"Y'all, stop... Look!" he said, pointing to what was happening with the moving convoy. "I think... It looks like they're...leaving!"

"Get out! Sparks! You're right," said Bethany. "They're turning around. They really *are* leaving! Yeah!"

"We did it, y'all! We sent them packing!" one of the youth cried out.

In ecstatic celebration, the teens began to hug, and some began to reach down for some snow, dumping it over each others' heads. Soon, a snowball extravaganza ensued, as the youth momentarily forgot that their real troubles were just about to begin.

Now standing just inside the closed exit way, Christensen heard the sound of youngish revelry, seemingly coming from just outside, behind the metal door.

"What's this?" he said to himself, as he cautiously opened the door.

Peering outside, he recognized the youth, including two of his own kids. He then pushed the door wide open. Catching the sight of Christensen, the teens immediately stopped their celebration and froze in place. A different kind of terror quickly overtook them.

"Uh-oh, we're busted," Gustavo remarked in obvious nervousness and dread.

"Can someone please explain to me what in the world is going on out here? Zeke, what is the meaning of this?" Christensen questioned, clearly vexed. "And where's the police?"

"Dad, they've left. We did it," Zeke said, trying to diffuse some of the righteous parental wrath he knew they certainly had coming to them.

"You did what? Get in here, all of you. Now!" Christensen said in a low but forcefully gruff voice, feeling all at the same time an indescribable sensation of justified rage and extraordinary relief.

Without hesitation, the teens rushed in.

"No...don't go out into the sanctuary. Get in backstage. We're all going to have a serious talk," he warned them, as he looked outside again, still trying to make sense of the strange, recent happenings. He soon realized the kids were right. For whatever reason, the police had pulled out. *But what, other than divine intervention, could explain all of this?* Christensen thought. Confused as he was, he hadn't the luxury of sweet contemplation over the apparently miraculous deliverance. His immediate attention had to be turned toward the absurdity and down right stupidity of the teenagers' perilous behavior that night.

Following the teens backstage, Christensen told them to sit down and wait for him to return. He then ran up on stage, where John was, and discretely informed him about their puzzling liberation.

"Tanner, are you absolutely certain of it?" John asked in disbelief.

"All I know, my brother, is that tonight we have been delivered from great evil. Thanks be to The Name," a relieved-looking Christensen said to his friend.

"That is marvelous. Praise The Name, for He's still doing miracles today!" John exclaimed. He then went on to jubilantly tell the crowd that everything was fine. "Tonight, we've all witnessed many great wonders, my friends."

While things were getting back to normal out in the sanctuary, a perplexed group of mostly parents and siblings were filing into the backstage area, to find a rather terrified group of youngsters. Before Christensen had a chance to begin the half-dozen or so interrogations in the presence of their family members, Zeke offered his explanation for their actions. A distraught parental bunch sat in utter bafflement.

"What in the world got into all of you? Do you not know what could have happened, The Name forbid?" a disgruntled parent said. "I don't know whether to hold you and never let go or ground you for the rest of your adolescence…"

"Dad, everyone, please don't be freak out. I'm truly sorry, and I take full responsibility for what we've done," a penitent Zeke said, offering what contrition he could muster, while still holding on to some inner sense of justification. "I just want you to know…This was not us kids against you. It was all of us against them."

"Looking back it does seem absolutely *loco*, I know," Gustavo said in his friend's defense, "I can't explain it. But at the time, it felt like something we just had to do."

As they sought a prayerful and just resolution to the difficult and unprecedented situation, the group of parents agreed on administering punishment, but with an adequately slight dose of grace. The youth were to be grounded for the next two months, while they performed services for the Community of Brethren, in addition to coming before the assembly at their next gathering to ask for forgiveness and reconciliation. The still lingering collective sense of shock on the part of the families backstage was now blended with unbelievable joy and an uncomfortably guilty sense of pride in their kids. But then again, all the night's events became part of a growing sense among them that they stood together, inseparable, as spiritual brethren facing a common but worsening tribulation, against which they had to help one another to take courage, and to jointly struggle to overcome, with the help of The Name.

Finally being able to breathe a sigh of relief, Christensen dismissed the group back to the sanctuary and began to take inventory of their situation in the midst of an apparent, if short lived, respite from unavoidable opposition by the Federation.

"Are you all right, Tan?" Claire asked, being the last one from the group to head back out to the sanctuary.

"I'm okay. Just trying to figure out how to find out more about what's happened here tonight. We're beyond visualization signal out here, and there's no working televisor... I feel marooned." He then said, "Maybe it's better not to know, at this point."

"Hey," Claire said, trying to lift Christensen's spirits, "we've had a great harvest tonight. And Alyssa made a personal decision to follow The Name."

"That's wonderful, Claire. Really wonderful. This night will go down for us as an unforgettable rollercoaster ride."

"The ride's not over, yet. We've got baptisms to do," Claire reminded her weary husband.

Twenty-Eight

Baptisms

As the main part of that evening's program was drawing to a close, the time had now come for those gathered there to transition into the baptismal ceremony involving those who had received the *Evangel* and come to faith. At that point, with the power still cut off and with candles yet burning, John announced that baptisms would follow, but that for those who did not wish to stay for the ceremony, transportation would be available shortly for them to leave, just as soon as the buses and vans had been cleared from all the snow on their windows. While much of the crowd began to shuffle, in preparation for departure, Christensen walked up on stage from the backstage area, to make brief announcements and give instructions for how the baptisms would be conducted, right after a short break.

Soon thereafter, a now much more intimate group of members, as well as some three-hundred new Believers, nearly six-hundred in all, were gathered around the baptistery in expectant celebration. As the leaders routed the candidates for baptism, in groups of twenty, around through the backstage area, where they put on their white robes in gender-separate stalls, and up through the front stage, the first few candidates made their way down and lined up before the still waters of the pool. Members of the band and gospel choir also assembled down below, softly joining together in contained acoustic rhapsody.

Alyssa came out with the first group to be baptized that evening. With the soft glow of candlelight shimmering and dancing on their faces and gowns, she and the other excited, white clad new converts could not help but resemble a collection of angelic hosts. Alyssa, one of the many younger members of this first group, alternated between talking with the others in the line up and looking over at the Christensen clan, who smiled back at her as they looked on.

"Momma, doesn't Alyssa look like an angel, standing there?" Holly remarked.

"She does. They all do," Claire replied. "And you know what?"

"What?"

"Tonight, a great celebration is certainly going on among the angels in heaven."

"Wow..." Holly responded, vividly imagining the joyous heavenly scene.

By now, feeling a lot more calm and collected after the eventful moments that preceded that evening, Zeke began to realize and be able to appreciate the significance of what he was about to witness in Alyssa's baptism. The spiritual chasm between them had finally been closed. Both he and the young lady were now kindred in the Lord. His heart began to beat faster with that new realization, as he savored every moment, and thought about just what he could say and do about his heart's helplessly rising desire. Could he dare to imagine the normal course of a developing courting relationship with Alyssa, even as the fate of the faithful appeared to increasingly hang on a balance? Whatever his conclusion at that moment, all progress regarding his intentions toward Alyssa, and her feelings in return, would have to wait. For he could expect no mercy after the stunt he and the others had pulled that night. To him, still a young heart, a two-month wait would surely feel like time without end, eternity and infinity cruelly mended together. Yet, he stood convinced that Alyssa was definitely worth the long, excruciating wait.

Before the actual baptisms got underway, John "the Baptist" Waters stood next to the candidates and spoke a few words about the symbolic significance of that ancient ceremony:

"As has been done among the faithful for over two millennia now, your baptism in these waters is an outward sign of your internal transformation, based on what the Anointed One already accomplished for you on the cross. Your obedience unto baptism also serves as a public profession to the body of saints and witnesses here gathered about your commitment to The Name, to following His Son, and to living through and being purified in the Spirit of Truth, in Whom you've been sealed forever against spiritual perdition." John then added, "Through baptism, you are identifying with the death, the burial, and the bodily resurrection of the Anointed One and are being water-marked as a member of the Community of Brethren all over the world and in times past, present, and future, and as co-heirs with us and Him of everlasting life and eternal communion with The Name and all His saints."

In saying this, John "the Baptist" Waters, himself now wearing a white robe, entered into the pool, indicating with a slight facial contortion the rather cold initial feel of the water. Then, he jokingly said, "By now, I should be used to this. After all, I've got a nickname to live up to. But the truth is, the pool heater is not working right now, and you're really going to have to think…summer," he said, addressing the group lined up to enter into the pool. The onlookers chuckled a bit. "C'mon, Tanner. You're in here with me," he said, gesturing for a robed Christensen to get in, having been assigned that evening to aid with the baptisms.

"This is getting really primitive," Christensen said, joking along.

With his arms extended to receive the first one in line, John took the young man by the hand and led him to Christensen, who shivering a bit stood a few feet away on the opposite side of the rectangular pool. John then took the second in line, the young Alyssa, and helped her into the now moving waters and positioned her sideways and in front of him. Both candidates had opted earlier for baptism by full emersion. As both John and Christensen placed their left hand on each candidate's shoulder, and raised their right hand, John said, "Based on your profession of faith, my sister and brother, we now baptize you in The Name, in His Son, and in the Spirit of Truth." Bringing their right hand down and covering the candidates' nose and mouth with a white, disposable cloth, they gently lowered the two down beneath the waters and brought them back up, to the applause and cheering of the surrounding crowd.

The Dreamers of Allianz

At that moment, under the glowing ember hues of the many flickering flames still lighting the dark sanctuary and all around the pool area, the mood of the place, once somber, turned ecstatic. Overjoyed, Claire, Zeke, Bethany, and Holly jumped up and shouted, "Way to go, Alyssa," who then waived back, shaking a little and wiping water from her face, as she headed out the other end of the pool, making room for the next in line. As she exited the waters, Alyssa was welcomed by a group of smiling helpers, holding outstretched towels.

Two-by-two, all new Believers that night were baptized into the worldwide family of the faithful, and they all joined together in a celebration of the Lord's Supper. As the ceremony ended, and all were departing into the now clear night, the Christensens, along with Alyssa and the Waters, stayed behind to close down the place. The time was now almost 11:30 p.m., and all was still well. All candles extinguished, but all spirits still on fire, they walked out together, exhausted and feeling hungry, but also at peace, toward their lonely vehicles, seeing no sign of police presence anywhere. The snow had ceased falling, and the sounds of already melting snow from the warming temperatures outside punctuated the otherwise silent night, as the wet drips fell interspersed from the large pavilion's sloping roof.

On their quiet ride home, while the others fell asleep in their seats, Christensen's mind was being continually filled with many haunting, but also exhilarating images from the hours that went before, even as he noticed the many fresh, extra wide tread marks on the snow covered roads, likely left there by the intimidating cog convoy. They reminded him that dark menace truly had visited them that night. In so many important ways, it had been a perfect night. In so many others, a night they might, if at all possible, prefer to forget. But as the ruddy *"Fuel Low"* warning on his dashboard called to him in the stillness of the moment, Christensen was again reminded of the nightmarish predicament in which they found themselves as Believers, and the real tenuousness of their condition under the seriously radicalizing Allianz system. Their immediate future seemed like anybody's guess, now that they had come face-to-face with terrifying evil.

Twenty-Nine

Reality Check and Dreaming Isaiah

By the early hours of the morning, the big picture had come into sharper focus for Christensen. He nervously managed to follow the still recent and disturbing media footage from the Federation's aggression in the Charlotte and Atlanta areas, the night before. *We were going to be next*, he grimly deduced, as shivers ran up and down his spine, just thinking about how closely they had come to being attacked, themselves.

While Claire and the kids slept, Christensen had spent much of the wee Monday morning hours in his basement bunker, in constant contact with John and others in the Children of the Promise group. Together they tried to analyze the fantastic course of events they had collectively witnessed and sought mutual support in the face of the tragedies affecting the other members of the Community of Brethren. An influx of new messages from concerned Resistance members throughout the South and from across many parts of the globe had been accumulating overnight and clogging up Christensen's dated communications network. Distressing thoughts of what might be the fate of their brethren in the Southeast, now in the hands of the Federation, and of how they in Tennessee were inexplicably delivered from the same tragic end, were almost too much to bear. But their anguish was made even worse by the awful sense of survivor's guilt that Christensen and the others began to taste, as they realized the evil which had passed over their own gathering, but which had evidently not spared their brethren, as the media replays so frightfully reminded them. Little sense could be made of it, except to say that for reasons which perhaps only the angels in heaven were privy to, their turn to be dealt the enemy's destructive blow – even a final one – was not yet to be.

The heart-wrenching question of what to do next – to continue with the gatherings and face grave danger, or to retreat to safety and face condemnation by their own conscience – still needed to be answered. In the midst of that painful moment, however, resolving the impasse seemed less important and necessary than to pray and grieve over their brethren's losses. With sinking hearts, they struggled to return to any semblance of normalcy, as the new day began. How could they, after the dreadful events of just hours before? But Christensen, for one, would have to force himself to revive. He still had a job which he, for some odd reason, could not simply desert, even if his dismissal from it appeared all but certain, indeed. Perhaps, the security of quotidian routine was what he desperately needed at that moment. Thus, as if engaging into autopilot, Christensen began to ready himself for the long and uncertain day ahead.

It was not quite 5:00 a.m., when Claire awoke to the loud utterances coming from Zeke's room, next door.

"Tanner? Zeke?" she said, still dazed and half asleep.

Regaining some coherence of thought, and with no sign of Christensen nearby, she hurried, taking a few steps down the hall toward Zeke's room. As she entered his room, Claire soon verified that her son, once again, appeared to be receiving Spirit dreams. Now talking more clearly than ever, despite his unconsciousness, Zeke's recitation was surely coming, Claire discerned, word for word, from the sixth chapter of the Old Testament book of Isaiah.

"…'Holy, holy, holy is the Lord Almighty; the whole earth is full of his glory'… 'Woe to me!' I cried. 'I am ruined! For I am a man of unclean lips, and I live among a people of unclean lips, and my eyes have seen the King, the Lord Almighty'… 'See, this has touched your lips; your guilt is taken away and your sin atoned for.'... Then I heard the voice of the Lord saying, 'Whom shall I send? And who will go for us?' And I said, 'Here am I. Send me!'..." Zeke continued articulating in his sleep.

The thought of recording those words, or at least taking them down in writing, as a way of preserving the precious material now being uttered in its entirety, crossed Claire's mind numerous times while she sat in unbridled, if quiet amazement. But her son was moving so quickly through the verses, that it would seem futile to try to hastily produce a recorder, even if she knew where one were to be found at that point. And at any rate, Claire questioned the wisdom of creating such a record, as important as that might be, given the delicate state of affairs in which they found themselves presently, relative to the Federation.

In a different time, and under different circumstances, she would not have hesitated for a moment, but not now. Her motherly concern instinctively moved her to want protection for her son from being found out as the perpetrator of what would certainly be regarded as a religiously entrenched act of subversion, no doubt condemnable by the Allianz Code. They had had more than enough danger and excitement to last a long while, she felt. Claire opted, therefore, to simply remain there with Zeke, watching over him as he unwittingly spoke the very words breathed into the minds of the prophets and the ancients, thousands of years before.

What a gift, this seemed to her, although perhaps a curse to many others. What a thing to behold; her own son, being most assuredly divinely elected as a mysterious instrument of The Name's glory. *But why? Why Zeke? And why now?* she wondered. Such a normal boy, he was, in just about every way. As she now lay next to her son, Claire secretly pondered these things, as the sonic rhythms of his Scriptural narration brought a sudden and wonderful peace over her, and eventually lulled her irresistibly to sleep.

A couple of hours later, Zeke woke up. Seeing his mother next to him once again, he knew what this meant, which also helped explain why he felt such great thirst.

"Mom, my throat's so dry. I really need some water. There's an empty cup on my desk," Zeke indicated, pointing toward the wall opposite them.

"All right, honey, I'll get you some water. I'll be right back," Claire replied, as she woke up from her deep sleep.

"Thanks," Zeke said, putting his hand to his throat and struggling as he swallowed dry.

As Claire worked her way downstairs, after tending to her son, she found Christensen dressed for work, sitting quietly in his usual spot in the den, and staring out the window. Over the years, the old armchair upholstery had gotten worn and branded with his body's imprint, after so many mornings of reliable devotions, which had long been part of his work pre-departure ritual. Amid trials of many kinds, Christensen had come to greatly depend on that quiet time with the Lord, for comfort and for gaining perspective on the day ahead. That early morning, perhaps more than ever, those moments of prayer and meditation were a necessity, and how he searched for that true intimacy and fellowship with The Name, longing for His mercies to be renewed, as promised in the few psalms Christensen had memorized as a younger man.

"Hey, Tan," Claire greeted him.

"Hi, blondie. Good morning."

"Good morning to you, too. Have you been up long?" she asked.

"I never really went to bed. I spent most of the night trying to follow the news and visualizing John and others in the group," he disclosed.

"Oh, honey…I worry about you. How long can you keep this up?" Claire said, voicing deep concern over Christensen's almost sleepless schedule.

"For as long as the Lord energizes me."

"I do hope you don't fall ill. You should at least take a good lunch with you to work."

"Look at it this way, honey. No sleep, no nightmares, right?" Christensen halfway kidded.

"If only the nightmares came just while we slept…" Claire fatalistically uttered.

"I know. I'm still in shock over last night and over the tragedies out East," Christensen admitted.

"I just can't believe it, still… Have you heard any more about it?" she asked.

"Very little that's new. But word has it that, though there were many arrests, no one got seriously hurt during the ordeal," he replied.

"That's very good news. So what happens to them now, Tanner?"

"No clue. The cogs apparently took away truckloads of Believers, and there's yet to be any confirmation about their fate or whereabouts, since the arrests. That really irks me. But there's really nothing much anyone can do to help. We don't even know where they were taken."

"Gosh. That's so awful. What are you and John thinking? You know, about the gatherings and all?" Claire had to know.

"Only the Lord knows, at this point. But if there's any way, we'll try to press on, especially with Easter being just around the corner. Over the years, that's been a time of great soul harvest for us."

"I know, Tan, but …"

"Claire, listen. We can't just run away from our destiny. We've all been given a role for such a time as this. And we have to remain faithful," Christensen concluded.

"I know you're right. But that doesn't make it any easier. I'm just having to choose to trust…in you…in The Name," Claire responded.

"That's how I get by, too…total dependence on Him." Then he said, on a lighter note, "I'm trusting The Name for a nice catnap on the WormRail ride to the airport."

"You do that, honey. You've got to get some rest, sometime," Claire urged her husband.

"Time... For everything, there's a time..." Christensen said, recalling the old passage in the book of Ecclesiastes. "It is written, 'I know that everything The Name does will endure forever; nothing can be added to it and nothing taken from it. The Name does it so that men will revere Him'..." he quoted from memory.

"Yes, but according to King Solomon isn't everything meaningless? Just vanity, as he said it over and over again?" Claire asked.

"True. But I believe King Solomon, in his wisdom, was referring to life on this earth. Yet, he had to know that there's another reality."

"What do you mean, Tan?"

"The Kingdom of The Name has drawn near to us and we've been taught about love. We can push forward because of love, Claire. Love of The Name. Love for others... We have a new covenant through the cross of Calvary. And it's based on love. And through that love, we'll be saved on the day of His appearing," Christensen answered.

"Come quickly, Lord. Come quickly," Claire prayed. "In the meantime, grant us wisdom and grace."

"That's a great prayer, Claire. So simple... But, still, a great prayer."

Claire then switched to another subject of great import and urgency. "Tan, Zeke continues to dream. Somehow I still think it has something to do with what's been happening in the big picture. You know, all of the opposition against us?" Claire commented.

"Claire, there is definitely a great stirring in the waters. I can feel it. It's all coming to a head, somehow. I don't exactly know how our son or we fit in all of this, but I am certain of one thing. Whenever evil is present, grace abounds all the more, the Word of Truth promises us. And evil clearly is upon us," Christensen said, "so The Name must also be moving in all of this. He's bending His bow."

"So, what are *we* supposed to do now?" Claire asked in frustration.

"Wait on Him."

"I don't know if I have that much faith," Claire said, as she sat down on the floor, between Christensen's feet, and with her back against the seat of his armchair.

"Claire, we walk by faith, not by sight…remember?" Christensen said, gently covering her eyes. "We might not see clearly in front of us, but when we look back, we can see the numerous blessings, providential protection, and the faithfulness of the Lord. Seeing that should give us strength to trust Him with our future, even when we cannot see it with clarity."

Claire then confessed, "I wish you could stay home, Tan. Every time I stop and think about last night, I get so afraid and so panicky."

"I know. But just give me a few days to see how things will shape up at work. You might have me home full-time soon," he said, knowing from the recent news at work that his days at his job were shortly numbered.

"The kids would actually love that, you know? Me, too."

"Yeah. But it can't last forever… Speaking of kids, are they up, yet? I've got to get going," Christensen mentioned.

"I'm letting them sleep in this morning. But they'll be up soon. We've got some serious schooling to do," Claire indicated. "I just hope we can concentrate."

"You're amazing, Claire. Just amazing."

"You're too kind, Tan. I don't feel so amazing. But…thanks, anyway."

Thirty

Horn's Strategy

Upon learning about Dariah's decision regarding the Children of the Promise gathering, Adammus Horn did not wait long before trying to reach her via PSS connection. Anticipating Horn's disdainful reaction, Dariah avoided answering his call that morning, while she rehearsed a defensible account and mastered the subtleties of the face-work she would have to present to him during the unpleasantly expected visualization. Dariah knew she only had a couple of hours to spare before having to face Horn. She was also certain Horn would savor every minute of his anticipated and incisively directed condescension. He was a hard man.

Yet, in a bizarre way, which continually surprised even her most sober sensibilities, it had always been Horn's carefully applied arrogance and masterful sense of self, and his own unyielding power in the most challenging of situations, that had so intensely and irresistibly drawn her to him in the first place. Even as a sharp, young law student, Dariah thought, there was something intoxicating about Horn, a certain *je ne sais quoi* that exuded tremendously alluring power. If there had ever been, in fact, a quintessential embodiment of the male power-mystique, Horn was it to perfection. In this, Dariah knew herself all too well. She had, almost tragically, a seemingly insatiable appetite for absolute power. And while Horn had frequently managed to infuriate her over the years, nevertheless Dariah often found herself craving his attention, approval, affections, and his very presence. This was so even though she could reason that on most occasions she was left wanting, frustrated, and perennially unsatisfied in their rather imperfect connection.

Much to her surprise, this time Horn was refreshingly sanguine. No doubt, another functional dimension of his manipulative and seductive persona. Such versatility, so craftily employed over several years of evident institutional ascent, had crucially assisted him in achieving significant and uncontested preeminence in the Allianz law enforcement establishment. It had also gained him unmatched influence over the highest governance body in all of Allianz, the Council of Regents.

Finally reaching Dariah, Horn made his views clear. "I was disappointed, Misha. But I can't say I didn't see it coming," Horn candidly commented regarding Dariah's dealings with the Children of the Promise group, as he began the visualization. "I'm not giving up on you yet, though. I'm giving you another opportunity to show me the special talents for which I nominated you for American Marshall."

Disarmed by his surprising and uncharacteristic amiability, Dariah once again found herself at a loss for words in trying to communicate to Horn the rehearsed and official-sounding response in her defense. Instead, she dangerously revealed, "Horn, I just couldn't go forward with it, once I gained personal knowledge of who would be targeted. I don't know why it mattered to me so much in this particular instance, but what's done is done, and I take full responsibility for it."

"Oh, the slippery slope of sympathy and compassion…" Horn replied. "You know, Misha, in this business we can't afford to cultivate pity. A tender heart makes you a weak target, and then you get trampled on mercilessly by your enemies. Once crushed, you're ineffective, and before you know it, you're looking at the world through the sorry space between two metal bars, if you're spared at all, by your political adversaries."

"I know it sounds weak, Horn. I know it sounds pathetic. But I just had to pull out… Don't worry, though. I'm not yet finished with this project. Misha Dariah will not be discounted. I will get the job done. And the next time we go up against the Resistance, personal ties or not, I will put a stop to their operations and come out the undisputed victor," Dariah vowed.

"It's very good to hear that, Misha." Horn then went on to illustrate, "You know, when I was still at Harvard Law, I remember one of my favorite professors once told us a story about the *misericord*. It was a dagger used to give an injured knight his death wound. In that story, however, compassion, or *misericord*, meant death."

"I see."

"Don't let that be your fate, Misha. I'm warning you...as a friend," Horn said. Dariah hesitated, but then boldly countered, "A friend? That's not a term I've heard you utter about me in years."

"Misha, let's not pretend. I still remember who we once were together. We'll always have that in our common past. But I'm not the same person I was then. I didn't get to where I am today by letting my focus slip."

"You mean like I did? Is that what you're saying?" Dariah challenged him.

"Don't take it personally, darling," Horn replied. "I never do. It's best that way."

"So, that's all I can expect out of you, Horn? The comfort of the all but forgotten past and that soothing, impersonal touch you offer me?" she sarcastically asked.

"Misha, look...I'm going to help you, okay?" Horn said, knowing just when and how to deflect tension in a conversation, and showing his exacting ability to maintain the upper hand in dialogue.

"Help me?" she responded, annoyed.

"Yes...I'm going to turn your little flirtation with pity into a profitable venture for you and for me, Marshall," Horn proposed.

"I'm not sure I follow your logic, here."

"Let me ask you something... When was the last time we took a trip together, you and me?" Horn asked.

"What? What are you talking about?" Dariah replied in confusion, for it had been several years since they had even been together in person.

"I knew you'd be shocked," he replied. "But you know I haven't been away all these years by my own volition. The Court has kept me tied up in hundreds of key trials."

"Of course."

"Now, I want you to listen to me carefully."

At that point, Horn went on to explain the scheme he had concocted. Horn and the Allianz delegation were going to arrive in the American Province on Tuesday evening, a day earlier than expected, and together, on Wednesday morning, he and Dariah were to pay a special, personal visit to a particular individual of interest in the South.

"I want to use him, Misha. He could be of incalculable worth to us. So I need you to tempt him with an irresistible offer," Horn instructed.

"What makes you so sure Christensen will cooperate? He's obviously a man of strong convictions," Dariah questioned.

"I'll leave that up to you, Marshall. He's your problem. Make full use of your persuasive resources. You just make sure you close the deal for us," Horn answered. "I'll see you tomorrow night, in D.C., Misha. Bye, darling."

"Yes, tomorrow... Uh, safe travels," Dariah replied, and the visualization ended.

To get her mind around what had just been discussed, Dariah paused for a moment. Suddenly, nervousness gave way to anxiety, anxiety to fear, and fear to dread. *What if I fail him appallingly? What if I let Horn down, yet again?*

Although Dariah liked to think that she had meritoriously earned her position, the truth was that Horn had essentially handed it to her on a silver platter, by personally nominating her before the General Parliament in Paris. And, knowing him, Horn would not hesitate to take it away from her, if once again disappointed in her. To make matters worse, the thought of personally seeing Horn, after almost five years, provoked her worst insecurities. She wondered how to present herself – as Misha or as Marshall. She couldn't imagine their long awaited rendezvous happening at a less opportune moment, and in a more uncomfortable circumstance. But if there was one thing Dariah knew for sure, it was that tomorrow would arrive soon enough, and she *was* the American Marshall. Therefore, in light of this illustrious visit by the Federation's own Prosecutor General, she had better make sure to deliver on behalf of Allianz. No other outcome would suffice, or she might lose her post, as well as Horn's already waning respect, forever. With not a moment to spare, Dariah proceeded to make her own plans to ensure her success.

Thirty-One

Andrus' Counsel

It was now already Monday evening in the district of Paris. Adammus Horn and the ten members of the Council of Regents were being debriefed by a team of high-level government functionaries on the state of the Federation. Also present were the members of the Allianz delegation who would accompany Horn on his imminent trip to the American Province, as well as High Sage Andrus, who would be bringing a plenary address highlighting the truly remarkable global growth of the Path of Transcienz. Following this meeting, the much larger General Parliament would convene, as bi-weekly scheduled, in order to receive a simplified and censored version of the overall report, typically delivered in the form of parliamentary policy recommendations to be ratified by the Parliament's body of Allianz Nobles.

At the top of the agenda for the initial debriefing meeting were environmental and metropolitan overpopulation concerns, as well as the latest Federation-sponsored crackdowns against the worldwide Resistance movement. The continued mysterious disappearances of Believer families, now totaling sixty-two in almost as many countries, continued to represent a puzzling development for the government, especially as more attention was being paid by the populace to the lack of an official public pronouncement about the strange vanishings.

The high point of the evening, however, came courtesy of the vibrant and loquacious High Sage Andrus. Wearing a silver-colored, fabric headdress and a gaudy, amethyst talisman around his neck, he epitomized mystical extravagance. Andrus' long and shimmering, silver and purple-accented, white robe moved fluidly around his full figure. His exquisite garment touched the floor and hid his leg movements, giving the audience the impression that the High Sage floated effortlessly, as he paced gracefully across the center platform of the palatial main chamber in the Allianz Palace. His jet-black beard curved softly to a fine point, extending several inches out beyond his chin. As he spoke, the point of his dark beard fluttered, like a precision needle busily recording seismic activity on a graph.

Engaging as ever, Andrus delivered his riveting address:

"Esteemed co-stewards of our Federation's promising and bright future... Vigor to Allianz," he began. "It is indeed my great pleasure, tonight, to unveil for you the most excellent news that, according to our very carefully maintained registry of inter-provincial membership in our enlightened Path, we have now reached the four and a half billion mark. Thus, we are approaching the seventy percent threshold for the entire globe's population, well before the established GDM-20 goal. Our predictions are that, barring any unforeseen challenges, we are poised to reach the eighty percent mark in the next three years, thus exceeding our GDM-20 ambitions by a significant margin of ten percent of the total population," Andrus announced to the audience's standing ovation. "Furthermore, I am overjoyed to inform this distinguished assembly that, as our records indicate, we are now dream connecting, on a daily basis, around a billion individuals worldwide. And as you know, dear friends, a metaphysically involved populace means a continuously thriving Allianz system. I, your humble servant, bring you this good news in hopes of fostering an ever-mutually prospering relationship between Allianz and Transcienz." The transcendent High Sage then continued in his address, nearly mesmerizing the audience, including the Prosecutor General.

The speech by Andrus was indeed a momentous one that evidenced the strategic alliance between politics and religion under Allianz. As the effective guardian and the main communicator of the popular Transcienz teachings, Andrus never squandered an opportunity to take credit for the Path's staggering momentum around the world. To be sure, his exuberance in style and in speech made him a rising Allianz icon, and the recognition he continually gained from the Council of Regents, and especially from Horn, afforded him the access to power he needed to secure his place as the Federation's top mystic.

Horn, thrilled by the welcome news from Andrus, descended to the center platform to personally congratulate him. The High Sage then took the opportunity to counsel Horn on the crucially important visit to the American Province.

"My beloved in the enlightened Path," Andrus said somberly, in mid embrace, "the voice of our most adored antecedents bring you an oracle through your loyal servant about the leadership in Washington, D.C."

"I am listening."

"The destiny of that great province hangs on a balance," Andrus cautioned. 'It is time to deepen your ties with Dariah and to test her commitment to Allianz. You must tell her about the **Great Catacombs Program**, and take her to North Africa, as soon as possible. Her partial knowledge, at this point, is not likely to secure her total loyalty to Paris for long. She must fully learn about the substance and magnitude of the **Great Allianz Directive** if we are to be certain of her devotion to our objectives. This weekend, I shall be in Damascus for a Transcienz tour. You may visualize me there, should you require further counsel on this matter… The eyes of our ancestors will be upon you."

"I understand, my most trusted counselor," Horn responded. "I will make preparations to undertake this important endeavor. I am grateful for your service and will see to it that you are granted the appropriations needed to complete your Transcienz Hall projects underway in the Rome and Istanbul districts."

"I am truly touched and made exceedingly glad by your kind demonstration of gratitude, Your Grace, and am absolutely certain that your investment in the great Path will return to you manifold," said the demagogical High Sage, as he bowed respectfully. Soon after, Horn departed to finalize the preparations for his trip to D.C., just a few short hours away.

Thirty-Two

Uncertainties

At the Memphis Inter-Provincial Airport, that Monday afternoon, Christensen sat with about twenty other implanted and non-implanted air traffic controllers, at a meeting with the airport superintendent, who, for the sake of the handful of non-implanted employees present, spoke in English. Changes in their sector were going into effect later that week, and three-quarters of the controller force was being discharged as soon as Wednesday, when a program review by Allianz Federation representatives was going to be conducted, in preparation for an imminent visit by the Paris delegation.

As the superintendent read the alphabetical list of names of those being let go, "Al-Hammamet, Christensen, Conrad, Ephraim, Mathison, Nageeb, Nguyen, Peters, Sanchez..." it became obvious to those present at the meeting that all five of the non-implants in that sector were being removed from their jobs, along with a number of implants, totaling eighteen names. Though they had tried to prepare themselves for the inevitable, the official announcement hit all of them hard, but especially the non-implants, who had few other employment prospects. For these few, the news reached them like an inescapable avalanche that might very possibly bury them and their families alive.

"Ladies and gentlemen, your last workday will be this Wednesday," the superintendent announced. "You are expected to have collected all of your belongings by that day, as well as to

The Dreamers of Allianz

have your access cards and ID tags turned in and accounted for. On your way out, at the end of your half-day Wednesday work shift, you will be handed your severance pay stub. From that point on, you are not to return to the tower for any reason whatsoever, and if you are seen there, or caught attempting to enter the premises, you will be immediately detained. Is that understood?" Most of the men and women gathered there nodded in acknowledgement. Christensen and two other non-implants shook their heads in contempt.

"Christensen...care to let us know what the problem is?" their boss inquired.

"Sir, it's just that the first we heard about all of this was not even a week ago," Christensen replied. "It just doesn't seem right for us to receive such short notice, basically a day and a half, on something of this magnitude. Some of us, like myself, have been with this airport for nearly a decade..."

"I realize that, Christensen, but these are the orders I've been given. And it looks like this comes from very high up, in D.C. This really is out of my hands, and I'm sorry. If I don't follow through, it's my neck we're talking about," explained the superintendent. He then continued, "But I want you to know how appreciative I've been of you all's service here, over the years. We haven't had a single serious air traffic-related incident at this airport in over eight years... But times are changing, and we must comply with the new demands and expectations for our facilities. I wish things were different, but..." he said, shaking his head.

As the meeting concluded, and the staff returned to their posts, the five non-implants huddled around Christensen's desk, the senior controller in the group. With heavy hearts, they feebly tried to console each other.

"What now?" asked one of them, as the others just stood there, speechless.

"Well, Roy. It's the end of an era," said Christensen.

"Do you have any plans?" a female controller asked their senior colleague.

"I'm going to go home, kiss my wife and kids, and then lose myself in what I've still got that's good and precious to me...my faith, my family," Christensen replied. "After that, it's just a day at a time for me. I'll probably sleep more, that's for sure."

"Well, I should be so lucky," another controller, the youngest among them, remarked. "I've got no wife and no kids. My job's all I've got...and now it's history."

"Gabe, how's your spiritual life these days?" Christensen asked him, knowing the young man to have sporadically attended Brethren Gatherings in the past, although he was not aware of any conversion experience by this man.

"Honestly? Lukewarm, at best."

"Well, friend, this would be a good time to change that. If at any point our faith should really matter, this is the time," Christensen said.

"I've been sort of taking some time off, you know?" the young man explained, referring to his less than active faith life.

"Gabe...if things seem different now, and you're feeling distant from The Name, let me tell you something, it's not The Name that has changed. It's you. He never changes. Remember that."

"Thanks, Christensen. I'll give it some thought."

As they disbanded, each went about the painful task of beginning to clear their individual work areas of, in some cases, years of materials, personal artifacts, mementos and memories. Gabe, the young controller, secretly began entertaining the idea of getting implanted. He was young and just starting out. He did not really know The Name. And life without the implant was beginning to cost him too much.

The next morning, the Christensens had a brief but sobering family talk over breakfast about the even more uncertain days ahead. Following that, Christensen departed for his final full day at work. Soon thereafter, Claire received a visualization from Alyssa's mother, who was hard-pressed to request an important favor. She was going to have to leave on a two-day, work-related trip on

Wednesday and had been counting on Alyssa's being able to stay over at the Christensens for a night. Having learned recently that the scheduled slumber party had been canceled, due to Zeke's and Bethany's punishment for their reckless conduct at the Brethren Gathering, Ms. Lorentz called to plead for a small exception to be made, since, being new to the area, they really did not have too many other possibilities for finding another family to help them on such short notice.

"I'll need to double-check with my husband, Ms. Lorentz," Claire replied, "and I'll let you know as soon as I possibly can. On my part, I would be willing to make an exception in this case. You know, we are really fond of Alyssa and wouldn't want for her to be put in a tight spot because of something that wasn't her fault."

"I appreciate that, Ms. Christensen, and do thank you for the way you've welcomed Alyssa in your family. You know, last night we spoke about her baptism experience, and I must say I'm quite pleased with how she's developing new and exciting interests. Things have been tough for her, since the familial covenant between her father and I was legally terminated, six months ago. Then, having to move to a new place and a new school, in the middle of the academic year, was another difficult adjustment for her," Alyssa's mother commented. "But your family has been a real source of comfort over the past couple of months, and I'm so thankful."

"What about you, Ms. Lorentz?" Claire boldly asked. "How do you find support through all of it?"

"Well, as you know, I don't quite see things as you do. I find refreshment through Transcienz dreaming."

"Of course."

"I mean no disrespect by this, Mrs. Christensen, but…"

"Please, call me Claire."

"Okay…Claire. What I was saying was, I fail to understand why anyone would want to waste, I mean…spend, *any* time with deity ideations."

"I see," said Claire, knowing that offering an explanation would yield no effect on an implanted individual who had chosen activation, which was the case with Alyssa's mother.

"I've often asked Alyssa to consider activation and seeking the Path of Transcienz. I think just the language benefit by itself would be a huge relief for her. But considering the circumstances, I've decided not to keep pressuring her with one more thing," explained Alyssa's mother.

Ms. Lorentz had not yet realized the profound consequences of Alyssa's conversion. She had not yet been made fully aware of the significant challenges the prior evening's decision at the Brethren Gathering would present for her daughter; from the counter-effects on her implant, to the danger she would be exposed to as a new Believer under the growing threat coming from the Federation's repressive apparatus against the Community of Brethren. The truth, in effect, was that no one, not even Believers, knew the full extent of the spiritual, physical, or social ramifications of such a transformation. All they knew was that, once activated, one's implant appeared to have a detrimental effect on one's will to seek after or desire to know The Name. And that signified reason enough for the Resistance to galvanize their efforts around reaching the lost for Spirit-sealing.

That afternoon, as Christensen and Claire briefly spoke via PSS, he conceded to Ms. Lorentz's special request, provided that Zeke, especially, would remain incommunicado as far as Alyssa was concerned.

Thirty-Three

Les Invalides II

At 9 p.m., Paris time, Adammus Horn and the Federation's delegation to the American Province were onboard a departing, three-hour supersonic flight to Washington, D.C., due to arrive at their destination just after 5 p.m., local time. The Allianz Federation's official aircraft, part of the sizeable and newest official fleet of twenty giant A-999s, soared to its space orbit, which was pre-programmed for its CyberSat-navigated, partial trek around the globe. Encountering mild storms as it cruised through the mezzo-atmospheric range, the large, CyberSat-auto-piloted A-999 handled the turbulence expertly. The crew mainly functioned to meticulously tend to the comfort and convenience of the nearly one hundred self-important passengers. Inside the roomy and well-appointed main cabin, it was business as usual, as Horn and the other top Allianz officials convened in the luxurious conference room inside the plane's multi-functional, partitioned interior. Together the officials became abreast of the many facts and figures on the still significant world player, the American Province.

Among other items in their agenda, one unusual but highly significant line item was *Les Invalides* **II Program**, or **LI-II**, located in Washington, D.C., and initiated by the Allianz Federation in GDM-9. The secret Federation initiative, which received its title after the 17th century military hospital, built by Louis XIV on the left banks of the Seine River, did not share in the original Parisian establishment's mission, as a place to care for wounded French soldiers. Quite on the contrary, it involved a Machiavellian plan to institutionalize implanted Allianz citizens who suffered from any yet incurable infirmities or significant physical or mental handicaps, and who would willingly surrender themselves, personally or by proxy, for the benefit of scientific study.

Their seemingly noble gesture, however, was most likely derived from false-consciousness and unthinkable deception by the government. For what appeared to be a willing consent to donate their bodies for the sake of the potential well-being of humanity, was in fact an implant-induced impulse that would render them victims of a monstrous prototypical program developed by the Federation. The altruistic aims of that scientific institution were in fact a cover for an unprecedented plan that envisioned the permanent and uninterrupted mass harnessing of brain energy from a vast population of donors. Furthermore, many of the still surviving implanted victims of the devastating cancerous plague, were also being used in this terrifying plot, along with an army of infants and youth, cloned from the DNA material of these patients; all helpless donors of their brain energy and unconscious contributors to the maintenance of CyberSat and the might of Allianz.

This program, now in its fifth year, became the testing ground and direct progenitor of the more recent and even more abominable and secretive Great Catacombs Program, which was to ultimately fulfill the Great Allianz Directive. Knowledge of the true goals of LI-II and of the very existence of the Great Catacombs Program had, up until then, been a privilege of a mere dozen or so of the world's most elite scientists and only the top-clearance status officials in all of Allianz. At that point in time, not even the American Marshall possessed such exclusive government knowledge. She was an unsuspecting – though not powerless – accomplice, an entangled marionette in this convoluted Allianz pantomime. But soon, that was about to change for her, and on her response to Horn's disclosure about the programs hinged the very fate of the Resistance.

While the Allianz delegation was still first learning about these classified and grotesquely utilitarian plans, their aircraft was initiating its descent and final approach for landing at D.C.'s **Allianz Marshall Air Base.**

Thirty-Four

Horn and Dariah Meet Again

The Federation's A-999 touched down at the air base in D.C. at precisely 5:06 p.m., with no unexpected problems, despite the strong, gusting winds. Dariah and her cabinet members waited near the arrival gate, along with the assembled press and a substantial number of cog security personnel, formally arranged behind them. As the announcement was made that the Prosecutor General and the Allianz Delegation were about to deplane, Dariah took a deep breath, trying her best not to betray her nervousness and sweaty palms behind her fully uniformed, official decorum.

Having fully covered all crucial details on this momentous visit with top province officials and her White House staff, Dariah knew she would lack no support for what was to be, perhaps to date, the most consequential performance of her political career. With Horn, however, there was always the danger of the unexpected. He was a man of many surprises when it came to maintaining his political supremacy, and because of the certainty of the unknowns she had better be prepared for any and all eventualities. One thing was certain; Adammus Horn was not one to take a power backseat to anyone. He was going to establish his dominance, and it was all Dariah could do not to let herself be blindsided by his larger-than-life persona, or his self-exalting ambition to assert his preeminence wherever he went, throughout the dominion.

"Marshall Dariah, presenting the Prosecutor General and the Allianz Federation Delegates to the American Province," the ushering cog announced, just before the translucent gates at the end of the skyway that lead the passengers away from the aircraft were opened.

"Atten-tion!" Dariah called out, prompting the sizeable American Province entourage and the extensive cog presence to tighten up their formation. At that point, the gates were opened, and a detachment of four armed cogs marched through. Behind them, and leading the considerable multitude of Allianz delegates, was the Prosecutor General, himself. Wearing a black suit and overcoat, Adammus Horn appeared taller, more svelte, and more imposing than Dariah had remembered, as he moved with arresting poise directly toward her. Dariah swallowed hard.

Seeing Horn face-to-face, though still at a distance, actually did something to Dariah. Unexpectedly, she felt her body flirt with a welcome feeling of relaxation. She sensed her chest less tight and was pleasantly able to breathe more deeply and with greater tranquility. Perhaps the grueling anticipation of that moment had been worse than the real thing, she reasoned, and now she needn't worry any longer. Yes, suddenly she found herself more confident than ever. The illustrious American Province Marshall was ready to stand shoulder to shoulder, as it were, with Allianz's most intrepid Ambassador. Dariah's shining moment had finally come, before the scrutinizing stares of the entire American Allianz establishment. They were about to witness her crowning moment, as the top host to the distinguished emissaries of the world's supreme governing power. Dariah had never felt so in control. Holding her arms up, to where her fists touched each other in front of her chest, thus forming an "A," she self-assuredly signed the "Vigor to Allianz" insignia. Then, taking one step toward the fast approaching Horn, Dariah extended her right hand to shake his.

In that instant, and to her utter astonishment, the completely unexpected happened. She just could not believe it. Horn had done it once again...

"Come here, darling," he uttered, as he leaned in and grabbed her by the small of her back, landing an astoundingly indiscrete kiss on her horrified, open lips, widely visible to all who helplessly gawked at the surreal and rather unbefitting sentimental display.

What was she to do? How could she possibly save face in front of the onlookers, whose befuddled reaction she could hear, in mid kiss? Horn had her right where he wanted her. If she fought back, she would risk an even worse and more mortifying scene. If she did nothing at all, she would jeopardize her authority and stature, being demeaned and ridiculed in front of all her subordinates and possibly spectators from all around the globe, who might be tuned in to the live welcoming ceremony. *Did I really invite the press to this? How could I have been so stupid?* were the first thoughts that flashed through her mind, as the brief seconds felt to her like an unending and malicious travesty. As the shockingly surprising scene unfolded, audible mumbling was intensifying in the ranks. Finally, with throats clearing in their vicinity, Horn disengaged, sporting a perversely self-amusing grin, so classic for him, Dariah recalled, as she now blushed conspicuously.

Dariah was beside herself. Harsh and cruel expletives flooded her thoughts, but she fought hard not to lose what was left of her dignity. She had never been one to mince words, yet all the baffled Marshall could appropriately muster in response, as she tried to regain her composure, was a feeble, "Um…On behalf of the American Province and its citizens, Mr. Prosecutor General, I welcome you." To which he replied, "My Parisian greetings to you, Marshall." He then turned to the perplexed cabinet members standing close by and said, "And to you, faithful servants…Vigor to Allianz."

As the brief ceremonial welcoming was concluded, the entire group left the cavernous arrival atrium and moved out toward the line of black-colored, official limousines and mini-buses, waiting just outside the sprawling main air base building. Flanked by countless cog security detail vehicles, the stationary convoy gave away the paramount importance of the approaching political personalities. Dariah, still fuming from the humiliating stunt, in which she had been an unwilling participant, struggled to stick to the protocol conversation. She could not even bring herself to look at the tall, black-clad, dark and handsome figure walking just to her left. Saving some choice words for a less public moment with Horn, Dariah forced herself to act her part, despite Horn's persistent advances.

"Impressive form, Marshall," said Horn. "I'd love to conduct a *personal* inspection…"

Instantly picking up on his tasteless *double-entendre*, Dariah quickly deflected Horn's offensive, stating coldly, "Our cogs constitute the best trained police force in the Federation. I can guarantee you that a personal *inspection* is a waste of your valuable time in the American Province."

"We shall see, Marshall. The night is still *beautifully* young..."

Again redirecting the conversation, Dariah outlined for Horn the program scheduled for that evening. "Mr. Prosecutor General, our official convoy will take us to the White House immediately. At eight o'clock, a banquet will be served in your honor, in the Great Ballroom on the grounds."

"Wonderful. Dinner with my old partner in crime," he said.

"Right...and don't forget the other four hundred or so of our closest friends," she sarcastically remarked.

"I had planned on conversing politics with a few dignitaries tonight, but not a chance. My eyes will be fixed on the stunning American Marshall... Wow, Misha. It's really been too long for us," Horn commented, laying aside all of the impersonal etiquette and protocol, as he attempted what to Dariah sounded like his unimpressively common and shallow flattery.

"*My* eyes will be fixed on the clock, sir," she countered, as she continued in her brisk pace, still avoiding even the slightest hint of eye contact with him.

As they arrived outside, Dariah's petite frame struggled against the strengthening wind gusts. But she was not going to be helped by Horn. Even as he played the debonair gentlemen, gesturing for her to get into the limousine ahead of him, she resisted, bracing herself against the wind.

"I'm fine. You first, sir," she said upon reaching their vehicle, positioned third in a long line of transports.

As the two of them entered the middle section of the stretch-limousine and sat down opposite each other, the doors were closed by cog security. Horn and Dariah now found themselves secluded and completely alone with each other. Protected by privacy soundproofing glass, the prominent Allianz officials might as well have been worlds away from the security cogs sitting in both the front and back compartments of their limousine. To the cogs' amusing advantage, those privacy barriers allowed them now to freely speculate on, and collectively joke about, what might be happening just beyond the dark, dividing glass walls. And given the passionate embrace they had witnessed just minutes earlier between their notable passengers, they had every reason to feel titillated by their imaginative innuendo. But their hopeful insinuations could not be farther from reality, for icy and tense were better mood descriptors for capturing what was truly taking place inside the secluded limousine cabin.

"My Misha...beautiful and captivating as ever... The Visuals really did not do you any justice," he persisted in his smooth overtures, as the convoy set out toward the White House.

Dariah offered no response, as her eyes were stubbornly fixed on the moving scenery, now speeding past her window. In her mind, though she could not get away from Horn's insufferable presence at that moment, she wished she were on the other side of the Potomac, with miles separating her from the cause of her irksome feelings. After the uncomfortable recent spectacle, how tragically ironic it was for Dariah to think that she had actually long fantasized about her rendezvous with Horn. For her, now, the distance between naïve fantasy and exasperating reality could in fact only be measured in light years.

"Aww, come now, Misha. You're not *really* upset about that kiss back there, are you?" Horn patronized. "Frankly, I thought it was a fitting tribute to us, after all these years. Quite sweet, I would say," he added those words, finally hitting a nerve and instigating her firm response.

With piercing intensity, Dariah looked at Horn and angrily replied, "What? *Sweet*, you would say? Listen to me, Horn. I don't know who you think you are, pulling a vile stunt like that on my turf and probably in front of the entire world... Actually, I know exactly who you *think* you are, but I am neither amused, nor impressed. And if you even so much as come within three feet of me from now on, I swear I will create such a stir and smack you so hard, that you'll wish you had never been born a man. So, get a clue and get over yourself!" she ranted. "And if you even hint at publicly embarrassing me like that again, I swear to you, I..."

"Whoa...calm yourself, darling. You obviously didn't enjoy it as much as I did, but for crying out loud, don't overdo it. We've got some serious intercultural misunderstanding going on here..."

"No, Horn. I understand. I understand completely. But I'm warning you..."

"All right, all right...I get the message, darling. I'll be civil. Just don't freak out on me, okay? It was just an innocent kiss," Horn disingenuously replied.

"Hhh!" Dariah hissed under her breath, still upset, as she again looked away from him.

Her righteous indignation was always in the past dismissed by Horn as "freaking out" or "emotional and hormonal overreaction." His utter contempt for her true feelings, whenever she reacted – admittedly harshly, at times – against his complete lack of judgment or sensibleness when it came to their interpersonal rapport, was intolerable. It had been years and, clearly, the man had never matured personally, she discerned. To Dariah, though she had always felt irresistibly attracted, like a moth to a blazing flame, to Horn's virility in the public arena, his juvenile macho episodes in the context of their personal relationship had ceased being endearing to her – if they ever really were – eons ago.

Yet, somehow, Horn still found use for this side of himself, as he continually pursued his cheap serial conquests. Emotionally, Horn acknowledged, he and Dariah now seemed as synthesized as vinegar could be to oil. He knew he might ultimately have to appeal to her other powerful drives, in order to make this a fruitful visit to that vitally important Allianz province. But he was not giving up on wooing her just yet.

Thirty-Five

Estrangement

Later that evening, the banquet commenced. In typical Washington style, unless a propitious situation presented itself, the gala event was more of an opportunity to see and be seen, than an occasion for serious political deal making. Horn mainly kept to his statement made earlier to Dariah. His attention was clearly focused on the Marshall, even as he delivered a brief speech, thanking the distinguished public figures and billionaires and trillionaires there present, for their devotion to Allianz, and for their hosts' warm welcome and gracious attention to the delegation's every need. Horn then again sat down, front and center, next to Dariah.

"Delightful little party," he remarked, raising his glass in a complimentary toast to his attractive hostess. "One would almost think it was in honor of a close, dear friend."

"Don't flatter yourself, Horn. You and I both know we need each other…politically, that is. As far as the other thing, take my word for it. I can stomach it about as well as I can these repulsive fish eggs," she replied, looking down at the caviar spread, left still untouched on her appetizer plate.

"One of these days, Misha, you'll learn to appreciate how politics and pleasure can be the best of allies."

"I thought *you* were the one who advised me not to take things personally, and that you never did. 'It's better this way,' I seem to recall you saying, quite recently, in fact."

"Misha, I would gladly eat my words for you, if you graciously allowed me the honor of starting over, tonight," the suave Prosecutor General said, reaching out and touching Dariah's hand.

"Three feet, Horn. Keep away from me. I may be playing docile right now, but I don't easily forget it when I've been wronged. And you've got 'Mr. Wrong' written all over your face," she said in her witty return, removing her hand from under his.

At this, the noticeably annoyed and frustrated Horn leaned back on his chair and turned toward the distinguished madam seated to his left, no doubt a more convivial conversation partner than the obstinately unforgiving Marshall had turned out to be, that evening. For her part, Dariah gloried in her small but still thoroughly satisfying countermove against Horn. His greatest weakness was again laid fully bare before her; the female allure.

Minutes later, a high-ranking cog official approached Dariah and, trying not to cause too much of a stir, delivered an urgent message into her right ear. The Marshall's countenance shifted dramatically, catching Horn's attention.

"What is it, Misha?" he asked, presuming something was wrong.

"We've uh..."

"We've what? What's wrong?" Horn insisted.

"We've got company..." Dariah replied. "Demonstrators. Lot's of them...outside."

"Well... How nice of them to drop by," Horn uttered, facetiously.

"Shoot! I was wondering when we'd see trouble. But I certainly didn't expect it so soon after you arrived. You are definitely a loved and hated man, Horn. That's for sure. Do you always pack trouble in your suitcase?"

"Seriously... You know, Misha, back home we have some very persuasive ways of discouraging protests. You would profit much by learning this from the temperament of the French."

"Don't worry, Your Excellence. I'll handle this. I'll have it all under control," she tried to reassure him.

The pressure was on for Dariah to prove herself to Allianz after the compassionate reluctance she had displayed against the Children of the Promise group. It was also her opportunity to regain the high level of respect she felt had suffered in the eyes of her cabinet and other officials due to the kissing incident at the air base. To her, this was a do-or-die situation, and failure on her part was not an option.

Indeed, a lively crowd of demonstrators, about four hundred in all, had marched up Pennsylvania Avenue and gathered just outside the great, clear dome, which had been providing a protective shield for the White House ever since GDM-Minus-9. The shield served as a way of thwarting terrorist attacks against it. The crowd of non-implanted protesters boldly shouted incendiary slogans and carried signs that said, "*Go Home, Persecutor General!*" and "*Puppet Dariah Kills for Allianz's Approval!*" aiming at generating public awareness of the evil that had befallen religious groups of all types over the years, but especially the Community of Brethren.

In their majority, these men and women were members of that community of faith, though part of a much smaller and particularly militant sect, known for its significantly more radical and outspoken slant. They were not, however, carrying with them firearms or lethal weapons of any kind. This was not meant to be an act of war, but rather a calculated act of civil disobedience in the exercise of a long revoked right of free speech. It was a righteous sense of indignation toward appalling injustice, not an irrational, mob-like need to lash out, that compelled this admittedly radicalized small segment of the Community of Brethren to demonstrate against Allianz. But they were, in fact, violating the Allianz *status quo*, and the Federation was not about to dismiss the opportunity to label these dissenters as deviant and even nefarious criminals and to use them as an example before the eyes of the world.

As part of their repertoire of collective action, a large number of the protesters lining up in front of the picketing group were carrying wooden walking sticks. Together, they began rhythmically banging their sticks on the crystalline dome, making a boisterous noise, loud enough that it reverberated all through the stately government mansion, sounding to the banquet frequenters rather like powerfully rhythmic native drumbeats, stereotypically known to announce war among some indigenous groups. The strange and fearful noise was now reaching into the ballroom, creating a frightful commotion among the guests.

All eyes were now on Dariah, who stormed out of the grand banquet hall, with Horn following closely after her. In haste, she trotted down a windowless internal hallway which led to the only above ground control room inside the White House. From there, they would be able to watch, via security monitors, the troubling developments outside.

"Misha, wait," Horn said, as he reached her just inside the control room.

"I don't have time for this, Horn."

"No, of course. But, Misha, this is a time for drastic action. Or this will quickly spread like yeast and become unmanageable."

"I told you, I'll handle it," she said, turning around to view the monitors capturing the protesters.

"Look at them," Horn alerted. "They accuse you of being an Allianz puppet and a killer. Are you going to let them have the last word?" he pressured her.

"Major," she called out to the ranking cog official in the room. "I want them surrounded and arrested. Take them to the 8th Cog Precinct and book them."

"Yes, sir," he answered her.

"Wait one minute, Major," Horn called out.

"Sir?" the cog officer replied, confused. "Whose orders am I following, Commander Dariah?"

Turning to the imposing presence in the room, she said, "Horn! You are a guest here tonight. I'm in charge. Is that clear?" Dariah immediately chastised.

"Granted. But if I might make a suggestion for an alternate course of action..." he uttered.

The Marshall paused for a moment, and then said, "I'm listening."

Horn then proceeded to lay out his plan. While the banquet continued on, a small cog detachment was to leave toward the demonstration, and from behind the crowd and in concealment they were to fire a few live mortar rounds against the White House. The shots would not be sufficiently powerful to penetrate the protective and resistant polycarbonate-based dome, but if executed just right, the attack would appear to come from the large crowd of protesters. The plan to frame the demonstrators would give just cause for an armed counter attack and would culminate in the arrests of the protesters for the much more serious offense of terrorism, and not simply for lesser charges of disorderly and threatening civil misconduct. The arrests would thus appear completely justified and would cause a favorable assessment of the Federation's offensive, whose proverbial hand would be forcibly moved to deter these insurgents from further and more violent actions. It was a cunningly sinister plan. But then again, that was Horn's specialty.

"But don't take them to jail," Horn instructed.

"What do you mean? What are we going to do with them?" Dariah replied.

"Oh, Marshall. Do I really need to spell everything out for you?" Horn rhetorically asked.

"You're going to have them executed, in cold blood?" she asked in alarm.

"Don't be naïve. What have we done following the other arrests, Marshall?" Horn inquired, referring to the recent Federation interventions against the Brethren Gatherings in the Southeast.

"They're in jail. They're all in jail," she replied.

"Are they? Are you certain of it?"

"Horn. What is going on here? I gave specific orders…"

"Desperate times call for final measures," Horn said. "It is my duty, as Allianz Prosecutor General, to safeguard the well-being of the Federation. I had to rescind your orders…"

"You did *what*?" Dariah exclaimed, in shock.

"They were taken away to the *Les Invalides* II site," Horn revealed.

"Horn, that's a hospital. Why were they sent there?"

"It's a medical research institute, darling."

"This is insane! I don't believe you!" She then addressed the cog officer, in direct terms, "Major, do you know about this?" Offering only a reluctant, silent nod, the officer looked to Horn for some pronouncement in his defense.

"Do not condemn the police, Marshall. They were following *my* direct orders. I deemed those interventions as a top Federation priority, and enacted my powers to take over those operations."

"*You...*" she cried out, in angry disbelief.

"The stakes are high, Misha. They are higher than ever. One foolish misstep and we could lose control of the Federation."

"But what about...the Tennessee gathering. Don't tell me, you..."

"I just had to watch what you would do, Marshall. And, regrettably, my suspicions were confirmed," Horn replied.

Scandalized, Dariah slapped Horn hard across his face and began to retreat, stepping backward and looking at Horn at first, and then turning and running toward the Oval Office. Horn, touching his left cheek, regained his composure, and yelled, "Don't go too far, Misha. You and I have unfinished business to discuss, tonight." But Dariah kept on running, soon disappearing after turning down another hallway on the right.

Addressing the cog officer, who was still standing there, speechless, Horn gave his orders, "Major, we will proceed with my plan. I want it put into effect immediately. They will be silenced...for good."

"Right away, Mr. Prosecutor General," the Major replied in a nervous salute.

Over the next hour and a half, tumult and mayhem overtook the demonstration outside. By the end of the struggle, sixty people among the demonstrators were dead, and upwards of three hundred others were arrested and subsequently taken north, to the location of the *Les Invalides* II institute, built on the grounds of the fully remodeled Walter Reed Army Medical Center, renamed in GDM-10 as, Allianz Forces Medical Research Hospital.

Thirty-Six

More Vanishings

Back in Midville, Christensen and Claire had been following the developments in D.C., as they were unfolding. Bethany was in her room, reading, while Holly already lay asleep on her bed. Zeke was still finishing up his Aikido workout in the basement. Unable to understand the news in precise enough detail, due to the impossible language barrier, Christensen and Claire nonetheless managed to deduce that something horrific, involving a group of Believers, had just taken place in D.C., that evening. A cog official appeared to be providing the basic run down on the events, and based on his demeanor and body language, Christensen could discern that the Federation was presenting a well-prepared justification for the cog course of action.

"This is more than I can bear to watch, Tanner," said Claire.

"Something is definitely not right about this. How could these demonstrators have the artillery resources necessary to conduct this attack on the White House? That's just not like the Resistance, even for these militant groups. It would be a major departure from the usual *modus operandi*. I'm almost sure they were framed, Claire," reasoned Christensen.

As they continued to watch the distressing images on their hyaline televisor, Zeke came upstairs and briefly joined them. "What's going on, Dad. Where's that?" he said, referring to the news coverage.

"It's in D.C., son. It looks like the Federation has targeted another group of Believers."

"A gathering? On a Tuesday night?" Zeke inquired.

"No. This was a group of demonstrators protesting just outside the White House," Claire explained.

"Did people get hurt?"

"Yeah. Afraid so. It looks pretty ugly. There have been deaths," Christensen replied.

"Zeke, I'm feeling uneasy about you seeing this. This is live coverage, and some of it may not really be age-appropriate," Clare commented.

"Mom, I'm sixteen. I can handle it. Besides, I need to be aware of this. It was almost us just a couple of day s ago," Zeke pointed out.

"I know, honey," Claire responded, "but hopefully you won't need to worry about being caught in something like this. This was a confrontational bunch. They took a risk, and they paid the price. Now, all we can do is pray for them."

"But, Mom, how can we just watch this and not want to do something about it? If we just sit here and take it, we will most likely end up like them. I don't want us to go down without a fight," Zeke declared with typical teenage zeal.

"Zeke," his father cautioned, "we can't let our emotions control our reactions. Sensei always said that we must face every situation with stillness, without tension. Our reflexes won't be as sharp if we tense up. We do have a defense prepared inside of us, but we must let it harmonize with the attack. Move too soon and they'll track us. Move too slow and they'll crush us. Trust in The Name and in His perfect timing. He will work through us and help us move with precision if and when the time comes."

"And speaking of that, my young warrior," Claire interjected, "I want you to move upstairs to get cleaned up with precision and then harmonize with your bed, zip-zip."

"Hhh," Zeke sighed forcefully in frustration. "Mom, what do I need to do to prove to you that I'm grown up enough to be included in serious matters?"

"That will come in time. It's inevitable. But that involves good timing, too. Now go, before I show you *my* sharp reflexes," his mother replied, jokingly.

"Good night, y'all."

"Good night, son. Sleep well," said Christensen.

"That'd be nice," Zeke replied, as he walked up the stairs. "Feel free to check in on my recitation tonight…"

"Don't worry, son. We'll be watching over you," Claire answered.

By now, Zeke's nightly dreaming episodes were beginning to attain an ordinary sort of feel. Outside of a clear purpose for the Spirit dreams, they were possibly starting to seem rather random to the Christensens, a sort of odd religious relic whose consequence for the times was unclear, if of much use, other than for their own appreciation.

Just then, the focus of the news was shifted to what appeared to be a story about yet another case resembling the vanishings, whose stories had been surfacing with greater frequency, as of late. This time, the images were from a village in the Province of Tanzania, in the African Southeast, although the Christensens could only guess Sub-Saharan Africa.

"This poor man seems to be relating something about a disappearance," Christensen pointed out. "He seems to be a relative or a neighbor."

The images showed the inside of a family's hut, which looked as if it had been abandoned suddenly. The dinner pot was still on the fire, and other food items apparently only half prepared, some having fallen on the ground inside the humble, one-room dwelling. An open wooden hope chest lay on its side on the ground, near the wide open door. Other items looked to be out of place, seemingly indicating some sort of struggle. As the news camera then changed angles, the image revealed a telling object hanging on the wall of that hut.

"Tanner! Do you see that?"

"What?"

"Look, right there," Claire said, pointing on the televisor screen to an object hanging on an internal wall of that hut.

"It looks like a cross," Christensen noticed.

"It is. This is yet another family of Believers that has vanished.," Claire said. Christensen, sliding his right hand over his forehead and graying hair, closed his eyes and shook his head. "They were targeted for it, Claire...for their faith in The Name," Christensen concluded. Claire then turned to Christensen and embraced him.

"Tanner, how can this be happening? Is this really the end?"

"It's the beginning, Claire. I feel it's only the beginning, as Scripture warned us."

"Lord, help us all," Claire uttered.

Thirty-Seven

Confrontation

Feeling satisfied with the outcome of the cog response against the demonstrators, Horn returned to the banquet hall, where the festivities continued on into the night. While working his charm around the still crowded ballroom, Horn looked for any sign of Dariah, but his search was in vain. She was nowhere to be found, and he astutely guessed that the Marshall had burrowed herself inside the solitary confines of the well-guarded Oval Office. He waited for an opportune moment to excuse himself from the tiresome and generally useless hobnobbing, and left in search of the American Marshall.

"Sir," one of several security officers addressed Horn, as he walked down the corridor leading straight to the Oval Office, "I am sorry, sir, but no one is to go past this point. These are direct orders."

Indignant, Horn countered, "Young man, I'm in no mood for your antics. Do you know who you're talking to?"

"Once again, sir, I must ask you to back away. My orders are to allow no one to pass…"

Closing his eyes, Horn raised his left hand and nervously rubbed his own forehead, betraying his impatience. In mid sentence, this officer and the five others standing guard there fell into some sort of strange trance, as if they suffered from an acute and sudden catatonic spell.

Horn had used his occult, supernatural resources before. From this moment on, however, he would resort to using them with greater frequency and intensity, for his own unfolding sinister purposes.

"Sorry, boys. You shouldn't try my patience," Horn said, as he proceeded, walking past the seemingly frozen officers. "You will have no recollection of this when you snap out of it."

Suddenly, the Oval Office security system alerted, "*Warning! You are trespassing officially secured space. Do not proceed.*" Simply ignoring the alert, Horn continued on until he came within a few feet of the Oval Office's main door. "*Warning! You are now in breech of officially secured space. Stop immediately or you will be neutralized.*"

Impatient, Horn yelled, "Misha, I know you can hear me. Open up. It's no use hiding."

Hearing no answer, Horn stepped forward, setting off a screeching Oval Office alarm. "*Warning! System armed.*" With one look, Horn instantly disengaged the system, and yelled out, "Misha, I'm not going to ask again…" At once, the door was automatically unlocked and opened.

"*Oval Office access granted*," announced the security system. Horn walked in to find Dariah behind her desk, looking thoroughly dejected and feeling absolutely violated, but quickly turning her discouragement into fuming rage.

"How did you get past the guards?" Dariah exclaimed.

"Let's just say I had a paralyzing effect on them," Horn replied.

"What kind of a monster are you?" she asked in disgust.

Looking straight at her, Horn slowly paced forward, toward Dariah's desk and replied, "It is because of monsters like me, Marshall, that you even have the luxury of running this province and sitting behind that very desk. Don't forget, Misha, I made you who you are, and I can take you down."

"You may take it all away from me, Horn, but with all due respect, I prefer to believe that I've worked my tail off to earn my position. But for whatever reason, when you look at me with those dark eyes of yours, you still see me as a helpless little woman."

Laughing, Horn walked over and sat down in a stately high-back leather chair, positioned just a few feet away, to the right of Dariah's desk, and said, "Helpless? No. But too angry and sentimental to be effective."

"Don't you even go there, Horn. I find this highly suspect coming from you. Your character judgments seriously lack in credibility, especially considering your eagerness to sabotage me at every turn, just to prove me wrong," Dariah replied.

"Things don't need to go on this way, Misha. After all these years, I should be entitled to more trust from you."

"Trust? How can you expect me to trust you, Horn? Every chance you get, you persist with denigrating any and all authority that Allianz has itself given me. And for what? Just to satisfy your ego? To ensure your superiority? Since when am I your competition? Why should my authority be threatening to the great Prosecutor General, who for all intents and purposes runs the entire Federation? You're the *de facto* ruler of entire Allianz empire."

"Thank you, but it is not your authority that concerns me, Misha. It's your loyalty, your heart."

"My heart has been behind every decision I've ever made for Allianz, Horn, and I'm darn proud of that. That is how I function, and I make no apologies for it," Dariah replied.

"I shouldn't have to point out to you, darling, that the heart can be an untamable involuntary muscle. You're better off basing your decisions on more reliable muscles."

"The brain, right?" Dariah offered with disdain. "Excuse me, Mr. Prosecutor General, but I've yet to meet anyone who can operate in as cunning and unfeeling a manner as you do. So much for brain power."

"Brain power certainly has its place in Allianz, Misha. But it's not the brain I'm referring to. It's the fist," he corrected her.

"Horn, I've had enough of your demonstrations of force. There's only so much indiscriminate muscle flexing you can do, before you begin to be seen as a ruthless tyrant. You may have your reasons to despise democracy, but Allianz cannot survive without a healthy dose of public support and approval. And you can't just force that on people. You can't manufacture it, either. It's been tried before, and it has always failed," she said.

"Clearly, you mistake me, my dear," Horn countered, as he stood up and approached Dariah's desk. "I'm a man of the people. And beyond that, I came here wanting to help you. But unfortunately, sometimes those who stand in greatest need of help are often too desperate to recognize or even accept a helping hand. And desperate people must be helped, Misha, before they're no longer able to see clearly whose side they're really on."

"Haven't I proven myself to Allianz for over a decade?" Dariah asked rhetorically. "Don't you think you're taking this loyalty thing a bit too far?"

"Loyalty is the life-blood of this system, Misha. And, more than commitment, it demands constant proof. What I want to know is, are you ready to go to any and all lengths to defend the Code?" Horn challenged her.

"Don't count me out just yet, Horn. You don't know me as well as you think," she assured him, trying desperately to keep her whole world from collapsing all around her.

"Soon enough, darling, you'll have a chance to prove your loyalty to Allianz. It's now time for you to dazzle us and offer further, irrefutable proof of your loyalty. That is, *if* you're really up to it."

"Bring it on, Horn. You don't know who you're playing with. I'll take your challenges any day over your insulting disregard for my authority."

"That's my Misha. It didn't take you too long to come around, now did it? Come with me now, darling. We've got a special visit to make before the night is over."

"What are you talking about?" Dariah reacted. "I've really had enough of your surprises for one night."

"Trust me, my petite. You won't want to miss this," Horn said, as he got up and led the way out of the Oval Office. Then, speaking to the revived officers standing guard just outside the Marshall's office, he ordered an immediate transport to take him and Dariah to *Les Invalides* II.

Thirty-Eight

The Great Allianz Directive Revealed

Following the same route North, taken earlier by the convoy of cog vehicles carrying the arrested demonstrators, Horn and Dariah headed toward the Allianz Forces Medical Research Hospital complex, where *Les Invalides* II was housed. It was late, and the wind had picked up considerably since the early evening. As they were nearing their destination, their vehicle and their cog escort transports suddenly came to an abrupt stop. A large, ancient elm tree had toppled onto the road, its trunk traversed across the way, impeding passage up to the hospital compound. Jostled a bit inside the official limousine, Horn spoke via intercom with the driver.

"What in the world just happened?" Horn inquired.

"Sir, I apologize for the rough stop. But a large object, apparently a fallen tree, is obstructing our passage up ahead," answered the chauffeur. "It looks like we'll need to wait until a road crew arrives to clear up this mess. It may take several minutes to an hour. It's a massive elm, and there appears to be no clearance on either side of it for our vehicles to get around."

"What now, Horn?" Dariah asked, betraying her amusement. "This is man versus nature, and it looks like in GDM-13 nature's still ahead on the score cards, no matter how hard we may try to master it."

"Don't be so sure of it, my dear. Nature has a way of disposing of its dead. And that tree is out of time. But we, we have a destiny to fulfill. And soon, even nature will take a backseat to the glory of man," Horn spoke mysteriously.

"Horn, your hopeful hyperbole does little to improve our current situation. Maybe you ought to step out and tell it to that tree," Dariah said, mockingly.

"You know, that's not a bad idea," Horn replied.

Opening the limousine door, Horn stepped out, but stood next to the vehicle, holding on to the door.

"Horn!" Dariah yelled, "I was just joking. Get back in here. Security will go nuts."

"Ah, let them."

With the wind gusting against him, Horn looked intently at the obstruction. Suddenly, as if out of thin air, a bright flash, like a powerful electrical discharge, ripped through the sky, striking the tree's trunk, splitting it to smithereens, and throwing the burning debris clear off the road. The deafening noise and intense vibration from the explosion made the vehicles tremble, startling Dariah, while the cog officers just watched the whole thing in total astonishment.

"Horn! Watch out!" Dariah exclaimed. "What the heck was that?"

Looking inside the vehicle at Dariah, Horn smiled and answered, "That was nature, taking a backseat to the glory of man."

"What just happened, here?" Dariah asked.

"Never mind, darling. We'll be moving again soon," Horn answered, getting back into the limousine and closing the door. "Let's move," Horn commanded the driver, via the intercom.

"Yes, sir. Did you just see that, sir? It was amazing," responded the chauffeur.

As the convoy moved forward, passing by the now incandescent, scattered piles of hot, burning wood, Dariah watched in bewilderment. She then looked at Horn and said, "You're an enigma, Horn. I don't know what the heck that was back there...but why do I have a feeling that you had something to do with it?" Wearing a mysterious grin, Horn did not bother to respond. Unwilling to fess up to his peculiar, supernatural abilities, he preferred to keep Dariah guessing.

Having cleared through all of the security checkpoints at the hospital complex, their convoy finally arrived at site of *Les Invalides* II for their morbid tour. Once inside the building, the warden, having already been briefed on the purpose for their late night visit, led Horn and Dariah to a sort of inner sanctum, from where they would have a privileged view of ongoing operations via numerous windows and monitors. Beholding the gruesome view of thousands of apparently dormant patients, along with several hundreds more being processed at that facility, Dariah revealed her distress.

"Why are you showing me this, Horn? Where are the demonstrators? Who are all these people in these beds? Are they sick? Are they dead?" she asked.

"These are dreamers, Marshall…the dreamers of Allianz," Horn replied, wide-eyed and wearing a mysterious grin.

"What do you mean?"

Stunned, Dariah listened to Horn explain how the Federation, in pursuit of making the Great Allianz Directive operational, had built this place as a prototypical project for population testing, using terminally ill volunteers, among them many of the elderly stricken with the great cancerous plague, as well as many convicted and apprehended criminals, including previously arrested members of the Community of Brethren, and even a large number of politicians who had been prosecuted and sentenced on corruption charges.

"Testing for what?" she pressed him.

"Dream State permanence," he answered. "We've been able to maintain these individuals in an indefinite comatose state, while they charitably surrender their brainwaves for the good of CyberSat and, ultimately, Allianz."

"Wait a minute. I had knowledge about the connection between Transcienz and CyberSat. But you're telling me that there's more?" Dariah commented.

"Lots more, darling. And eventually, when they are utterly brain dead, they must be replaced with others still."

"You said this is a prototype. A prototype for what?" she asked, troubled yet intrigued.

"If I told you at this point, you would pose too great a risk for Allianz," he revealed.

The Dreamers of Allianz

"Horn, you didn't bring me all the way here to show me this and not tell me what is really going on," she replied in evident disaffection.

"No. No, I didn't," he confessed. "I was just wanting to see your reaction."

"Hhh! No mind games, Horn. What is this really all about?"

"Well, there is this place in North Africa. Allianz has been top secretly building it over the last few years. It is called the Great Catacombs Project," he said. "That program is the real deal. And it makes this look absolutely miniscule by comparison. Finally, the ultimate fulfillment of the Great Allianz Directive is at hand."

"There's no other way to put it, Horn. This is positively diabolical," Dariah replied.

"Genghis Khan, Alexander, Caesar, DaVinci, Einstein, Gates, Jobs... All the world's greatest minds were at some point considered maniacal. But, ultimately, they were celebrated as unprecedented geniuses of their age," Horn went on. "And the brilliance and scope of this unparalleled program are nothing short of absolute genius."

"What are we talking about? Hundreds of thousands?"

"No. Millions. And potentially billions of permanent dreamers globally," Horn finally revealed. "And you and I will go there to see it, Misha...soon."

"But why? Why me? I'm the American Marshall. Why do you want to include me in this?" she asked.

"Simple. I want you to be convinced that the best way for Allianz to use society's rejects is put them to sleep. Let's just say it's their way of paying back their debts to the system," Horn replied. "I also want you to realize that the very position and future you hold in the Federation depend on this. These dreamers are CyberSat's life force. And CyberSat is Allianz's life force. You see, it's all connected. It's the very circle of life for Allianz, for you, and for me. It's arresting, really. The whole thing rests on these who are resting," Horn whimsically added in self-amusement.

"But, Horn. Why North Africa?" she wondered.

"Space. We needed lots of space," Horn explained. "Our geological surveys indicated that the subsoil beneath that region is an immense, dry aquifer complex, which extends from the Province of

The Dreamers of Allianz

Algeria all the way to Egypt, and down below the Sahara to its southernmost reaches, from Mali to the Sudanese Province. Construction began at a frantic pace about two years ago. Our point of entry will be the Province of Tunisia, from the old Roman city of Carthage. From there, we will be able to access the already completed sections of the Great Catacombs, and I guarantee you, darling, once you see it, you'll never be the same."

"This is unbelievable, Horn," Dariah said.

"Seeing is believing, darling. And after seeing it, you *will* believe," Horn affirmed, not realizing how prophetic his own statement would really turn out to be, but in a totally unexpected way for him.

It was after midnight when Horn and Dariah left the LI-II site and returned to the White House. By then, the old enemy, jet lag, was powerfully affecting Horn's disposition. And the otherwise potent Prosecutor General was quickly feeling like a beached jellyfish.

"I would invite you into my room for a night cap, darling. But for once, I am utterly spent."

"Good. You should save your strength for Christensen, tomorrow," she suggested.

"Right, our special friend in Tennessee..." he said facetiously. " I will see you bright and early."

"I'm sure you will, Horn. Good night."

"Yes. And a good night to you, my beautiful Misha," he said, before turning in.

Retiring to her chambers, it was not long before Dariah lay on her bed. Unable to fall asleep at first, she tried to take in all of what she had seen and heard that night. A great sense of admiration for the might of Allianz, but a sudden fear of it as well, came over her. It felt to her as if she had awakened to a new reality, one that went beyond simply playing politics and going after the bad guys. As she tossed and turned, she began to realize the weight of her new knowledge. With great angst, she contemplated the dramatic ramifications for the world and its inhabitants of the course on which the entire Federation had set for itself under Adammus Horn's de facto command. She found herself helplessly adrift in the turbulent, rapid waters of a world system so powerful that even she, the eminent American Marshall, had only two choices before her; to give into the overpowering flow, or to face certain demise under its exhausting, unrelenting torrents.

As for her feelings for Horn, Dariah simply felt numb. If anything, meeting him again face-to-face after all these years made her finally realize that the romantic notions she had been carrying inside of her, even subconsciously at times, had certainly found no grounding in her new reality check. In fact, there was something she saw in Horn that was beginning to greatly afflict and even frighten her. Although he was much the same as he was before, there was a new side of him that made him seem like an unknowable stranger. She felt as if she could no longer separate her notion of Horn as a man from the Allianz juggernaut. It was as if he had now come to fully embody the system. Strangely, to her, Horn had somehow become more of an institution than simply an actual person. Furthermore, her recent exchanges with him were taking an undeniably corrosive toll on her very soul. In her place of political preeminence, however, there was simply no getting away from Adammus Horn. In Allianz, he was all-powerful, all-consuming, all-infecting.

"Adammus...Horn...Adammus...Horn," she repeatedly whispered. *Huh... Man...Power...Man of Power? Or rather...The Power of Man*, she thought. Then she said to herself, "I never really took notice..."

As Dariah wrestled with these thoughts, a nervous chill and a sensation of complete loneliness came over her. Lying there, she suddenly felt like a defenseless little girl, lost and scared, on a cold, dark night. Feeling helplessly afraid, she pulled her covers over her head. Paralyzed by fear, but expending all the energy she had left fighting the uncontrollable shivers, Dariah slowly weakened, and eventually gave into the heaviness of exhaustion.

Thirty-Nine

Christensen's Despair

It was early Wednesday morning, and once again Christensen's sojourned in his bunker for most of the night, only to wake up to the sound of another urgent, incoming message from me, on the Resistance's clandestine network. The message read:

"We have confirmed widespread reports of coerced implantations on arrested members the Community of Brethren. We have learned that thousands of Believers have been taken to locations in D.C. and North Africa, and are being forced into comatose states and being indefinitely kept in individual pods for some sort of scientific experiment by Federation specialists. We do not know for certain what the nature and purpose of these experiments really are, but we do believe that among the captives are many women and children, as well, and great evil has come upon them. Tanner-san, I would not be exaggerating if I said to you that terrible darkness is now upon us all. We may be very near the point where the sign will be given for us as a people of The Name to take cover. Please stand by, pray, and be on full guard, for we do not know from moment to moment how things will look for us. Your leadership in the South is needed now more than ever. Please admonish our faithful brothers and sisters there, and may The Name keep us in His care. Your friend, Dr. C."

Once he finished reading the message, Christensen finally broke down. Feelings of fear, rage, desperation, sorrow, and self-doubt assailed his mind, soul, and body. He felt too frail to even be able to stand and take any action on behalf of his community of Believers. How was he to lead and encourage, when his very existence and sense of self were so embattled with the overwhelming taste of defeat and death? Overcome with grief and exhaustion from his tearful reaction, Christensen succumbed to the urge for a cathartic sleep escape from the seemingly hopeless situation. But it was no use. Even in his dreams, he could not run from the trouble that persecuted him at that moment.

In another intense dream, Christensen found himself watching helplessly behind clear, fortified doors, struggling to view his family through the gaps between the cogs guarding the entrance to a procedure room. He fought in vain to free himself from the tight fasteners that restrained his erect body. His screams were unheard and only served as release for his rage; rage for what they were about to do to his wife and daughters. He could barely make out what was happening behind those translucent doors, but his height was an advantage, as the straps gave slightly and he managed to push up against the wall behind him. Now a few inches higher he was able to glance at the seats in which Claire, Bethany, and Holly were to be forcibly placed for the procedure. As his strength began to leave him, he could do nothing but watch the quick and virtually painless application of the Forehead Cognit Implant on his wife and daughters. But what of Zeke, who had last been seen running away after freeing himself from the grip of a cog? There was now no way to know his whereabouts. Escorted by cogs, his wife and daughters seemed to resist, as they were placed on their seats and were harnessed to the hardware. Surrendering all to their faith, Claire and the girls took one last look at each other. Claire closed her eyes as if to indicate and transmit to her girls her trust in The Name.

"*Be still. Do not move, or the implantation could be fatal,*" repeated the instruction of the unfittingly calm, female voice coming from the implanting apparatus.

The automated arm closed in toward their heads, pointing an emerald-green beam of light to the space between and above their eyebrows. Christensen screamed again, "No! You barbarians... stop!" That haunting image was indelibly burned in his brain. The bright procedure room darkened. In seconds, the implantation was complete. Lights came back on, and the new, alloy-made Allianz "A" implant on his wife's and daughters' foreheads glimmered in the light. At that moment Christensen knew he stood permanently separated from his implanted wife and daughters, who would soon begin to dream indefinitely.

"Oh, Lord!" he clamored.

"Dad?" Zeke uttered, interrupting Christensen's nightmare. "Are you okay?"

"Zeke, where's Mom? Where are the girls?" Christensen asked, still breathing hard and feeling quite disoriented.

"Dad, everyone's upstairs, still asleep. I was lying in bed and just couldn't get back to sleep. So, I came down to the kitchen to grab a small bite of something, thinking that maybe I couldn't fall asleep because I was feeling hungry," Zeke explained. "Then I heard you down here, and..." Christensen then fully realized he had fallen asleep and had experienced another frightening dream.

"I see. I guess I was just dreaming."

"You mean you were having a nightmare..."

"Yeah... I suppose Dr. C's message got to me," said Christensen. He then turned to his son, giving him a somber gaze, and said, "Son, there's something you need to know."

"Dad, what's the matter?" Zeke asked, seeing that his dad was dreadfully serious and sensing he was deeply troubled.

At that moment, Christensen felt an urgency he had not felt before to really sit down with Zeke and, for the first time, bare his soul; not as father and son, but as brothers in The Name. Driven by a pressing sense of clear and present danger, Christensen needed to count on Zeke to help him watch over and take care of their family.

"Zeke, I want you to listen to me very carefully, son."

"Okay, Dad."

"You know by now that really bad things are happening to Believers just about all over the world. It's getting to the point where I really don't know what to expect, anymore. Even though we've been praying, I don't think that humanly any of us can truly feel safe, with the way things have been going."

"Dad, why are you telling me this?" Zeke questioned, still unsure of what was on his father's mind.

"Son, I have to leave you for a while today. This will be my last day at work, and after today, only The Name knows how things will be for us," said Christensen. "But, Zeke, I want you to take care of Mom and your sisters, if anything should happen to me."

"Dad, what's going on? You sound like you think something bad is going to happen to you."

"There's no telling what troubles lie ahead. And maybe nothing at all will happen. But I just have a bad feeling in my gut about today, for some strange reason. It's as if I'm about to face something very, very difficult, and..."

"But, Dad, you already know it. It's your job. Remember?" Zeke offered.

"Yes. And maybe that's all it is. But even if all goes as expected today, I just feel that we need to be prepared for any eventuality, if and when I go missing."

"Missing? What do you mean? Why are you saying this, Dad?" asked the boy, suddenly anxious about the way his father was acting.

"Son, don't be worried. We'll continue to put our trust in The Name. But you must be ready to help your mother take some action in my absence, if that should occur. Now, pay close attention..." Christensen then went on to tell Zeke about the Global Exodus plan, which had been in the works for over a decade. After that, Christensen accessed a small keyboard, hidden in a concealed compartment, located inside an air vent on the bunker ceiling, on which he typed the letters, *"S-D-G,"* for *"Soli Deo Gloria,"* and the numbers, *"1-7-5,"* for *"The Name's perfect grace,"* in biblical numerology.

No sooner had he finished typing, than a secret floor hatch was opened in the center of the room, revealing a dimly lit passageway that led, via a mechanical underground transport, to a sanctuary cavern somewhere down below the surface, several miles away.

"Whoa! What *is* that, Dad?"

"An escape hatch, for when our disappearance into the underground sanctuary becomes necessary. I want you to remember this secret code and to be ready to assist Mom and the girls, in case I'm unable to do it," explained Christensen.

"Wow, this seems like something out of a science fiction story, or an adventure flick."

"Unfortunately, son, this is not fiction. The reality of our indefinite retreat may be much closer than we imagine. And if things really start to go down, I want you to be wise about seeking help. Don't trust anyone with an implant," Christensen cautioned him.

"No one? What about, you know, Alyssa?"

"That's different. We know she's been Spirit-sealed. But don't take chances with anyone else. And, son…if you have to, don't be afraid to make use of your Aikido training. It might come in handy, if you know what I mean…"

"Dad, this is getting scary," said Zeke.

"I know, son. But I need you to trust me in this. Things might get really bad. Things may look dark for a time. But I want you to know that we, who believe in The Name, have been given a promise that He will neither leave us, nor forsake us. He will make it all turn to good, in the end," Christensen said, in exhortation.

"But how can you be so sure? Can we really, truly know that things will work out?" Zeke pressed his father.

"No question about it," Christensen affirmed.

He then picked up a model airplane he had sitting on his desk, and holding up a miniature replica of a vintage Boeing 747, he said, "You know, son, back when pilots still flew most commercial aircraft, they soared far above the clouds and the often turbulent weather conditions. Even during the daytime, if the visibility was poor, they had to rely on instruments that told them how to guide their planes. Pilots had to go by what they knew was reliable and true, not by what they saw or couldn't see. But on their ascent, as soon as they would break through the clouds, there they would encounter perfectly blue skies and the sun shinning brightly. Zeke, the sun was always there. It had never left the sky. In the same way, the Son is always there. He hasn't left his throne and, He is coming in the clouds. The Name is still sovereign, and we too must trust in what we know is reliable and true," Christensen said, trying to soothe his son's concerns.

"I understand, Dad," Zeke replied. "I'll be ready to do it, if I have to, but..."

"Yeah?"

"Don't leave us just yet, okay?" Zeke pleaded, embracing his father.

"I'll do my very best, son, to be right here with you, your sisters, and Mom when you need me. I cannot promise you, but I'll do my very best." He then said, "Now, let's get on upstairs. It's time for me to get ready. For what, exactly, I don't know..."

Christensen felt oppressed inside, physically, emotionally, spiritually, the way he had felt before, when getting ready for a funeral. He remembered Claire's mother's mournful goodbye, just about one year earlier, and how he struggled with the finality of it all. Mrs. Woods had been the last surviving parent for both he and Claire, and a strong spiritual and emotional pillar for them. Her loss made them feel truly alone in the world. The comfort and security of her voice of wisdom and hard-earned patience were never again to be felt, as when she used to utter those soothing words, *It's going to be all right, dear*, which so often meant so much to them over the years of their difficult apprenticeship, as a young couple and later as parents.

Her silence was painful. The same heavy sensation of loss weighed down Christensen's entire body all over again and produced a kind of mental and physical lethargy that slowed his senses. This time, it was his professional and financial pillars that were crumbling, and Christensen wondered how much longer it would be, how many more pillars he would see collapse, before his whole life came crashing down. Still, he found strength to ready himself and venture out, if only because he did not know what else he could do. Losing his job, nay his career, was a certainty, and he might as well not delay the unavoidable.

Forty

Strange Last Day

Christensen's WormRail ride to work that morning was uneventful. Just as he had done for years, he exited the shuttle and hopped onto the moving sidewalks that led to the main airport terminal. Scanning his employee ID tag, perhaps for the last time, he accessed the underground corridor, which ended in the controller complex beneath the airport tower. If the eerie feeling of no longer belonging to that familiar air-traffic terrain wasn't enough, the strange stares from his about-to-be ex-co-workers made him feel like a real odd item in that implant-dominated environment. Was he just feeling so self-conscious that morning that he was imagining there to be more to those stares than there really was? Or were the strange gazes all part of the uncomfortable and awkward employment termination ritual, one he was experiencing for the first time in his almost decade-long tenure at the Memphis Inter-Provincial Airport? Whatever it was, there seemed to be something truly peculiar going on that morning.

Arriving at his now almost barren and unrecognizable workstation, Christensen noticed the presence of increased airport security all around his department, along with a number of cog officials crowding the narrow hallways of that complex. As he methodically gathered up a few last things that belonged to him, Christensen slowly wiped off the dusty layers before placing each item in a box. With every memento, came an opportunity to recall the specific stories and events that spanned some of the most turbulent, though

The Dreamers of Allianz

meaningful years of his life. No sooner had Christensen put away the last collectible vestige of his now defunct career, a miniature airport tower, than a nervous co-worker, also on his last day of work, came up to him from behind and urgently whispered, "Tanner…"

"Roy! For heaven's sake, man, what's going on?" Christensen asked, startled and now picking up on the high tension that was thick in the air.

"Tanner, listen. In all my years in the tower, I've never seen this place so infested with security personnel and cogs."

"So, what do you suppose is the matter?" Christensen inquired.

"From what I've gathered, it has something to do with the visit by the Allianz official delegation, this Friday," Christensen's colleague suspected.

"Yeah?" Christensen replied, sensing that something else was on his friend's mind.

"Yeah. And uh…I'm afraid it also has something to do with you."

"Me?" exclaimed Christensen.

"Afraid so, brother. The 'super' has been looking for you since earlier this morning. It sounds really urgent," his worried friend explained.

"The boss? Looking for me? Urgent? What in the world could it possibly be?" Christensen wondered aloud.

"Just hear me on this, Tanner. You need to get over there to see him this instant," Roy admonished him. "Just give me your box, and I'll hold it for you 'til you get back. Now get on over there."

Feeling at a loss, now more than ever, and quite disturbed by all of the ubiquitous police presence, Christensen hastened to make his way over to the main office and found his boss wide-eyed and obviously agitated.

"Christensen, you haven't a moment to lose. You're to get up to the sixth floor conference room immediately," instructed his boss, in a disconcertingly grave tone.

"The executive boardroom? What for?" Christensen asked, intrigued. "What about the dismissal protocol I'm supposed to go through today?"

"Never mind that, for right now," said his boss. "These are extremely unusual circumstances. That's all I'm able to tell you at this point. And you'd better not delay." He then added, "And when you're through, come see me right away. I also want to know what the heck this is all about."

"Based on your tone and by what I'm seeing around here, I don't suppose I'm about to receive a distinguished service award, am I?" Christensen joked, trying to diffuse the tension and seriousness of the situation.

"I'd say you're right about that, Christensen. But I've got a feeling that this may turn out to be a once-in-a-lifetime day for you, nonetheless," his boss offered in mystifying response.

Following his boss' instructions, Christensen reluctantly took the elevator to the sixth floor. Alone for the short ride, Christensen felt fear creeping in, as he struggled to understand what was behind all the suspense. He could think of nothing that could explain the rationale for being singled out in this manner. After all, other than the fact that he was a non-implant, he mostly blended right in with all the other controllers in his department. But since the other non-implants seemed to have been left alone, he deduced that his non-implant status could not explain the situation either. Unable to come up with satisfactory answer, he took a moment to pray. Within seconds, the elevator signaled its arrival at the executive floor. The double-doors opened up to reveal a squad of armed cogs, waiting just in front of the elevator doors.

"Mr. Christensen, come with us," one of the officers said.

The cogs then escorted him over to the main boardroom. As he entered the room, Christensen saw the silhouette of a person standing in the glare of the large windows that faced east. As he moved off the line of the glaring sunrays to catch a better view of the individual standing there, he heard the doors shut behind him.

"Mr. Christensen," he heard a female voice say, as she turned around to face him. "Welcome. It's been a long time." Struggling to make out who she was, Christensen replied, "Excuse me, uh… do I know you?" Stepping forward, into the room's light, the woman's face and her green and black uniform were at once clearly revealed.

"I believe you do know me, Mr. Christensen. I am Marshall and Commander Misha Dariah."

Forty-One

Fateful Showdown

Christensen stood there, speechless. The silence persisted and, for a moment, all time seemed to stand still. His immediate reaction was to doubt the whole thing, wondering if perhaps he had been the victim of a tasteless, albeit well orchestrated, farewell, practical joke. Yet the woman standing in front of him did carry a striking resemblance to the leader of the American Province. But what possible reason could the American Marshall have to come there, specifically looking for him? Unable to get past the unlikely scenario, yet succumbing to the pressure of the awkward silence, Christensen voiced a tentative, "I…I'm not sure I understand."

"I see you are in disbelief, Mr. Christensen. I certainly understand it if you're wondering about the genuineness of this unexpected meeting. But I can assure you, this is not a charade."

"Uh, forgive me if I seem perplexed ma'am," Christensen replied, still unable to make sense of the surreal situation, "but I fail to comprehend the logic of this very strange situation." He then asked, "Why am I here?"

"You're an intelligent man, Mr. Christensen. Surely you can appreciate how singular this occasion truly is. You have caught the attention of the government, and I have come here to discuss with you matters of utmost importance to both you and the Federation."

"I'm sorry. I'm not following you," he responded, now even more dumbfounded. "How could I possibly be of any interest to the Federation? Are you sure you have the right man?"

"Positive. There's no mistake. Now, Mr. Christensen, if you would just sit down and relax," Dariah invited him, "I will be more than happy to explain to you why indeed I am here. I think you will see that there's no need to feel apprehensive about this, and I hope we can establish a sound and positive rapport, as a result of what I am about to share with you."

Acquiescing, Christensen groped for a chair next to him, and sat down without taking his eyes off of Dariah. Although the reality of the situation was beginning to sink in, he remained confounded by it nonetheless, unable to come to grips with the fact that this was Commander Dariah, the archenemy and persecutor of the American Community of Brethren.

"Marshall Dariah, I uh…can't at all conceive of what interest you might have in me, particularly. As I'm sure you're aware, as of noon today a number of us air traffic controllers will be out of a job. What could I possibly have to offer to you?"

"Mr. Christensen, I am fully aware of your situation," Dariah replied. "You do have my sympathies. But times are changing fast, and it is paramount to the security of Allianz that the entire aerospace industry conform to the new operational demands of our world system. Assimilation to the implant protocol is a basic requirement for functioning under the newest industry matrix. The resulting impact on the non-implanted and under-prepared members of the workforce is of necessity. I do believe you understand."

"You'll have to pardon me, Marshall, but I find it extremely difficult to believe that you do in fact concern yourself with the human fallout from this shake up," Christensen countered. "I don't pretend to think that the impact of this on mine and many other families really even registers on your radar, to use the vernacular from my line of work… Former line of work, that is."

"Fair enough, Mr. Christensen," she said. "Then, why don't you allow me to get straight to the point."

"Please…"

"Mr. Christensen, you may not recall, but we have a bit of history together."

"Uh, yes, of course. I do remember you...Misha Dariah. You were one of my students at MIT," he affirmed. "Some students, you just don't forget that easily. I'd say you fall in that category."

"Thank you. It's nice to be remembered," said Dariah. "We were fellow 'beavers' at MIT, and you were my TA for a term...Earth and Space Science, if I recall correctly."

"Yes, so much for our little school reunion... But I'm going to take a wild guess that that's not exactly why we're here." Christensen remarked.

"Very perceptive of you, Mr. Christensen," Dariah replied. "In fact, we'll need to leave our reminiscing about the old days for a more opportune moment."

"Aw, just when I was beginning to feel the warm fuzzys..." Christensen nervously joked.

"Yes, nevertheless..." said Dariah. She then continued, "Mr. Christensen, as you know, the Federation has, for years, been resolute in our enforcement of the Allianz Code. We have sought to eradicate non-compliance and deviant disorder in all sectors of the Federation, and this has meant having to go up against groups that have been defiant against the status quo, whatever their ideological persuasion may happen to be."

"I'm well aware of that," Christensen said, intently listening to Dariah, as she paced in front on him, on the other side of the boardroom table.

"During my tenure, as the American Marshall and Commander, perhaps no other group has so intrigued and, to be perfectly honest, vexed me, as the one known as the Community of Brethren Resistance."

Upon hearing these words, Christensen suddenly realized the degree of danger that he faced just being there, in the presence of Marshall Dariah. Yet, he very much felt he was being held captive; if not by the fact that armed guards stood just outside that room, then by what he discerned to be a divinely appointed encounter. All of a sudden, he understood the real reason for his unsettling feelings earlier that morning. The mystery, however, was not yet fully unveiled, for he did not know what ultimately awaited him in this fateful meeting.

"Mr. Christensen, let me be absolutely plain with you," Dariah said. She then revealed, "I am well aware of your significant involvement with the Resistance in the American South."

Christensen, as if moved by an impulse or a self-preservation instinct, jumped up from his chair. His body began to tremble, and he began to walk slowly toward the door, with his gaze helplessly fixed on the American Marshall.

"I wouldn't go out there if I were you, Mr. Christensen," Dariah warned him. "My guards have orders to apprehend you, should you be seen trying to leave this room unaccompanied by me or without my authorization."

"Am I your prisoner, Marshall? Is that what you're saying?" Christensen asked with indignation.

"Absolutely not. I am simply ensuring that you do not leave here before you have a chance to seriously evaluate your very few options. What I have to tell you, Mr. Christensen, no doubt can significantly impact your future, as well as that of your family, even that of the Children of the Promise group. That *is* what you call you yourselves, is it not?"

"It is."

"I do urge you, then, not to act foolishly, and prematurely walk away from here, turning your back on my proposition without giving it careful consideration."

"Proposition? What proposition?" he inquired with a mixture of relief and derision.

"Mr. Christensen, last Sunday evening, I instructed my forces to stage interventions at three large Community of Brethren gatherings out East and here in the South. Their orders were to move to neutralize the activities of those groups and to detain Resistance cadres responsible for organizing and conducting those subversive gatherings. Two of the cog missions were accomplished successfully. The third operation, however, was ultimately aborted," Dariah disclosed. "Do you know why, Mr. Christensen?"

Christensen then walked back over to his chair and sat down. The haunting memories of that evening were still fresh on his mind, and he knew full well that it was his group that was to be the third target. Looking down, he then recalled, murmuring, "It was a terrifying ordeal. We thought we were under attack and in grave danger. At that time, no one had any idea that there had been attacks elsewhere that evening. Nothing made too much sense, except that we had been alerted to the possibility that you were preparing to oppose us in the South. We just didn't know when or how."

"Perfect intelligence *is* a hard art to master, isn't it?" Dariah commented. "I think we both understand that all too well.'

"We struggled to know what to do," he went on. "What ever *could* we do? We were surrounded, while thousands of people were gathered in the sanctuary, completely unaware of the danger they were in, but surely sensing that something was wrong. It could have been a catastrophe," Christensen acknowledged. "But then my son and his friends secretly thought up a truly harebrained idea, to hurl snowballs at the cog forces."

"Yes!" Dariah exclaimed in response. "That was truly amazing. I found myself terribly amused," she admitted.

"Many of us prayed for deliverance. And deliverance did come," said Christensen, as he looked up at Dariah. "All of a sudden, they were gone. The cogs left as unannounced as they had arrived. That was, without a doubt, one of the most remarkable evenings I have ever lived through. Darkness turned to light, and hundreds of people believed and were baptized."

"Deliverance did come, indeed, Mr. Christensen. But do you know why I aborted the whole operation?" she asked.

"I believe our prayers were answered, Marshall. Exactly how or why danger was averted, we may never really know until glory," Christensen replied. "But all we knew was that our prayers were faithfully answered."

"I don't mean to burst your religious bubble. But, quite frankly, Mr. Christensen, there was one, single reason for why you were spared that night," Dariah said.

"And what might that be, Marshall?"

"It was only because of my prior acquaintance with you, remote as it may be, that I halted the operation, sparing you and your group's gathering last Sunday," Dariah related.

Skeptical of Dariah's account, Christensen replied, "Marshall Dariah, do you really expect me to believe that somehow our barely existent prior acquaintance, of two decades ago, was so significant to you that you decided to take pity on me and my group and abandon your mission to destroy us? No disrespect, but that seems absurdly far-fetched, coming from the all-powerful American Marshall."

"I know this may come to you as a shock, but that is precisely the case," declared Dariah. "You see, Mr. Christensen, at first I called off the intervention on some sort of visceral response I myself failed to fully understand, simply on account of knowing you. However, since then, I have come to appreciate the possibility of your true worth to our operations in the province. With your background, you have the potential to develop into a valuable member of our strategic planning team." Finally she said, "I have come here to offer you a prominent place in the top levels of our government, helping us to track down and stop Resistance activities in the province."

"Wait a minute, Marshall. Let me get this straight," Christensen reacted. "First you come here and tell me that you were compelled to spare me and my fellow brethren from calamity because of our prior acquaintance. And now, you're recruiting me to finish your dirty job and turn against my own people? What kind of an idiot do you take me for?"

"Not at all, Mr. Christensen. I would not presume to think of you that way. But you do understand that you have everything to gain by joining us, and everything to lose by rejecting my offer. It is just a matter of time before the Resistance is finished and done with. You do realize that, do you not?" said Dariah.

"And if I do refuse?" Christensen asked.

"Before I answer that, I want to clearly communicate to you the terms of my proposition," Dariah replied. "Mr. Christensen, I am prepared to ensure that you and your family are well provided for. I know that life as a non-implant has become one of increasing sacrifices. You can hardly manage to buy food or fuel for you family anymore, and the walls are closing in on you. If you accept my offer, Mr. Christensen, all of that would change instantly. Life would be sweet again. Think of how your wife and children would benefit from it. They would again be able to enjoy the pleasure of something as basic as good food."

"Marshall Dariah, you underestimate your opponent," countered Christensen. Feeling suddenly filled with the Spirit of Truth, he said, "Long ago, it was written that man shall not live by bread alone, but by every word that comes from The Name. My family and I depend on Him alone for our provision. We have secret food that you know nothing about. And, furthermore, no matter how much our stomachs tried to tempt and rule over us, any food would taste bitterly, knowing that other fellow believers hungered and struggled, while we feasted on your despicable Allianz delicacies."

"Very well then, Mr. Christensen," Dariah replied. "But what if I told you that I would ensure not just your safety and that of your family? What if, because of your service to us, your entire group, the Children of the Promise group, would be allowed full amnesty and would remain completely untouched by our forces? In fact, we would allow them to continue to perform their religious rituals in total safety, as long as no further recruitment activities were sought. Surely you would not want to be responsible for denying them this tremendous privilege, would you? How would your master not be pleased with such altruistic service on your part?"

"Up to your old tricks again, old tempter…" Christensen uttered under his breath. He then said, "I will not tempt my Lord that way. Only He can grant us security."

"Ahh, of course. I should have guessed that you religious types are eternal optimists. Realistic? No. But certainly hopeless optimists."

"With all due respect, Marshall Dariah, this hopeful fool believes you are wasting your time here. Nothing I have heard so far sounds anything but insulting to me. And even the absurdity of what I think you are proposing to me pales in comparison to your petulance in so much as implying that I have any inclination or desire to serve a system that I find to be so oppressively evil and detestable," Christensen answered with growing boldness.

"I didn't think this would be easy, Mr. Christensen," Dariah admitted. "But you must not forget that you were spared last Sunday evening. Spared of a catastrophic end to your subversive gatherings. I really don't think you have fully appreciated how close your group

The Dreamers of Allianz

came to sharing the same fate as the other gatherings out East. You could have all been arrested, or worse."

"Arrested? Is that what you're threatening us with?" Christensen challenged her. "I thought the Federation was in the vanishing business, all over the globe, as a matter of fact."

"If that is what you truly believe, Mr. Christensen, then shouldn't that worry you? That countless numbers are suffering because of a worthless ideology cultivated by all of you in the Resistance leadership?" Dariah insinuated.

"I don't expect you to admire our cause, Marshall. But you cannot escape the blame for trampling on completely innocent, good people, in your indiscriminate opposition to the Resistance? You are responsible for the mistreatment and killings of these countless many that you, yourself, have mentioned," accused Christensen.

"Innocence is not mine to determine," she asserted impatiently. "My mandate is to secure order, to uphold the Code. One cannot worry about fish, when running a dam. They must exist within the confines of a system that is concerned with a higher aim, the greater good."

"Greater good? That's a matter of perspective, wouldn't you say?" Christensen contested.

"Exactly. And from my perspective, resistance is futile. Dissenters are precisely the kind of fish that must be sacrificed for the ultimate good of the system."

"So why did you decide stop to your operation against my group? And why did you come here to see one fish?"

"I, too, have a heart, Mr. Christensen. Let's just say I wanted to do it for a fellow MIT beaver. I had hoped to convince you to consider a better, and certainly more viable and promising perspective in the long run. And to give you fair warning of what will unavoidably come, if you do not cease and desist."

"Fear not he who can kill the body but then can do nothing else to it, but fear Him who can kill you and throw your soul into hell," Christensen said, alluding to Holy Scripture.

"Please, Mr. Christensen," she replied condescendingly, "save your toxic, dogmatic poetry for willing ears. I am sure I have no clue what you are talking about."

"What I am talking about, Marshall, is that there are more determined fish in this ocean than you realize. We will not succumb to your terror campaign."

"I had hoped to reason with you, Mr. Christensen. But I can see it has been a waste of my time. Fish are not creatures one's mercy is well spent on," Dariah scornfully concluded.

At that point, as Dariah fully realized she had labored to no avail to produce the desired response in Christensen, she decided to ask one last question, this time not for the purpose of persuading Christensen, but simply to satisfy her own curiosity.

"Mr. Christensen, I have to believe that you do in fact take your convictions seriously. I'm beginning to understand that you must see no choice in the matter. After all, who would choose to believe as you do, and have to endure all of the hardship involved with the way of life associated with the Resistance?"

"No, Marshall Dariah. You are absolutely wrong," Christensen replied. "Everything that is most precious to me hinges on this choice to resist. It is not something I was born with. It is a complete, willful surrender to what is true and eternal. We're not victims of an ideology. Rather, it is our doxology that compels us to defend the Truth."

"Interesting rhetoric," Dariah commented. "But rhetoric only goes so far in filling one's stomach. So why not at least receive the implant and end the heavy burden?"

"Have you not heard, Marshall? His yoke is easy, and His burden is light, the Anointed One once said. But the Resistance is also convinced that your alternative means the end of our earthly existence, for those who believe in The Name. For we now know that if I, a Believer, receive the implant, I will go into a coma, and will ultimately die," said Christensen.

Just then, a disembodied, male voice, came from the far side of the boardroom. The chair at the head of the elongated conference table then spun slowly around, revealing a man, who had been present during the entire exchange.

"You will not surely die, Mr. Christensen."

"What? Who said that? Who's there?" Christensen exclaimed.

"Permit me introduce myself, Mr. Christensen. I am Adammus Horn...Allianz Federation Prosecutor General."

Forty-Two

Fleeing the Tempter

That morning was a trying one for Claire Christensen, as well. She wondered why her husband had not yet made contact with her. Giving into her anxious thoughts, she tried to visualize Christensen, but his malfunctioning PSS was not responding. She then tried reaching the airport Visual, in hopes of any news about her husband. Finally being routed to his department, Claire inquired with the floor manager as to her husband's whereabouts.

"Christensen… Tanner Daniel Christensen," she requested. "I wasn't able to reach him on his PSS. Would you help me locate him?"

"Ma'am, he no longer works here." Then, looking at the data file, he said, "Our records show he's already been processed for dismissal," informed the floor manager.

"Pardon me, please. I'm not trying to be pushy," Claire said, "but it's just that I know this is his last day of work. Normally I would have heard from him by now, and I'm a little worried, you know? I was hoping to be able to speak to him. I knew this was going to be a difficult day."

"I'm sorry, ma'am. I would let you talk with him, if he were here. But his workstation has been cleared, and there really is no sign of him anywhere."

"Well, then can you at least tell me whether he's left for home yet? I mean, it's not like he's gone missing or anything, right?" Claire asked, worried.

"This is all I can tell you, Mrs. Christensen. Perhaps he'll visualize you soon, and I'm sure everything will be just fine," he replied.

"Oh, all right," she answered with some hesitation. "I guess I'll give him a little while longer. Thanks."

"No problem, ma'am."

The visualization ended, leaving Claire even more puzzled and concerned. In fact, what the floor manager had told her was indeed true, to the best of his knowledge. Christensen's dismissal had in fact been fully processed by the superintendent, without Christensen being present, and as far as most of his co-workers knew it, Christensen had already left the tower for good, despite having left behind a box of his personal belongings.

Meanwhile, the meeting between Christensen, Dariah, and Horn continued, taking on an even more dramatic turn. As Horn approached Christensen on his own side of the table, Christensen stood up. This time, every sense available to him told him that evil was present there. On the surface, however, there was nothing particularly odd about Horn's appearance that would indicate this. He sported his usual black suit and carried himself with refined etiquette. Yet, there was something paralyzing about Horn's dark eyes. They somehow felt bitterly cold to Christensen, and for a moment sent a desperately agonizing chill up and down his entire body. Though he felt weak, Christensen resisted the urge to take a seat again. Drawing residual strength from somewhere deep within his soul, he strained but managed to spew out of his mouth something that actually stopped Horn dead in his tracks.

"In the name of the Anointed One, I greet you, Mr. Prosecutor General."

Those words almost unwittingly leapt from Christensen's mouth, as if someone else was speaking for him. Horn, quickly recovering from a slight loss of balance, masterfully controlled his face-work in order to hide his momentary distress.

"Oh, yes. How quaint of Mr. Christensen, isn't it Marshall Dariah," Horn responded. "I, too, offer greetings to you, from the Allianz Federation's headquarters. Now then, since we're so comfortable with each other, why don't we continue this conversation over some cocktails? Suddenly, I'm thirsty."

"Don't mind if I decline, Mr. Horn. I believe Marshall Dariah was just about to let me go," replied Christensen.

"Mr. Christensen, Marshall Dariah did a fine job expressing to you our very good intentions," Horn said. "However, there's one more item I feel we've yet to discuss, before we can conclude this meeting."

"Mr. Horn, I'm really not…"

"No, Mr. Christensen, I think you will be very much interested in what I have to offer you."

"I really don't think so," Christensen sternly reaffirmed.

"Oh, but I do. You see, Mr. Christensen, Marshall Dariah was able to offer you the basics of good food and safety. And although nowadays they are nothing to sneer at for someone in your situation, I should have known that a man of your caliber must be dealt with accordingly."

Noticing Horn's patronizing tone, Christensen replied, "Is that right?"

"Indeed… But make no mistake about it, Mr. Christensen. What I have to offer you, only *I* can offer you. And *that* is nothing less than *the world*," Horn stated.

"Impressive," Christensen responded facetiously.

"Scoff, if you must, Mr. Christensen. After all, I *have* known men, not unlike yourself, whose deep convictions were able to carry them through long hunger strikes and to lead them to take tremendous risks for the sake of their cause. But I have never met a single man who, when offered extreme power, did not at least pause to dream about the possibilities."

Christensen stood silent, struggling to keep his mind from wandering and gravitating toward Horn's statement.

"Ahh, yes, Mr. Christensen… Let us imagine all that could be yours."

"I can't, I..." Christensen struggled to resist the strangely powerful suggestion.

"Oh yes, you can. For it comes so easily you see. Like you, I once dared to imagine myself in high and lofty places," Horn tempted him. "But every man has his own vision of what that is. And you and I both know how much more you feel you deserve in your life... A career at NASA, perhaps? As a decorated and celebrated astronaut hero?" Horn insightfully suggested.

Feeling helpless to fight against the alluring imagery, Christensen began to give into his imagination.

"Oh, but I see more, Mr. Christensen...much more."

"Huh?" Christensen's interest was peaked as he listened, mesmerized.

"Oh, yes. Let us not stop there. For, truly, I have the authority to take you even higher, and to name you head of the entire Space Program under Allianz. Imagine, you, at the helm of the world's most daring, futuristic, and top-secret space exploration projects; even CyberSat's Project Red Dragon, the Federation's most ambitious space program yet. Yes, Mr. Christensen, you can have it all. All you need to do is join us, reveal to us all you know about the Resistance, and submit to me and to my authority. And as far as the implant you will receive, it is completely harmless, I assure you. Although...I am sure that your old mentor in the Resistance would have you believe otherwise. Croce is his name, is it not?" He said, mentioning my surname.

"What? How do know about Dr..." Christensen reacted in puzzlement.

"Ahh... Such inaccurate fables he has helped propagate... I know my competition well, Mr. Christensen... I can assure you, however, that the Allianz top government-issued implant would carry no risk to you whatsoever. Isn't that right, Marshall?" Horn said, turning toward Dariah. "I mean, when was the last time you craved a Transcienz fix?"

"He's right, Mr. Christensen," Dariah corroborated. "Our implants *are* different."

Indeed, by design, the very top-level Allianz politicians and officers did not experience the same Transcienz-related effects the general population did. Although in such cases the implant would suppress some consciousness and the desire for The Name, the interest in Transcienz Dream States were only felt with the standard-issue implants, administered to the population at large.

By now, Christensen could feel his mind swaying to the enticing sound waves in Horn's speech, and he began to experience an almost trance-like sensation. Horn had cunningly zeroed in on a soft spot in Christensen's psyche, as if a well-guarded secret had been astutely decoded, opening up a myriad of tantalizing desires, long suppressed by a man who, while fully realizing his great potential, had resigned himself, due to the demands of his work in the Resistance, to being satisfied professionally with so much less.

Trying hard to hide his impatience, Horn uttered, "So, Mr. Christensen, you can picture it, can't you? Now, all you have to do is capably assist us in our pursuits..."

Christensen opened his mouth, as if to say something.

"Yes?" anticipated Horn.

But then, something strange and unexpected came out of Christensen's mouth. He softly uttered it, appearing to be guided by his subconscious mind.

"Ar-ka-daş..."

"What was that, Mr. Christensen? What did you say?" Horn attempted to clarify.

Misha Dariah, who was still standing there, equally mesmerized by Horn's amazing persuasive powers, said, "Cash... I think he said, '*I want cash.*' He's asking for money!"

"What? You imbecile!" Horn harshly yelled out, further alienating Dariah. "Mr. Christensen, could you repeat that, please?"

"Arkadaş...I said, Arkadaş," he again spoke, sounding surprised at his own words and now fully coming back to his conscious self. "Arkadaş. What have you done with him? And all the others."

"Are you hallucinating, Mr. Christensen?" replied Horn. "Who is this Arkadaş you are referring to?"

"Arkadaş Izmir. He was a young pastor...in Istanbul. He was arrested by cogs, over a week ago, and has not been heard from since. He's disappeared. What have you done with him?"

"Ah, yes. I do remotely remember a Mr. Izmir, in the district of Istanbul. A zealous young man, he was, if I recall correctly. Too zealous, in fact, for his own good," Horn acknowledged.

"Was?" Christensen said, horrified. "What do you mean, *was*?"

"I am so sorry, Mr. Christensen. He obviously was an acquaintance of yours. Unfortunately, he was also a convicted criminal, and his fate has already been sealed."

"How could you? He was just a..."

"A subversive, a schemer, a foolish proselytizer," Horn interrupted him. "And it was the Federation's prerogative to put an end to it. It was as simple as that. It was not personal, Mr. Christensen. It never is." Horn then pressed Christensen on the matters at hand, saying, "Now, Mr. Christensen, I have made you an offer that's truly out of this world, and I have exercised a tremendous amount of restraint in patiently awaiting your response. I now require an answer from you. What will it be? Time is running out."

"You're right... Time *is* running out."

"Marvelous. We agree, then."

"My answer, Mr. Horn, is this; I will submit to no authority, but that of The Name, and I will serve no one, but *Him*." Christensen continued, "You're game is almost over, Mr. Horn. For we both know that these days we are living in are the Last Days of the end times."

"Last Days?" Horn replied, cackling. "Mr. Christensen, may I submit to you that indeed these are *not* the *last days*, as you so charmingly call them. In fact, evolutionarily speaking, humanity is only in its infancy. There's so much to perfect, even more to discover...about ourselves, the world, the universe. Don't be so naïve, Mr. Christensen. At least allow the one you call *creator* the simple dignity of seeing this cruel little experiment all the way through to its final conclusion." Horn then admitted, "Oh, Mr. Christensen...I, too, once sought the primal comforts of religion and blind faith. In fact, I had a short fling with the Unity Church, when I was at Harvard Law. But after enduring a year of meaningless, shallow rituals, and hypocritical preachers and their gullible followers, I gave it up for something I could truly believe in... I live in the real world, Mr. Christensen. And in this world, the name of the game is *power*...absolute power. And that's the only master, the only might, I care to take seriously."

"And are you prepared, Mr. Horn, to follow that idol blindly, down to its ultimate and final demise?"

"*My* final question to *you*, Mr. Christensen, is are *you* prepared to turn your back on this concrete, once-in-a-lifetime opportunity, and take your family and your brethren down with you?"

"Mr. Horn," Christensen replied with a kind of uncommon assertiveness that could only have emanated from the actual utterances of the Spirit of Truth, which in that moment strongly energized him, "you may be the most powerful man in all of Allianz. But I do prophecy, here and now, that as surely as I stand before you this very moment, one day sooner or later, the powers and principalities that give you all your perverse authority to influence and rule on the earth will be mightily overthrown. And you, along with them, will know everlasting torment, the likes of which no living creature has ever, *ever* known..." Then, Christensen said, "...And on that great day of utter humiliation and overthrow, a great cloud of glorified witnesses will surely watch the dominion of darkness unravel and perish, utterly crushed under the sure and heavy foot of the Lord Almighty Himself... I pity you, Mr. Horn. Despite myself, I pity you."

In that very instant, a terrible and incomparable feeling of desperation came over Adammus Horn and, for a brief second, he felt as if eternal, raging blazes were scorching him from the inside. Immediately reacting to the bizarre experience, Horn was overcome with intense fury, and impetuously lunged forward, rushing toward Christensen, as if propelled through the air by some sort of invisible power, his hands pointed directly at his intended victim's throat.

"Horn!" screamed Dariah. But in a rapid reflex, Christensen blended with the vicious aggression, moving off the line of attack. Instantly grabbing on to Horn's wrists, Christensen applied a *kokyunage* move from his Aikido training, powerfully pivoting and throwing his infuriated attacker in the same direction he was headed. Horn violently crashed upside down against the wall, and the force of the impact caused the room to quake.

"Guards!" yelled Dariah.

Immediately the doors were thrown open and, seeing the Prosecutor General collapsed on the floor, the cogs quickly evaluated the situation to be cause for using lethal force. Moving directly toward Christensen, the team of cogs drew their weapons. But Dariah immediately shouted, "No! Hold your fire! You are not to kill him!"

Capitalizing on the brief moment of confusion and hesitation on the part of the cogs, Christensen was able to plow through them, his right hand extended, shoving one of them aside by his face, and causing that cog to slam down on the floor, as Christensen ran past the first group of guards.

At once, reinforcements were called in, and a general alarm was sounded throughout the tower building. Christensen ran for his life, soon encountering more armed guards in the main hallway who, dropping to one knee, pointed their weapons at him.

"Our orders are to capture him alive! Use the stun cycle in your cog-blazers!" loudly instructed the leading officer in the group. "Freeze, you are under arrest!" he then yelled out.

Christensen instinctively stopped. Yet, as two cogs quickly approached and barely lay hands on him, he again saw an opportunity to employ his Aikido defenses in order to evade capture and escape. Cross-grabbing the hand that held his right wrist and turning it so as to extend the arm forward and between the two cogs, Christensen flowed into a *shihonage*. Still holding on to that extended arm, he quickly passed underneath it and pivoted swiftly. In doing so the cog was thrown completely off balance, while Christensen then quickly brought that wrist up toward the cogs shoulder, causing the cog's left arm to bend. Then, in a split second, by vigorously curling the cog's wrist and driving his bent arm back and down toward his left shoulder blade, Christensen created enough momentum and torque to actually flip the guard over himself, painfully leading his airborne body to collide with the second cog, before either cog knew what had happened.

Christensen was free again. Changing directions, he dashed full-speed away from the aim of the cog-blazers, whose stun cycle he heard firing consistently behind him. Before he could even blink, Christensen had dived diagonally, and then Aikido-rolled on the ground, away from the bright electrical flashes that zoomed toward and past him, narrowly missing their target. Knowing he had just seconds before the cog-blazers fully powered up again, and seeing the incoming cogs rushing toward him, Christensen headed toward a secondary corridor which, miraculously, was still empty of any police presence.

Possessing a thorough knowledge of the building's design, Christensen hurried down the narrow passageway, aware that it led to an exit door that opened to a seldom-used, central stairwell.

"After him!" he heard a cog officer command her men.

Now with dozens of cogs and airport security in hot pursuit just brief seconds behind him, Christensen disappeared behind the exit door at the end of the corridor before more shots were fired.

"Quick, he went through that door!" yelled one of the cogs.

Arriving at the closed door, the cogs tried to open it, but Christensen had managed to lock the door from the other side, using security latches.

Descending down the stairwell as fast as he could, Christensen knew he would not be able to make it to the ground floor without cogs coming up from below and intercepting his arrival. He instead chose to exit the stairwell on the 3rd floor, where the cafeteria and dining areas were located, and where the kitchen staff, still mostly unaware of the source or reason for the recent commotion, were busy with lunch preparations and did not pay much attention to Christensen, as he rapidly traversed through the dinning hall.

Turning into the loud and steamy kitchen area, Christensen ran toward the service deck in the back, heading straight to the loading dock zone. Hastily making his way past a number of large delivery vehicles, Christensen noticed one of them about to depart. Almost without thinking, Christensen leaped onto the moving truck's partially filled cargo area. Landing in a smooth forward roll, he quickly got up to a crouching position and did his best to conceal himself behind crates and boxes, as the transport drove down a long, spiraling ramp and out into daylight on the ground floor of the tower complex. Meanwhile, cogs and airport security scurried throughout the tower, still searching after their illusive fugitive.

Christensen's escape vehicle rolled quickly past the final airport exit, which was secured by unmanned gates that automatically opened to outbound traffic when a vehicle was sensed approaching the exit. Out of breath and feeling extremely disoriented inside that cargo compartment, after the fast, spiraling ramp descent, Christensen felt his head spinning. He struggled to comprehend the unfathomable series of events that had just preceded, from leaving for his dreaded last day at work and experiencing odd sights and exchanges as he arrived in the tower, to surreally coming face-to-face with none other than Marshall Dariah and the illustrious Horn, to dodging Horn's fury, to evading police capture, to finally making an audacious escape out of the airport.

Now daring to believe that he had managed to flee, the stunned and dismayed Christensen breathed a tentative sigh, only to be interrupted by the sudden terror that came over him, simply thinking about what might come next for him and especially his family. Completely unsure of where he was headed, he sat as a helpless stow-away in the back of a delivery truck. Feeling utterly at a loss about what to try next, Christensen succumbed to a moment of honest despair.

Soon after, and for the first time on that strangely eventful morning, Christensen realized he had not yet visualized Claire since he had left home that morning, and that surely his family must be worried sick about his lack of contact with them. As he reached for his PSS, his hopes were dashed again. He touched his left ear, feeling for his PSS, only to discover that his already unreliable communicator had in fact been lost, most probably having gotten knocked off his ear during the scuffle and tumult back at the tower complex.

From that moment on, only one thought persistently entered his troubled mind: *how can I warn and get to my family, before the forces of Allianz decisively move on them and seize them all.* Now committing himself to fervent prayer, perhaps more ardently than ever before in his entire life, Christensen surrendered all things into the hands of The Name, his Deliverer and now his only hope.

Forty-Three

No Word

It was already early afternoon on that fateful day, and still there had not been a single word from Christensen. Deep down, Claire knew something must have gone terribly wrong for her husband. She began to visualize the Waters and others in hopes of alerting them that their beloved brother in the faith might be in some serious kind of trouble, although, tragically, she was unable to offer any details beyond pure conjecture at that point.

"John, I just don't know where he could be. Now even the kids are getting upset, because we haven't heard from Tanner, at all," Claire told him via PSS.

"Claire, please try and remain calm. Do it for the kids, all right?" John pleaded with her. "I'll contact a few folks, and we'll do our best to find Tanner. Just stay home 'til you hear from him or from one of us. And if by chance he does show up or make contact with you, please let me know immediately, so I can tell the others."

"I sure will, John. Thanks. Thank you so much," she offered from the bottom of her heart.

With no clues to go on, however, the Christensen's friends found themselves impotent, unable to make any real progress or to offer any substantial assistance in finding Christensen. *Where could he possibly be? What could have taken place that morning?* Claire incessantly wondered, as if she owed herself and her children a viable explanation. Exhausted, she fell into weary sleep on the living room couch, holding tight to her PSS, which for now felt to her like her only lifeline.

Meanwhile, the children tried to pass the time together, not knowing what else to do but talk about what was on their hearts and minds, and occasionally glance at their televisor in hopes of gaining any helpful clues about their father's whereabouts.

"Zeke," whispered Bethany, "are you worried about Dad?"

"Actually, Beth, right now I'm more worried about Mom. I think Dad can take care of himself, for the most part, even though he's been very troubled lately."

"I hope you're right about that," Bethany said.

"I wish Daddy would come home soon," Holly uttered, looking for some comfort from her older siblings, whom she very much looked up to and saw as so grown up most of the time, relative to her.

"We all do, Holly," Bethany replied. "But don't be too worried. Who knows? Maybe he'll be here soon, and all of this will just pass, like a bad dream."

"Y'all, why don't we pray for Mom and Dad, right now?" Zeke suggested.

"Good idea," Bethany said, "You lead us, big brother."

The prayer the young Ezekiel uttered that time was not short, but it was basic, dry bones. No eloquence was called for at that moment. It was as if nothing else really mattered to them just then, save to simply focus intensely on their parents. Not knowing where their father was and unsure of what he might be going through, they offered a heart-wrenching supplication for his safe return home, as well as for all things to go back to at least a semblance of normalcy, although such a concept seemed more and more illusive as the days progressed.

Through their family routine, being homeschooled and spending much of their time as a family at the weekly meetings of the Children of the Promise group and its more formal gatherings, daily life for the Christensen kids, more often than not, had a way of finding them in each other's company. They had been taught to frequently pray together, for all kinds of reasons and in just about all circumstances. Though young in years, they had learned to depend on one another, that way. The closeness they shared with one another, and the common faith they each had professed from an early age, resulted in a kind of ease and synergy when it came to praying together. This meant that, at times, and this was definitely one of them, these three young people would weave in and out of corporate prayer, in the course of their conversation. Now, more than ever, joining forces again in holy petition was the obvious thing to do with their time, as they expectantly waited for their beloved dad to come through the front door.

"Hey, Holly," Bethany said, "I'm so looking forward to our slumber party with Alyssa, tonight. Are you?" she asked, trying to cheer her sister up.

"I guess," answered Holly, "but I sure wish Daddy would get home soon."

It just seemed impossible for these three to take the conversation anywhere for too long, before it would come back around to the pressing issue at hand; the fate of their dear father.

Forty-Four

The Great Escape

With the driver of the large truck in which Christensen hid completely unaware of his fugitive cargo, Christensen found himself still utterly clueless about his destination, even a half hour after his exodus from the tower. Having already crossed the borderline into the Provincial State of Mississippi, Christensen was being carried south, while a regional manhunt was about to intensify.

Back at the Memphis Inter-Provincial Airport, Horn had just recently been ably revived and given first aid by emergency airport medics who rushed to the scene, while a new team of doctors was arriving to run some tests on their illustrious patient. Still in the tower's boardroom and with a recuperating Horn vitally attached to a plethora of medical testing equipment, a cog officer went on to provide a highly anticipated security debriefing. Horn and Dariah listened carefully to the disappointing news:

"Sirs, airport surveillance cameras have captured these images of Mr. Christensen, during his escape." Pointing at some time-lapsed images displayed before them, the cog officer reported, "As you see here, Mr. Christensen seems to have boarded the cargo area of this food delivery transport and managed to escape undetected by our forces and airport security."

"And why was he not stopped immediately after he brutally assaulted me, and I blacked out?" Horn asked, angered by the undesirable course of events, and wasting no time before disingenuously spinning the embarrassing occurrence in his favor.

"Sir, we were ordered not to shoot!" was the officer's reply.

"What? Who issued that order? Bring him to me, immediately," commanded Horn. Fearful silence briefly followed.

"Uh, Mr. Prosecutor General, sir, uh…" the cog officer reluctantly attempted to answer.

"Yes? I'm waiting…" Horn impatiently said to him.

"Uh, sir…we were following Marshall Dariah's orders to neither shoot, nor kill Mr. Christensen."

"What? Marshall Dariah's orders?" Horn repeated, as he turned to Dariah. "Is this some kind of joke, Marshall? Explain yourself, at once," He directed.

"Negative, sir. The officer is being truthful and accurate. I did give orders not to shoot or kill him," she confirmed with some trepidation in her voice.

"This is outrageous! Did you not see what happened?"

"Yes, sir, I certainly did."

"Then why did you not have him stopped?"

"Well, sir, it all happened so fast, I…I saw you going after him, and uh…"

"Watch yourself, Marshall. You'd better get your facts straight… I was attacked!" Horn insisted, still entangled with the myriad of wires and electrodes attached to him.

"I'm afraid that's not what I saw, sir. I believe Christensen acted in self-defense," she said truthfully, but to Horn, defiantly.

"One more time, Marshall, watch yourself. You are swimming in treacherous waters, here."

Horn then looked directly and intently into Dariah's eyes, as if they were gateways into her mind, and supernaturally influenced her thoughts, suggesting, "The fact is, Marshall, I was viciously assailed, and ended up unconscious, on the floor. Meanwhile you just watched, and worse even, enabled him to escape, when protecting me was your primary duty, first and foremost. What were you thinking?" the disaffected Horn continued on in his barrage of questions. "What got into you, Marshall?"

"I…I'm not sure, I…" Dariah attempted a response, now feeling utterly confused.

The Dreamers of Allianz

"Marshall, I have no time for this. I expect you to explain yourself, at once!"

"I don't know!" she said, shouting back at Horn. "I believe what was going through my mind in the few moments when it all happened was that he was too valuable for us to just kill him. I had to make a split-second decision. I didn't think he would succeed in actually getting away," she feebly tried to justify herself.

"Of course, you didn't. Why is that not surprising?" Horn condescendingly replied, while Dariah just sat, silent. He then called out, "Lieutenant, I need a new PSS instantly. This one was most likely damaged in the struggle. I can't get it to uplink to my classified domain in CyberSat's Data-Realm," Horn said, handling his PSS.

"Sir, we've got spare units for just such emergencies. I can produce one here for you in a matter of minutes."

"Very well," Horn replied. The cog officer then contacted the logistics team and quickly provided a new PSS for Horn's use.

"Sir, here's the new PSS you've requested."

"Good work, Lieutenant. It'll just take me a minute here, and I'll be able to re-establish my classified uplink to CyberSat's Data-Realm," Horn said, as he appeared to be programming the new communications device.

"Horn, what are you trying to do?" asked Dariah, in a low voice.

Ignoring her, Horn continued, "...and there. Now, with direct CyberSat feed to my PSS, in just seconds I can pinpoint the exact location of Christensen's escape vehicle, and have a real-time, close-up satellite image of it," he explained.

"Brilliant, sir," replied the cog Lieutenant. "Our forces will intercept him, wherever you order them to go."

"Indeed, they will. But we've got to be patient. We don't want him to jump ship prematurely. Christensen has proven to be a resourceful escapee, and he might try to flee if he knows we're on his trail," Horn reasoned. "I've got a notion that..." he paused.

"Sir?" said the cog officer.

"...that driver is probably still unaware that Christensen's in his own cargo compartment. I want that driver instructed to turn back to the airport, but without giving away the fact that he's doing so. CyberSat will direct his return route, and Christensen will have no idea that he's being delivered right back into our hands. I want troops on the other side of the airport," Horn said, now viewing a PSS-generated holographic image of the airport grounds. "Based on this diagram, the truck will be arriving at the East-gate and will cross the parking lot where it looks like the small, private aircraft parking area is located."

"We'll be there, ready and waiting for him, sir," replied the Lieutenant. Horn then continued, "I want him apprehended as soon as he's inside the airport's perimeter."

"Yes, sir. Sir, are we to bring him to you, then?" asked the cog officer.

"No. Marshall Dariah and I are leaving here at once. As far as I'm concerned, I'm finished with Mr. Christensen."

In hearing this, Dariah asked, "Horn, isn't Christensen of use to us? Isn't he more valuable to us alive than dead?"

"Indeed, he is, darling. My plans are to do away with Mr. Christensen. Not to kill him," Horn told her in a foreboding tone. He then instructed the cog officer, "When he's in police custody, I want him sent to D.C., immediately."

"Horn, you don't mean..." Dariah exclaimed, reacting to Horn's Machiavellian plan.

"Yes, Marshall. You've guessed correctly. Christensen will join his comrades at *Les Invalides* II," Horn stated. "Now, Lieutenant, I want no errors this time, is that understood? And you be sure and notify me the moment he's been caught and also delivered in D.C. Is that clear?"

"That's affirmative, sir. We'll do it, and there will be no mistakes."

"Meanwhile, I want you to place immediate secret surveillance on Christensen's home. If something goes wrong, I want his family as a bargaining chip."

"Yes, sir," replied the cog officer.

"Dismissed," ordered Horn.

Turning to Dariah once again, he said, "My dear Marshall, after what has happened here, I believe I can no longer give you my unreserved vote of confidence. You are in imminent danger of being discharged from your duties. You now have no choice but to come with me. I'm not letting you out of my sight for one second. You will depart with me immediately to my next, overseas destination."

"Horn, what in the world do you mean? I've got a job to do here. What kind of an idea is that?"

"Marshall, I am relieving you of your duties in the American Province until further notice, and the province will be indefinitely turned over to the Deputy-Marshall. I am assigning you to accompany me to a place that will help me determine, once and for all, where your loyalties truly lie... We're to leave at once for North Africa."

While Horn and Dariah prepared to depart from Memphis, the cog forces were awaiting the imminent return of Christensen in the re-routed escape truck. At last, the vehicle was sighted, and it seemed that all was going according to Horn's plan. As the truck approached the East-gate, which began to open, Christensen, who had dozed off from exhaustion and worry inside the cargo compartment, suddenly awoke. Noticing that the vehicle was finally slowing to an almost halt, he got up and looked out to check his surroundings and probable location. To his utter despair, he realized he had just returned to the Memphis Inter-Provincial Airport, just as the truck was driving past the entrance gate.

"No," he said "It can't be."

A few yards away, a small battalion of cog troops stood ready to trap him.

Just as Christensen was about to resign himself to the fact that he had no choice but to turn himself in, he saw what was certain to be his only chance for deliverance. A few yards away, he spotted his colleague, Roy, who was making his way across the parking lot and seemed to be headed toward his personal aircraft, which he, residing several counties away in Tennessee, used to commute to and from work. Roy had just been terminated as an employee at the

The Dreamers of Allianz

airport tower, was headed home, and was completely unaware of Christensen's dire predicament. In an instant, Christensen jumped off the cargo compartment in which he hid, and bolted toward Roy, who turned around abruptly. Roy immediately recognized his friend and noticed that something was the matter.

"Tanner?" he exclaimed, surprised.

"Roy! There's no time to explain. I need your help, brother." Somehow instinctively discerning his friend was in grave danger and realizing the fateful moment in which he was caught, Roy replied, "Say no more. Take my Hummingbird. The Name be with you, my friend," and he handed Christensen the keys to his small but swift personal aircraft.

Noticing that Christensen was fleeing, the cogs charged in his direction. Quickly locating Roy's blue aircraft, Christensen, who had also been previously trained as a pilot while earning his air traffic controller license, started the Hummingbird, which was capable of vertical lift-off. Within seconds, he was airborne. Meanwhile, the cogs, arriving too late to intercept Christensen, encircled and apprehended Roy, who was subsequently taken in for questioning. For a second time that day Christensen left the airport commotion behind. As he did so, he was able to see his friend being seized and, weeping for him said, "Oh Roy, I'm so sorry. I'm so sorry, my brother. May The Name be with you."

Upon being interrogated, Roy was imprisoned. He never made it home that day and was never heard from after that incident. Roy's heroic act crucially gave Christensen a new opportunity to flee, and such sacrifice would not be forgotten. Within minutes after Christensen's new escape, cog aircraft had been dispatched in pursuit of the two-time runaway.

Forty-Five

Crashed?

Urgent word was sent out to Horn and Dariah about Christensen's capture fiasco. Meanwhile, flying manually in an indirect, erratic, and thus less predictable pattern, Christensen tried desperately to get to his family as fast as he possibly could. He pushed the Hummingbird personal aircraft to its velocity limits. Maintaining his friend's aircraft at a low altitude and flying below detection by air-traffic monitoring systems, he knew he could evade conventional radar capabilities. On Christensen's mind was also the high risk of being visually spotted by cog units, who would certainly be looking for him from their ground positions.

Now only about thirty miles from home, Christensen had miraculously managed to avoid contact with the police, and there was a good chance he might make it home soon. To his distress, however, Christensen felt a sudden jolt, followed by considerable loss of power in the aircraft. He immediately noticed that the Hummingbird was beginning to lose altitude. The ground was not far off to begin with, and he had to think very quickly. Oddly, all flight instruments seemed to be functioning normally and signaled no unusual power drop problems. Christensen felt at a total loss, completely unable to diagnose the source of the trouble.

Suddenly, the aircraft regained power, and a flashing message appeared on the instrument panel screen in front of him, which said, "*CyberSat Flight Navigation Engaged.*" Reading it, Christensen soon acknowledged he had lost all control of the aircraft, which was now being remotely guided by CyberSat's air-traffic overriding system. In fact, Horn, once having heard about Christensen's aerial escape, had moved to activate the overriding program via his PSS, and the Hummingbird was now in the process of being re-routed back to the airport.

"Prepare yourselves, ladies and gentlemen, for I am about to deliver Mr. Christensen into your hands," Horn boasted to the cog officials.

Christensen realized the aircraft was completing a wide u-turn, flying over open fields below. Within seconds, the aircraft was apparently headed back in the direction of the Memphis Inter-Provincial Airport. At that moment, Christensen knew that his only chance for reaching his family would be to eject from the Hummingbird. If he remained in the aircraft, his fate would surely be sealed. He also knew, however, that unless he managed to disable the CyberSat tracking signal, used to aid rescuers in finding the ejected pilot in the event of an accident, he would quickly be located and hunted down.

Tech savvy as he was, Christensen had to work as fast as he could to short-circuit his seat's tracking mechanism, taking advantage of the fact that the small airplane was now being remotely piloted. Sweating profusely from nervous tension, Christensen removed his flight helmet and work jacket and laid them aside. In a few short minutes he was able to disengage the seat's tracking system, which would enable him to eject without detection by CyberSat. Sitting down again, Christensen re-fastened his flight helmet and seat harness. But instead of ejecting and leaving the aircraft to return empty to the airport and instigating another search for him, Christensen came up with a daring plan. *If I crash this thing*, he thought to himself, *I could buy me some time before the cogs realize I've escaped.*

So, as a last but resourceful resort, Christensen shut off the engines of the small plane, deliberately causing it to get out of CyberSat's control and initiating a gradual nose-dive. He knew that within seconds the Hummingbird would plummet into a densely wooded forest preserve directly below it, so Christensen had to act fast to eject from the condemned air transport.

Pressing the "*Seat Ejection*" button, Christensen closed his eyes and waited for the powerful rocket boosters to thrust him out of the aircraft and safely into the air. But a split second became a couple of seconds, and he immediately realized that something had gone dreadfully wrong.

"What? No!" he said in utter desperation.

The top of the trees just below soon filled the entire field of vision through the plane's downward-turned front windshields. Christensen, now paralyzed with fear and out of time, simply closed his eyes once again, elevated his last thought to The Name, and braced himself for the likely fatal impact.

"Lord…" he whispered.

In what he could only attribute to sovereign, divine providence, the thrusters of his seat suddenly engaged, and in the last possible sliver of time, Christensen eluded the fiery crash, being propelled into the air with dizzying force. A huge ball of fire mushroomed from the crash site, and black smoke billowed noticeably, soon becoming visible from miles away, signaling the precise location of the downed plane. The fire burned intensely, rapidly consuming the wreckage. Little was apparently left of the fuselage, except smoldering, twisted metal and the charred contents from the interior of the plane. No one inside the Hummingbird could possibly have survived such a crash or its fantastic, flaming aftermath. Yet, completely undetected, Christensen had safely ejected by the narrowest of margins, as his seat actually brushed against the top leafage on the trees below, during the initial ejection.

Semi-conscious and feeling completely disoriented due to the powerful G-forces now acting against his body, all Christensen could do was hope that his seat's parachuting mechanism would soon engage for a smooth landing. But the conventional parachute landing never came, as the seat back thrusters continued to fire. Now regaining lucidity of thought, Christensen realized to his great surprise that he was actually attached to a rocket-propelled flight-pack. *How do you control this thing?* he wondered, still flying in a straight, upward trajectory.

Unable to recognize any control devices available to him, and with his hands firmly clasping the armrests of his now erect seat,

Christensen cogitated that he might, in fact, be holding on to the controls. He was right. As he moved his armrests up and down slightly, his rocket thrusters responded accordingly and he soon mastered its steering mechanism, rendering the machine fully navigable. Readjusting his trajectory by the sun's glare above the overcast sky, as well as by the angle of the main interstate nearby, Christensen was now headed toward Midville. Exactly how much time he had before his fuel ran out, however, was a matter of pure conjecture, as he flew at high velocity, gauging by the heavy road traffic down below, which he sped past.

As cog transports arrived at the crash scene, they contacted the cog officials back at the airport and proceeded to report on the plane crash.

"Can you confirm whether Mr. Christensen is found among the wreckage?" inquired one of the cog superiors.

"Impossible to know at this time, sir," informed a cog Sergeant at the crash scene. "The fire is burning intensely, and the jet fuel combustion has spread the fire to a large area all around the site of the crash. We'll need to put out this fire before we can safely inspect the wreckage and make a positive identification."

"Very well, then. Make it so, Sergeant," ordered the cog superior. "I'll debrief the Marshall and the Prosecutor General on this new development."

Forty-Six

Horn's Great Ambitions

Horn and Dariah had already boarded the official Allianz Federation airplane set to return to D.C., when they received the update on Christensen via PSS.

"Sir," informed the cog officer, "we've picked up no ejection signal from CyberSat. And based on the on-site reports, we believe that the chances of anyone surviving that type of crash impact or the jet fuel tank explosion itself, not to mention the intense heat from the ensuing fire, are virtually nil. We're conducting a full inspection of the site and a thorough investigation into the possible causes of the crash, but in all likelihood, sir, our fugitive has perished in that crash."

Christensen's fate, however, was by now of lesser concern to Horn, who had his sights intently set on North Africa. Their plane would soon take off for the American capital for a brief layover there, before their overseas departure the next morning. Turning to Dariah, Horn nonchalantly commented in response to the reports on Christensen, "Tragic, isn't it, Marshall. He had so much potential."

"Do you think Christensen's dead?" Dariah asked.

"I'd say he's finished," Horn replied. "Most likely dead, but even if he somehow manages to live, it's all over for him. Besides, how many lives can one man have?"

Secretly, Dariah hurt inside for Christensen, as she struggled to make sense of it all. But she just was not going to let Horn see her struggle, knowing that doing so would simply cause her already precarious situation with him to deteriorate further. In a matter of just a few days, her high status within Allianz and her future career prospects had most likely been irreversibly compromised, at least as far as Horn was concerned. Yet, she still sought answers for herself. There were things, many things, she did not understand, and her bright intellect would not rest or be satisfied until she had at least gained some perspicacity on what was really going on.

Tactfully, she calmly inquired of Horn, "Adammus, I haven't asked you this yet, but..."

"Adammus? I haven't heard you refer to me in this manner in a long time. I must say I like hearing you say my name. But, please, do go on, darling."

"Um, yes... What I'd like to understand is...what are you really seeking?" she asked, "I mean, what do you really desire for your future in the Federation?"

"Well, isn't it quite obvious, Misha, darling? I seek the highest heights, the very throne of Allianz, for I was born to rule from it."

"But the Allianz Council of Regents has already granted you all the power you could ever want," Dariah said. "Isn't that enough?" In a rare moment of unbridled candor, Horn then gave Dariah a glimpse into his ultimate vision for himself in Allianz.

"When I have achieved total and absolute domination, not only politically but also over the very souls of my subjects, then I will be venerated as I wish to be. And they will build a temple on the earth in my honor, where they will come worship the virtual image of their exalted king, dwelling on his high and lofty throne – CyberSat, itself. In essence, I and Cybersat will become one. And I will be their ultimate lawgiver. On bended knees they will bow down, and with their mouths they will kiss my image. *That* is the glory I truly seek. Nothing short of it will suffice. And I will not allow anything or anyone to spoil my plans or get in my way."

"CyberSat? You plan to dwell in space?" Dariah asked, absolutely dumbfounded.

"I did say the highest heights...didn't I, darling? For, where else should a supreme, idol master rightfully dwell and rule from?"

"Idolatry? You want to be idolized, Horn? Where are we? 1939, again?" challenged Dariah. "This is GDM-13, Horn. Do you actually believe you can coerce, or even expect that from the world again? Hasn't humanity plighted through enough self-absorbed and self-glorifying despots? I mean, do you really think you have the right to demand this type of subjection, which is tantamount to cultic adoration?"

"Don't I, my dear? Who, now tell me, has brought this world back to order from the very edge of the abyss of democratic false consciousness? Who, I ask you, has delivered lasting peace and has unified the world's peoples under a single Allianz banner, causing all wars to cease? Who, if not I? And who has hunted down unprincipled politicians and brought them swiftly to justice, after decades of shameless political scandals and state turmoil? Who has all but eradicated poverty and famine across the entire globe, and has practically ended crime? *I* did."

Dariah sat still, just staring at Horn.

"And further still," he continued, "because of the Virus and GDM, it was I who engineered the most significant revamping of the now thriving economic and labor markets on behalf of the clamoring masses everywhere. From my hands, darling, the world has received all these things. Now all I ask is for the world's all in return," Horn elucidated. "No, darling. No idol can fashion itself. If I am idolized, it is because I have offered something concrete to the world, something beyond empty promises and bankrupt ideologies, something that they can truly hold on to. And if the world now feels indebted to me and wishes to worship me, it is because a simple and timeless principle is at work: people seek out a hero, an idol to look up to. And, yes, I glory in it... But as for you, I feel sorry for you, Misha. For your vision has been blurred by misplaced sentiment and mixed emotions that have only jeopardized your place in Allianz. And for what?" Horn asked.

"I know that to you, Horn, it's all very black and white. But in my world I deal in complexities every day. That is why I just couldn't bring myself to go ahead with the attack in Tennessee. I wouldn't be able to live with myself if I simply disregarded the fact that someone I knew would be intentionally targeted without being given a chance. But, you? I thought I knew you. Yet, you have shown yourself to be ruthless, and I've lost the ability to simply follow you blindly, like I once did," Dariah replied. "I don't think I can help that, any more than you can quench that desire of yours for absolute power. More and more, I see we've become different, you and I...like intimate strangers.

"You're right, Misha. And what's most tragically ironic in all of this, is that today I see very little difference between you and that pathetic, deluded, idiot savant, Christensen. You are both hopelessly vain, stubbornly contemptuous, flawed, and deeply misguided. But at least *he* claims to live in service to his master. You, on the other hand...who do *you* serve, Marshall?"

"Not too long ago I thought I knew the answer to that. But now I find myself drifting against my own will, it seems. Plainly put, I'm unable to explain it."

"If I didn't know you better, darling, I would consider you a lost case. But all is not lost yet, Misha. There's still time," Horn told her. "You and I can still make a perfect match, and the place where we're going to, will force you to either come to your senses once and for all and reassume your rightful place in our Federation, with no reservations, or be lost forever in the maze of your own foolish vanity. The door is swinging shut, and very fast. I hope you choose wisely."

Hearing that, Dariah just sat there, silent. Soon their plane would be off, back to Washington, D.C., from where they would depart on a very early intercontinental flight to North Africa. Their African tour would commence in the Tunisian Province's capital district, Tunis, site of the famed, ancient Roman city of Carthage; their entryway into Allianz's Great Catacombs project. Looking out the jet's window, she watched the runway gradually drop down and away, and the scenery fade to white, beneath the dense, afternoon cloud cover.

Forty-Seven

Christensen Feared Dead

At the Christensen's home, a call came in on Claire's PSS, which abruptly awakened her.

"Hello, Tanner? Is that you, honey?"

But, actually, it was John, calling to alert the Christensen's to some disturbing breaking news footage he had just caught on ABN News.

"Claire, I know this will be difficult, but I really need you to try and remain calm," John told her in the most shepherding tone of voice he could muster.

"What? What is it? Did something happen to Tanner?"

"We're not sure. But by the images Shen-il and I are seeing, there appears to have been some kind of trouble with the police down at the airport. Tanner's picture was just flashed on the screen, and now they are transmitting images of some sort of airplane crash, somewhere between the airport and here…"

"Oh, my gosh, no!" Claire exclaimed.

"Claire, think carefully. Did Tanner tell you anything about an airplane that he might be in today?" John asked.

"No, absolutely not, John… But, then again, we should have heard from him by now," she despaired. "My heavens, what's happened to him?" she said, now bursting into tears.

After a few brief moments, John suggested, "Claire, you might want to look at the news, yourself. Maybe you can see something we can't."

"I just don't think I can bring myself to do it, John. I'm a nervous wreck," she replied.

"That's okay. Don't worry, Claire. I'll keep you posted, and I won't give up until I get some confirmation about Tanner; hopefully good news. Meanwhile, pray. I believe there's still hope," John said, trying to comfort her.

"John, I don't even know if I can concentrate enough to pray, right now. I don't know what I'll do if he's dead. I can't bear the thought of losing him! Not now, not like this," she said, sobbing. Empathizing, John offered to pray for Claire, and they joined together in prayer over the PSS.

Upon concluding that prayer, John told her, "Claire, I think Shenil and I need to come and be with you all. We'll be there tonight, or sooner if we can. Just hang on, my sister, and may The Name be with all of us."

"Thank you, John. We'll be here...waiting."

"In the meantime, Claire, remember... Trust in the Lord with all your heart and lean not on your own understanding. In all your ways acknowledge Him, and He will make your paths straight."

"Yeah," she said, recognizing the words from the third chapter of the book of Proverbs. "These words have been our mainstay for years, haven't they?"

"No doubt about it. And His promise still holds true now. He's faithful to keep it and to be glorified through it," John affirmed.

"I know," Claire whispered in reply. "Bye, John."

"Bye, now."

And they terminated their PSS connection.

Meanwhile, still some ten miles away from his home, the power in Christensen's rocket boosters began to diminish noticeably. He had to anticipate his descent, or he might risk a crash landing. Thus, he began preparing to land. Touching down, he rid himself of the rocket trappings, seat and all, and hid them along with the helmet he had been wearing among some brush covering a field adjacent to a neighborhood on the periphery of Midville.

Now on foot, he tried to think of a way he could proceed in his trek home more expediently than simply walking or running. He considered hitching a ride, but chances were he would be recognized and perhaps reported to the cog authorities, and that was a risk he just could not afford to take. Examining his immediate surroundings, he noticed a refuse dumpster sitting in an alley behind a residential complex about a block and a half away. Its items were about to be picked up by the automatic trash collection and scanning service. A more careful glance revealed an apparently discarded, rusty old bicycle leaning against the dumpster. *That's it. That's my transport home*, he thought to himself, beginning to feel somewhat relieved. Darting toward it, he arrived there just as the robotically driven waste management truck was about to scoop up the refuse. Acting quickly, however, Christensen succeeded in retrieving the bike, even as the mammoth and powerful mechanical arm, attached to the top of the truck, was reaching out toward the disposed two-wheeler.

Inspecting the junky-looking bicycle, Christensen noticed that its tires were completely flat and coming off the rims.

"Ahh, rats!" he reacted, "It will just have to do."

So, he pulled the dry and brittle tires off their rims and stood the bike up on its wobbly footrest. Then, taking off his top shirt, he ripped it, placing half of it on the torn bike seat, and with the other half he made a face covering for himself, to partially hide his face.

Christensen was hungry, thirsty, and worn out. But he had to continue on. After resting a short while, he was off on what he hoped was to be the final leg of his long, tortured journey home.

"Lord," he prayed, "grant me safe passage home, I beseech You, in Your holy name."

Forty-Eight

Alyssa Arrives

It was now 5 p.m. on that fateful Wednesday, and the Christensens awaited Alyssa's arrival. She was to come over late that afternoon, since her mother needed to leave town on her important business trip. The slumber party plans the girls had made had been spoiled by the worrisome mood of the day. But, somehow, having Alyssa there was something the Christensens wanted very much.

"Hi, guys," Alyssa said, as she entered their home. "Any news from your dad yet, Beth?" she asked, having already heard from Bethany about their onerous worries over Christensen, even though she and her mother had been out and had not tuned into the news at all.

"Nothing," replied Bethany, "but thanks for asking. I'm so glad you're here, Alyssa."

"I hope I can be of some help and not just get in the way," Alyssa expressed to her friend.

"You're fine," replied Bethany.

"Hello, dear," Claire greeted their guest, as she approached the young lady for a hug. "You know you're more than welcome at our home. And thank you for your concern."

"I see you brought your CogniToy with you," Holly chimed in, coming down the stairs into the living room. "Anything in there for a little cheering up?" the little one asked.

"Well, sure. Let me see. How about a round of miniature golf up in the playroom?" Alyssa suggested.

The Dreamers of Allianz

"Sparks!" cheered Holly.

"Zeke, want to come along?" Alyssa asked.

"I'm sorry, I can't," replied Zeke, standing nearby. "I'm not supposed to hang out with you guys. I'm seriously grounded... remember? And, anyway, I should probably stay down here with Mom...you know."

"Sure. That's fine. I'll see you, then," Alyssa replied, betraying slight disappointment.

"C'mon girls!" Holly called out.

Then, Alyssa remembered to tell them something and said, "By the way, Mrs. Christensen, I just saw some cog vehicles parked down the block as I walked over. I thought I should let you know that."

"Mom, do you think they're watching us?" asked Bethany, feeling scared.

"I don't know, dear. Anything's possible." Turning to Zeke, Claire then said, "Son, keep an eye out the window for us, would you please?"

"I will, Mom. Don't worry."

Zeke then moved toward the bay window facing the street, while the girls went upstairs. Claire walked into the kitchen to try, in her distress, to come up with something for her family to have for dinner.

With the cloud cover thickening and a light rain beginning to fall over Midville, daylight began to fade precipitously. Christensen continued riding his utterly inadequate and not exactly quiet, rickety transport. As he rode feverishly toward his home, still several miles away, he struggled to maintain good balance. Without good brakes and with much slipping and sliding he pressed on. He lacked adequate traction as the metal rims of the tireless bike spun against the now wet surface of the back ways and alleyways, which he opted to ride down, for security purposes. He hoped that keeping off the main roads would better ensure his inconspicuousness to strangers and cogs.

Forty-Nine

Zeke and Alyssa Captured

As dusk began to fall on the rainy southern town, something frightful was about to happen that would significantly alter the direction of things for the Christensen family. Due to a telling preliminary find at the Hummingbird's crash site, namely the identification of the charred remains of Christensen's work jacket, the cog stake out operation targeting the Christensen's home was indefinitely called off. In response, the cog vehicles positioned along the street began their move out, heading slowly down Juniper Drive, and filing loudly past the front of the Christensen home. The police fanfare caught Zeke's eye as he sat alone in his living room, intermittently monitoring what was going on outside the living-room window.

Springing to his feet, Zeke ran to the front-facing bay window. As he saw the cog transports departing, a profound sense of relief came over him until he found himself reliving the recent, dark experience of the previous Sunday evening. He wondered if tense encounters with the police had become the new norm for his family's life. It was a reality he did not wish to wake up to, especially now, with the uncertainty surrounding the fate of his father. Yet, lacking any other alternative, Zeke knew he had to resign to the fact that, in significant ways, his age of innocence, as it were, had come to an abrupt and seemingly irrevocable end.

All of a sudden, even as his face was still pressed against the window glass trying to track the exiting cog convoy now rounding the corner of their block, Zeke heard a distinct but muffled, low-frequency noise, unlike anything he had ever heard before. The increasing vibration that resulted from the alien sound indicated that whatever it was, it was definitely drawing closer.

Startled, Zeke yelled out, "Mom, come here! Please, hurry!"

Claire then came out of the kitchen, also concerned with the unfamiliar noise and the clatter it was causing inside the house.

"Zeke, what is that, son?" she nervously asked.

"I don't know. I just saw the cog vehicles leaving our street. This must be coming from somewhere or something else," he speculated.

Suddenly, while Zeke was still looking away from the window and toward Claire, he saw his mother's countenance turn ghost-like, with evident fear and awe.

"Mom?" he exclaimed.

Then, turning back toward the window, Zeke, too, reacted in dread, yelling out, "What in the world *is* that?"

Right before their disbelieving eyes, a dark, unidentified object, resembling some sort of spaceship, lowered itself down onto the street and right in front of their house. Soft, bluish lights shone from underneath it and, seeing something move on the side of the minibus-sized flying object, it appeared to Zeke as if a door or hatch of some type was about to be opened.

"Mom!" Zeke shouted, "Something's not right about this. Quick, get yourself and the girls down into the bunker…now! They're coming for us!"

"*Who's* coming for us, son?" asked Claire, worried.

"Cogs! They're still out there!"

Without delay, Claire sprinted upstairs and got the girls. Instantly, they all ran down to the basement.

"What's going on, Mrs. Christensen?" Alyssa asked, as they moved in haste.

"We're not sure, dear. But we're taking precautions, just in case. Please, hurry!"

Arriving at the far wall of the basement, Zeke located and pulled a secret lever, hidden in the floor, under the vase of a fake, ornamental plant. At once, the masked door to the bunker slid open, and Claire and the girls ran inside.

"Zeke, Alyssa, what are you waiting for? Get down in here!" yelled Claire.

"No, Mom," Zeke replied. "I have to stay back and protect you. I promised Dad I would."

Zeke quickly told his mom how to access the secret hatch in the bunker floor, just as his father had shown him that very morning, in the event that the situation called for an urgent escape from the house.

"Remember, Mom…*S-D-G* and *1-7-5*, for *Soli Deo Gloria* and *The Name's perfect grace!*"

"Got it, son."

"Alyssa, go. Get in there with them!" Zeke urged her.

"No way! I'm staying out here with you! And you can't make me change my mind!" she exclaimed.

Just then, they heard the sound of their front door being forced open, followed by the noise of the home security alarm, which briefly went off before going completely silent.

"Mom, I'm closing the bunker door…now! Stand back!" Zeke warned.

"But…what about Alyssa?" Claire cried out.

"No time, Mom…I love you all!"

Trying to avoid making any loud noise, Zeke gently closed the door to the bunker. Then, turning their attention to the creaking sound coming from upstairs, Zeke and Alyssa paused.

"Zeke, what *are we* going to do?" Alyssa asked, barely making any sound at all.

"*We*…are going to resist," Zeke answered, determined.

He immediately reached up above him on a wall shelf, where his father's live-blade, *samurai* sword lay on a stand. Grabbing a firm hold of it, he said, "Here, Alyssa. Use this."

"No, Zeke! I wouldn't know how! You take it. I've got another idea."

Then, handling her CogniToy, which was strapped across her left shoulder, Alyssa activated the realistic bow and arrow program. "Maybe I can fool them with this," she said.

"I hope it works, Alyssa… Now get ready. I hear them getting closer. Shhh," he signaled for them to be still.

"Wait, Zeke," she uttered.

Then, in a completely unexpected move, Alyssa stepped right up to Zeke and kissed him on the right cheek, saying, "That's for victory."

Surprised but thrilled, he answered, "Yes, *our* victory."

Just then, the door to the basement was opened, and from it emanated a burst of bright, white light, shining directly at them. Behind the blinding glare, the disoriented teens could see very little but what appeared to be three men in white garb.

"Don't move!" they heard one of them shouting, as footsteps rushed in toward the young pair.

"No!" Zeke yelled.

Fifty

Safe at Last?

Only minutes had passed since the start of the strange happenings at the Christensen home, and their beloved husband-father was now just a little over a mile from reaching his family. With a final jolt of adrenaline, he threw off his face cover and jumped off the old bicycle, which had given all it had to give. At long last, Christensen found himself on the familiar outskirts of his neighborhood of the last ten years. Feeling a bit encouraged, he left the old bike behind and took off running down the alleyway, toward Juniper Drive, now just a dozen or so blocks away.

Daylight had fled and dark was the night, as was the nagging, inescapable feeling in his heart. "Please, be okay," Christensen said to himself, as he thought of his dear family.

As he watched the surrounding, shadowy structures and scenery move past him while he ran, they only conspired to increase his somber sense of urgency. Looking for somewhat better outdoor lighting, he turned off the dark alley and into a parallel street. In minutes, Christensen would reach Juniper Drive on the very block where his house sat.

Suddenly, in the not-too-far off distance, Christensen spotted a slow-moving line of large vehicles headed up the street and directly toward him. The convoy was coming from the direction of his street, still blocks away. Though he did not know it yet, these were the cog transports which just minutes ago had been called off surveillance on his own home. As the distance between them quickly began to close, Christensen realized that these were actually police vehicles.

"Cogs?" he said in alarm.

Before he got too close to them, where the cogs might be able to clearly identify him with their bright headlights, Christensen turned quickly away from the street, cutting across a yard and toward another back alley. Dogs barked profusely at him.

"Hi, boys. Excuse me. Glad you're in your pens," he uttered softly, as he traversed all the way through the unknown backyard.

Then, stopping for a moment, he stared out of the darkness of the alleyway through the space between two homes and waited until he was certain that the cog transports had passed him by. As floodlights suddenly came on in his direction from behind one of the houses, Christensen ducked.

While the loud police vehicles were driving by on the street, only yards away from Christensen, another strange sound and dimly luminous sight caught his attention. Looking up toward the sky, he saw a low flying transport of sorts making a sharp turn almost directly above his head. *They're all around here*, he deduced, looking up at the strange flying transport. Refusing to dwell on the meaning of the cog presence in his neighborhood, he pressed on.

"I've got to get home," he said to himself, immediately re-taking his hurried course toward home.

A short while later, as he turned down his own street's back alley, his house finally came into view. The feeling was indescribable, and Christensen felt his whole body begin to quiver with layers of emotion. All at once, relief, consternation, fear, anger, and gratitude overwhelmed him. Panting and almost collapsing from overexertion, he entered his backyard and staggered directly toward the back door of his home.

From the outside looking in, nothing appeared out of the ordinary, except for the strange absence of any movement inside the house. Figuring that the voice-recognition home security alarm was on activated mode, Christensen announced himself audibly, "Tanner Christensen... Self-entry authorized," but there was no response, and the rear door remained closed. Testing it, however, he realized that the locking mechanism had been disengaged, and he was able to manually open the door.

"Gang, where are you? It's me...Dad," he called out softly, as he entered.

The sweetly familiar smell of his own home briefly transported him back to better times. A timeless flood of memories from his life with his wife and young children flashed before his eyes. In that split second he realized how much he had taken it for granted. Quickly coming back to himself, Christensen, now completely puzzled, stood in place inside the dining room of his home. Without the voices he knew so well, his house appeared empty, abandoned. Why was his family missing? Could Claire and the kids have gone to someone else's house? Perhaps the Waters' place? He could only guess.

Walking around to the living room, Christensen was stunned to discover that the front door had been left wide open. Suddenly, in a fearful realization, he put it all together. *The cog vehicles...the flying transport*, he remembered. *Am I too late to save my family?* he self-queried, afraid of contemplating the answer.

"Oh Lord, be not far from us," he frantically petitioned. Then, Christensen entertained a hopeful thought, *The bunker!*

Running down to the basement, he found undeniable evidence of foul play. His sword, lying on the Aikido mats and removed from its sheath, and other items out of place, clearly indicated to him that some unwanted presence had recently visited his home. He then recognized Alyssa's CogniToy, also dropped on the floor, and remembered that she was supposed to have spent the night with his family. *Oh Lord...what's happened here?* he thought, struggling to make sense of the chaotic scene in his home, and fearing the worst.

Walking toward the far wall of the basement, he geared himself up to find out if anyone was hiding in the bunker. *Please, be in there...safe*, he hoped.

In the darkness of the bunker, on the other side of the wall, Holly heard someone approaching the door to their hiding place.

"Mom," she whispered in alarm, "I think more of them are out there."

The Dreamers of Allianz

"Shhh. Don't say anything. They just might leave," Claire replied, as the three of them huddled together, trying their best to keep total silence, in hopes of not being found out.

"Mom, I'm afraid," whispered Beth, ever so lightly.

"Quick...into the hatch. Move slowly," Claire silently said, moving only her lips and gesturing for them to enter the already open escape way in the bunker floor.

Realizing she was out of time to enter the hatch herself, as the bunker door began to slide open, Claire quickly turned and grabbed a metal chair which sat nearby and prepared to use it as her defense weapon, while her girls watched fearfully from inside their hideout.

As the silhouette of a man appeared at the door, with the basement light shining in from behind him and flooding into the bunker, Holly let out a terrifying screech, "Ahhhh!" From the bunker floor below, Claire heroically flung the chair upward, against her perceived enemy, hitting Christensen right smack on his forehead as he came down the staircase, causing him to fall flat on his back. She then pounced on the intruder, attacking him fiercely using her natural weapons, the might of her teeth and nails.

"Ouch! Ahhh!" yelled Christensen, as he felt his assailant going for his flesh. Immediately, he cried out, "Stop...Claire! Kids...it's me, Dad!"

"Dad?" Beth shouted, in disbelief.

"Honey?" Claire yelled out, right away unclenching her nails from her husband's face and arms, and getting up off of him.

"Oh, Lord. Thank you," Christensen said, struggling to get up. "You're all okay..."

Feeling beaten to a pulp, he strained to reach for the light switch. When the room brightened, Christensen staggered down the steps, toward the girls.

"Daddy!" his daughters screamed in exhilaration.

"Tanner...oh, honey, are you okay?" said his wife, still in total shock at the mere thought of actually having mistakenly attacked her own husband. "I thought you were one of the... Oh, I'm so sorry, sweetie!"

"Claire, it's fine...it's okay. I'll be all right. It's just a few bruises, cuts, and scrapes," Christensen feebly reassured her, while assessing his miserable condition.

Claire then embraced her injured husband, as if years had kept them apart.

"Ahh! Not so tight, dear," he begged, "I'm barely holding together in one piece..."

"Tanner, I can't believe it. Is it really you?" Claire said in great relief. "I was so afraid you had..."

"Shhh...I know. Me, too," Christensen replied soberly, considering how close he had come to being captured, or even worse.

"Daddy, Daddy! I'm so glad you're okay!" Holly exclaimed. She then quickly remarked, "but, *man*! Are you stinky!"

"Thanks, Holly. That so...honest of you."

At that point, Bethany grabbed her father's arm and asked fearfully, "Dad, have you seen Zeke and Alyssa, out there?"

"What do you mean? No, I haven't," he answered.

"They didn't come in here with us, Dad" she told him. "They wanted to protect us...." Bethany said, now starting to cry.

"Tanner," Claire went on, "cogs came into the house. We didn't see them, but we heard them break in. We all ran down here as fast as we could, but Zeke and Alyssa...they stayed behind... Oh, Tanner, they were probably taken away."

In saying that, Claire broke down, agonizing about the fate of her son and Alyssa.

"I saw them, Claire. I saw the cogs. Their transports drove past me on my way here. I hid from them. I never imagined that they had any of you with them... What could I have done?" Christensen said to his inconsolable wife.

"Oh my son, my son..." Claire wailed, as Christensen's heart just sank, like a heavy anchor, dropping down unfettered on the seafloor. Devastated, all Christensen could do was hold his wife and daughters.

Just then, they heard voices coming from the main floor, upstairs.

"Claire? Girls? Are you down there?" a familiar voice uttered.

It was John "the Baptist" Waters and Shen-il, coming to be with them, as John had mentioned to Claire, earlier. Hearing his pastor's voice, Christensen answered, "John, we're down here!" Their friends then made their way down to the basement bunker.

"Tanner? Is that you?" John yelled out, quickly making his way down to the basement and toward the bunker door. "My brother, you're alive!" he marveled, as he saw his friend and then hugged him tightly, delivering another painful reminder to Christensen of state of his broken body, and heart.

"Ugh..."

"Praise The Name, Tanner!" John said. "But, look at you... You look just *awful!*"

"Don't ask, John. I couldn't begin to tell you..." replied Christensen, too weak and unable to recount the wild and unbelievable things he had been through that day.

"Claire...girls... I'm so glad to see you," Shen-il greeted them, as she filed in behind John.

Noticing that Zeke was evidently absent, Shen-il asked, "Where's Zeke?" Christensen then explained to the Waters what had likely happened to their son and to Alyssa.

Claire also added, "At first we heard the alarm go off. Then it stopped. After that, I heard almost nothing out there, except someone...Zeke, I think, yelling, 'No!' Then, I heard the thump of things dropping on the floor, but there was no noise indicating any real struggle after that... After a while, I heard a male voice ask, 'Are there others?'"

"In English?" Shen-il asked Claire.

"Right."

"Huh... That's really odd," Christensen remarked, sharing in Shen-il's puzzlement and confusion. "Why would the cogs be speaking English with each other"

"I don't know, Tan," answered Claire. "But, then, I heard nothing...nothing at all. Just total, eerie silence for what seemed like forever... The next thing we heard was you, Tanner, when you were coming down here."

"Oh, friends... What can we do?" asked John.

At that moment, in that old bunker, after all Christensen had lived through that day, he finally came to the end of his rope, and said, lowering his head, "I know what I need to do…"

"What? What do you mean, Tan?" fearfully asked Claire.

"I'm turning myself in…in exchange for getting Zeke and Alyssa back. This is entirely *my* fault. I shouldn't have laid such a heavy burden on Zeke's shoulders."

Christensen then went on to recount his dreadful experience that day, from the time he arrived at the airport that morning, to his ultimate air escape and journey home.

"Oh, honey…" Claire lamented.

What an impossible predicament for them. After enduring so much sacrifice and finally seeing Christensen's miraculous arrival home, how could this be happening? Yet, there was no question now in Christensen and Claire's mind. The trade off had to be made, before it was too late for their son and young Alyssa.

"John… Please, brother, hand me your PSS."

Needing to make doubly certain, John asked, "Tan, are you sure this is the right thing to do? I mean…isn't there any other way?"

Christensen offered no reply. He simply extended his open hand to receive John's PSS. Taking it, Christensen paused and took a deep breath, as if to build up the much-needed courage to do what was impossibly difficult, but absolutely necessary. John just could not bear to witness what was about to ensue, and he turned away, as the words from Holy Scripture echoed unrelentingly in his mind: *"Greater love has no one than this, that he lay down his life for his friends,"* or in that moment, for a beloved son and brand new sister in The Name.

With tears welling up in his eyes, John walked across the bunker floor, and reaching Christensen's control center, pulled a solitary chair out from under the small desk. John then sat down, directing his unfocused stare at the system screen, as if trying to escape the dire reality unfolding right behind him. On that time-weathered desk, sat Christensen's fragmented, old digital paraphernalia, still faithfully intercepting secret communiqués from Resistance outposts located throughout the global battlefield. Hearing the intensified weeping in the background, John knew his friend was undertaking the greatest, most costly act of love.

As Christensen pronounced himself with a frail "Hello?" John suddenly yelled out, "Stop! Don't do it!" This prompted his startled friend to terminate the barely established visualization.

"John, what in the world was that?" Christensen exclaimed, utterly frustrated.

"Look! It's a brand new message on your screen," John indicated, reading the blinking text on Christensen's messaging equipment.

"From who?" Claire inquired.

"It's from Dr. C! The title reads, *'Zeke and Alyssa Safe.'* I'm dead serious, Tan."

"What? Are you sure?" Christensen asked, quickly coming to check on it himself.   Indeed, just in a nick of time and by the sovereign grace of The Name, I had managed to send them the urgent message.

"How can this be?" Claire wondered out loud. "How can he know that for sure?"

Christensen read the content of the message out loud. They learned that I was briefly stationed on an island in northern Brazil, holding meetings with a persecuted group of Believers there, called *Itapoã*, which meant *Stony Point*, in the indigenous Amazonian *Tupi-Guarani* language. During one of those meetings, earlier that very day, I received a prophetic message from a young brother in The Name, who was part of that group. The message, from a vision and a dream, stated that Allianz did not have Tennessee's young man and woman. Zeke and Alyssa were well and being safely transported to a remote Resistance facility, called "The Red Monastery," located in the Province of Slovakia, near the border with the Polish Province, on the central part of the European continent.

"This is unbelievable," Christensen said, rejoicing.

"But, Tanner, how can we confirm that? How can we know for sure?" Shen-il inquired, always skeptical in good measure.

"We'll know soon," Christensen replied. He then pointed to the text and said "According to what it says here, he's already en route to America, and in one day…that's tomorrow…Dr. C will meet us at a predetermined location, near his secluded mountain hideaway, outside of Gatlinburg, in East Tennessee. Once we get there, he'll explain everything."

"We haven't seen him in years," Claire said. "This must mean something really big."

"What if it's a trap?" Shen-il considered.

"That's unlikely. But what other option do we have?" Christensen asked rhetorically.

"How are we getting there, Tanner?" Claire asked. "We don't have enough fuel to make it all the way across the state, and surely by now our van is marked by the police."

"Take *our* car," John offered, without hesitation. "It's a compact transport, and there's still more than enough fuel in it to get you all the way there. We'll ride home on the WormRail and keep an eye on things while you're gone." Then John commented, "You know, the Lord never ceases to amaze us. We've been taking the WormRail everywhere lately, because there just aren't that many fuel stations anymore that will sell to non-implants, and we've been trying to conserve our car's H-Pak. But today, for some reason, we really felt we needed to drive our car here. Now we know why..."

"Oh, John, Shen-il...how can we thank you two?" Claire said.

Shen-il then walked over and hugged Claire, saying, "You don't have to my sister. And here, Claire. Take these... We brought these munchies for you all. Take them with you on the road, and may The Name watch over you."

"Thank you."

"I just can't imagine what could have happened, if I had..." said Christensen, contemplating the worst – turning himself in.

"Don't, Tanner," John interrupted him. "Let's just put it behind us. And let's thank The Name."

"You're right. And let's not forget Dr. C. The old man's timing couldn't have been more precise."

Sharing profound relief, the group joined hands, right there in the bunker, and offered up to the Lord an ardent prayer of thanksgiving and a request for continued deliverance, especially on their journey east. John then told them, "Go in peace. I'll take care of everyone here."

Time was of the essence, and although Christensen felt like he had been put through the meat grinder several times over, the situation at hand left no time for sleeping and recharging. The family would have to leave immediately after Christensen had a chance to get cleaned up a bit. Perhaps, they all agreed, the overnight drive across the state would afford the weary Christensens some time to recover before their momentous next step.

Fifty-One

Leaving Home

It was already 8:00 p.m. when the Christensens finally left their home and headed eastward across the state. Although Claire had not voiced it at all, she somehow knew in her heart that their departure meant a one-way pilgrimage, tantamount to bidding a permanent farewell to their dwelling place of an entire decade. As she drove, her husband, well disguised under a hat and a fake mustache, had a sorely needed time of rest. Claire, who herself was sporting a long, brunette wig and a cap, thought about the life she was most likely leaving behind. A part of her struggled to let go of the sweet moments, such as when they first brought baby Holly home from the hospital. But then she recalled, still with some anguish, the horrid experience at the hospital, when the downright pushy medical personnel incessantly attempted to persuade her to implant her newborn. Just thinking about it sent nightmarish shivers down her spine.

Her mind then wandered to the time when, on a particular Mother's Day, Zeke and Bethany, at twelve and ten respectively, ventured to prepare their first surprise supper meal for their family. Claire remembered how, after the polite first few brave bites, the family unanimously agreed that they would be better off concluding their meal at the nearest McDonalds, after which they returned home and dynamically team-cleaned the kitchen for their mother, for the next three hours. Then, there were also the joys and sorrows of homeschooling, which for Claire commonly boiled down to a daily exercise in stubborn determination to inculcate into her children the meaning of excellence. She recalled how this process was often seasoned with her own character growth pains, while she slowly developed hair-pulling patience. Not to mention the almost daily pleas for an extra measure of grace from the Lord, just to make it through the insanely unrealistic homeschool curriculum demands, which now seemed so unfitting, so untimely. But Claire now amused herself, remembering the exact, triumphant moments when, at the same "magical" spot on the dining room table, each of her homeschoolers first learned how to read, write cursive, memorize math tables, and recite all of their Scripture memory verses. Time was kind to her recollections and, in hindsight, Claire acknowledged that the sweetness of those moments won out over the toils, trials and self-doubts she daily battled against, as a homeschooling mother.

But there were also memories she would just as soon forget. Over the course of the previous decade, she helplessly watched her husband be changed inside and out, as he spent time in that musty, old basement bunker. Only sporadic vestiges remained of the endearing, hopeful, and light-hearted man she had married. The Resistance work persistently absorbed the light out of him. Though she understood and accepted the crucial, even noble reasons why things must be so, that bunker had cruelly swallowed up the husband she once knew, only to spew him out again and again, allowing him to emerge broken, in the blackness of the late nights. He was more tech savvy, to be sure, yet also greyer, and more troubled and emotionally drained. As time went on her husband was almost unrecognizable as the companion she so yearned for and needed. But Claire forced herself to learn to pray alone, often asking the Lord to mend herself whole again for the next day, without Christensen.

No, these memories she would prefer to leave behind, perhaps locked inside the hermetic enclosure of the very bunker that spawned them. She could gladly give up that lovely home with its mixed bag of memories, if she could see her man be reborn, revived; older yes, but also enchanting to her again. Still, her heart, though hardened and calloused a bit around the edges, overflowed with thankfulness to The Name. She had learned over the years to intentionally count all of her blessings. Driving alone with her thoughts, as her family dozed off to the gentle humming of the highway lullaby, Claire Christensen, perhaps for the first time in years, felt the crackling sensation of icicles thawing around her heart. In some way she did not fully grasp, this road trip east symbolized for her a new beginning, or perhaps a new ending.

The stream of private thoughts and prayers at the wheel must have afforded Claire the therapy and serenity she needed to single-handedly take on all of the driving duty for that trip. It was almost 2:30 a.m., and to her amazement Claire had managed to follow the directions and carry her slumbering passengers almost all the way to their mountain destination. Realizing that they were nearing their Appalachian rendezvous location without suffering a single setback or dreaded run-in with the police, Claire breathed a sigh of relief.

Sensing the car slowing and swaying as it followed narrower, winding roads up the Smoky Mountain range, Christensen and the girls began to arise from their deep, invigorating sleep.

"Hi, honey. Where are we?" Christensen asked Claire, still feeling groggy from several hours of total mental respite from the cares of the world.

"Hey, Tan. I'd wish you a 'good morning,' but it's not even 3 a.m., yet... But I think we're almost there."

"Really? I must have completely passed out for hours."

"Six and a half hours, to be exact. How are you feeling?" she asked.

"Terribly sore all over," he groaned.

"That's not at all surprising, considering..."

Then, feeling curious, she asked, "Had any dreams?" Christensen gave it some thought, and then he answered, "You know, I can't remember a single dream I've had all night."

"Dreamless sleep, huh?" Claire commented. "That's sure a welcome change."

Straining to turn himself around in the tightness of the Waters' compact vehicle, Christensen peered into the backseat, where his daughters lay half-buried under a pile of favorite pillows, teddy-bears, and bunched up sleeping bags. Holly lay stretched out, her partly uncovered legs conveniently and comfortably resting on top

The Dreamers of Allianz

of her big sister's lap. Seeing Bethany's eyes opening, Christensen asked, "Hey, Beth. You're up, huh?"

"Oh, I guess," she offered, in yawning response. "Dad, I'm so glad you're here with us," the raspy, sleepy voice uttered.

"Thank you, sweetie. It's been a wild ride for all of us, I know. I'm very glad to be with you all, too," he replied, gently touching Claire on her right shoulder, as she continued to drive.

"How much longer 'til we get there, Mom?" Bethany wanted to know.

"Well, Dad's got the directions and the map in his hands, now," Claire replied. Christensen then read the ending portion of the directions they had received in my message, earlier. As he studied the map, he announced, "Well...based on this, we should be there just minutes from now... It looks like one more right turn about a mile up the road, where we're supposed to see a sign saying, '*Private Drive – No Trespassers Allowed*.' We'll then follow a dirt road for a couple more miles, until it ends on a private lake."

"A lake? Up on the mountain?" Bethany inquired, sounding quite intrigued.

"That's what it says here. And the map seems to concur," her dad replied. "It's probably a mountain lake."

"Then what do we do, Tan?" Claire asked.

"We wait. Dr. C says he'll meet us and pick us up there. I figure we should just take him at his word."

"How, Dad? How's he picking us up?" Bethany asked.

"He left that a mystery," answered Christensen, "and probably for good reason."

"Oooo...exciting," she said.

"I *really* hope this pans out," Claire responded.

"Well," Christensen replied, "so far, so good, right?"

"Hey, Mom. I'm hungry. How about I look for some snacks in these bags back here?" their eldest daughter proposed.

Suddenly, Holly, who was half awake, roused herself, saying, "Me, too! I'm starved."

"Sure, girls. Go ahead. I didn't even think to look in there, to see what Shen-il gave us, but I'm sure it will do... And I want to hear no complaints, ladies. Is that clear?" Claire forewarned.

"All right, Mom," Bethany replied, adding, "She's so sweet, isn't she?" referring to her voice teacher and friend.

"Can I see what's in these bags?" Holly said, grabbing one of them.

"Hey, slow down, missy!" her sister told her.

"Girls..." warned their dad.

"Okay, you first," Holly relented.

"Let's see... Anyone for some mouth-watering, congealed strawberry treats?" Bethany offered, facetiously.

"Yummy, my *fave*..." Christensen said, playing right along.

A few minutes later, upon reaching the dirt road, the car began to vigorously bounce up and dip down, following the uneven terrain. Although the night was clear and with good visibility, the vehicle's headlights left much to be desired when it came to identifying craters and road bumps before it was too late.

"Weee!" Holly shouted, as she flew freely in the backseat of the car.

"Mom, can you drive a little slower?" Bethany begged. "I'm hurting back here with all this bumpiness, and my stomach's not happy about this, after that *tasty treat*."

Looking out the back window, Holly was struck by the clear starry sky. The road ahead was illumined by the car lights, but the trail behind them was pitch dark, and rather scary-looking, if it were not for the majestic starry spectacle.

"That's so amazing, y'all!" Holly cried out in wonderment. "I've never seen so many stars! They're everywhere!"

"That's right, pumpkin," Claire responded, "the heavens do declare the glory of the Lord."

Within minutes, the road began to slope downward, and as they drove a bit further, there appeared on both sides of them a shimmering body of water.

"We're here. There's the lake," Claire pointed out.

Soon, having run out of road, they came to a full stop at the end of a small peninsula.

"It's so pretty, Mom," Holly said, looking out her window on the right side of the car.

"It sure is, sweetie."

"Now that we're here, how long do we have to wait?" asked Bethany.

"Not sure," answered Christensen. "We'll just sit still and see." Then, he added, "On second thought, how about us singing some good ole hymns of the faith, to help pass the time?"

"Uhh... Maybe I'll just go back to sleep..." The teenager uttered, halfway jokingly and giving into a bit of drowsiness-induced ennui.

"Now, now," her dad lightly chastised. "Such a budding singing talent can't just snub the old treasures of church music. Start warming up that sweet voice of yours, kiddo. Besides, just look at what a gorgeous night the Lord has blessed us with."

"Oh, fine," she agreed. "But I think it's safe enough out here for y'all to take off the silly wigs and hats, and that ugly fake mustache on you, Dad."

"Hey...I was beginning to get used to it," her dad teased.

"Yuck!" exclaimed Holly.

"All right, then. Off it comes." Removing his rather unbecoming disguise, Christensen then asked, "So...what shall we sing?"

"How about 'Great Is Thy Faithfulness'...my all-time top pick?" requested Claire, as she shut off the hydrogen-powered engine and turned off the headlights.

"Whoa! Now that's going *way* back, Mom," Bethany observed.

"I think that's a nice choice, honey," Christensen remarked. "And we all should know it pretty well, right? Ready?"

"Yep," replied the hardly enthused pair in the backseat.

"*Great is thy faithfulness oh Lord, my Father...*" they joined together in song.

Fifty-Two

Dariah Recommits

At 5 a.m. sharp, Washington time, Dariah and Horn were meeting for breakfast at the White House before their momentous voyage to North Africa. Dariah was packed and ready, but remained quiet, not uttering a single word to Horn since the time she coldly greeted him good morning.

"I see you're in a pensive mood this morning, Misha," Horn said, trying to initiate a dialogue.

"Uhum…"

"…And may I say, darling, that seeing you in civilian garb brings back to my mind a rush of sweet memories," he carried on, despite her disinterest. "Your uniform can seem like such a formal barrier between the two of us."

"Don't fool yourself, Horn," she finally engaged him. "I paid no mind to you in my choice of attire. This is going to be a long flight, and I'm trying for comfort. That's all there's to it."

"I see… Fair enough, fair enough."

"Besides, need I remind you that I'm your captive on this trip? This is *not* what I was counting on doing at this point in time… Although, I must say that the historic location has rather peaked my interest," she admitted.

"Historic, indeed, darling," said Horn. "More than you could ever imagine… Let us go, now. Our fate awaits us."

"*Our* fate?" she countered him.

"Yes...my glory. And if you so choose, yours, too, Misha... Allianz still needs you. And, personally, I hope to avoid having to appoint someone else to run America. But the ball is in your court."

At that moment, something resonated strongly with Dariah. Inside of her, a process of cognitive transformation began to take hold, as if she were beginning to awaken from a strange dream, in which the order of things in her life had been temporarily altered, suspended by some force unknown to her. *What am I doing?* she questioned herself, as she re-examined the sequence of events in the four days that had preceded. *Horn's right,* she concluded in her own mind. *I've been an idiot, letting myself be influenced by this ridiculous bunch of fanatical insurgents. What have I gained by giving into such sentimentality regarding Christensen, a common man I barely even know? Nothing but trouble and scorn, that's what.*

She then vowed to herself that, from that moment on, she would invest all of her energies and resources in regaining Horn's trust. Dariah's resolve to stand with Allianz would be unshakable, or she would be the first to resign from her prominent position and title of American Province Marshall and Commander.

"Horn, I deeply regret how I've acted in the past few days," Dariah began. "I will not let you or Allianz down again. From now on, I am redoubling my efforts to do all that is in my power to crack down on this asinine Resistance movement...Christensen or no Christensen. How can I apologize for my absurd mental lapse?"

"No apologies necessary, darling. I am ecstatic. Yet, I wonder if you are truly ready and determined to carry out your responsibilities..."

"I am... Count on it, or my name is not Misha Dariah," she asserted, pounding her fist on the breakfast table.

"Fabulous. This is indeed going to be a glorious day for us, and for the Federation. Let us not delay any longer."

"Of course," said Dariah. A few short minutes later, a cog officer announced, "Commander, Prosecutor General, your limousine awaits you to take you to the air base.

"After you, darling," Horn indicated.

"Thank you...Adammus."

Fifty-Three

Rendezvous with Dr. C

Cramped inside the compactness of their borrowed vehicle, after almost an hour of impromptu praise to The Name, one by one the Christensen clan surrendered to yet another snooze session. Unable to resist being lulled to sleep by the persistent croaking and hissing of nature's own praise and worship chorus, Christensen and his crew checked out until just before sunrise, when both their sleep and the serene surroundings were abruptly disturbed.

In the hazy blueness of the early morning hours, when the sun's tentative shine was still too timid to overtake the entire sky and eclipse the brightest nocturnal celestial bodies, not far from the edge of the peninsula, a strange movement, like that of water stirring, began to form in the otherwise placid lake. Christensen and his family sat perfectly still, fast asleep in their vehicle, when suddenly the sound of bubbling and gushing water grabbed Claire's attention, since she was the lightest sleeper in the bunch.

"Huh? What's that noise?" she said, as she opened her eyes and nudged Christensen, whispering, "Tanner, wake up."

"What? What's the matter?" he replied, feeling disoriented and looking around himself for signs of something amiss.

Rubbing off the sleep from their eyes and the condensation from the foggy windows, husband and wife searched together for the source of the odd disturbance.

"Look!" Claire exclaimed and pointed, detecting the strange phenomenon manifesting in the lake waters to the right of them.

"What is that?" Christensen said, gazing perplexed at the circling and white-foaming spot on the lake, now growing larger and more turbulent, ruffling the layers of light, low-lying fog hovering above it. It appeared as if something were pushing its way up to the surface from down below the waters.

Instantly, a large, smooth-lined, triangular object resembling some sort of submersible ship, thirty to forty feet in length, bounced up onto the water's surface. Rotating itself slowly in the direction of the peninsula, the floating transport suddenly turned on its lights. The brightness pierced the monochromatic pre-dawn shades that dominated the natural scenery. With audible trepidation in his voice, Christensen uttered, "I really do hope that it's you, old man."

"Girls, wake up," Claire said, nervously reaching back to prod Holly's legs to make sure her daughters would respond.

"Mommy, let me sleep. I'm cold," Holly pleaded in vain, from beneath her covers.

"I'm not here. I've gone off to look for a coffee shop," Bethany said, also to no avail.

"I'm serious, girls," their mom scolded. "Now, get up this instant!"

"It's the Loch Ness monster!" screamed Holly, referring to the still enduring Scottish legend, as she looked out her window.

"We're in the Appalachians, silly!" replied Bethany.

"Okay, but what if it has a hillbilly cousin?" Holly speculated.

"That's the most *idiotic*..." Bethany countered, being immediately interrupted by her mother saying, "Shhhh! Be quiet, you two."

"Everybody, stay calm," urged Christensen. "It's going to be okay."

As the Christensens watched mystified, the cruising ship reached the gently sloping banks of the peninsula and somehow began to slowly roll up out of the water until it rested almost entirely on dry land. Behind the dimming blue lights, the ship's name could be seen written on its bow.

"*The Weber*," Christensen read out loud, immediately making the sociological connection and feeling a great sense of relief.

"Y'all, you can relax, now. There's no question. That's good ole Dr. C, coming for us," he said.

"Tanner, I know I've seen one of those ships before… It was last night. It looks just like the transport that landed outside our front window at home, before Zeke and Alyssa were taken," Claire remembered.

"Are you sure, Mom?" Bethany asked.

"It was dark out, and it all happened so fast. But I'm almost positive that's right."

As a top hatch was then opened on the ship's middle section, there came up through the opening a familiar, broad-shouldered figure sporting, as always, a skipper's beret worn backwards and holding an unlit pipe in one hand. A deep, loud voice broke the early morning stillness of the wilderness, calling out, "Christensens… Ahoy there, mi friends!"

"C'mon, everyone. It's time to go," Christensen announced with anticipation and excitement in his voice. He quickly opened the door on his side and got out of the car.

The thrill of seeing his old mentor in person was sufficient to make Christensen forget all about his stiff joints. He blurted out, "Sensei!" meaning "Teacher," in Japanese, just the way he used to directly call me, both on and off the Aikido mat. Christensen walked out to greet me, as Claire and the girls got out of the car and began to gather their belongings. It had been ten long and transforming years since we had seen one another.

"Tanner-san!" I saluted him gleefully. "Is that really you, son? How you've aged."

"And you haven't changed a bit, Sensei."

"Well, your compliments just aren't enough to get this old man to climb down from here. Don't mind if I reserve my affections for when you're up onboard the ship."

"No worries. It's just so *good* to see you again, after all this time," Christensen said emphatically, his breath visibly leaving his mouth, then vaporizing in the cold mountain morning air.

"It's a thrill for me too, Tanner-san," I replied. "I only wish our reunion were under more propitious circumstances."

"I hear you," agreed Christensen. He then said, "You remember Claire…"

"Of course...lovely *Chiara*," I replied.

"And the girls..."

"Yes, of course. Though I haven't actually met your little one."

"Don't worry. Holly will not be ignored," said Christensen.

Back by the car, Bethany and Holly were brightening and already engaging in sisterly banter, drawn from their extensive repertoire of annoying exchanges.

"Hey, I can see my breath," Bethany remarked.

"I can smell it," Holly teased, unable to resist the perfect set up by her unsuspecting sister.

"Come here, you little twerp. You're gonna get it..."

"Girls, behave!" Claire warned. "We've got unloading to do." She then told Bethany, with a tone of protest in her voice, "Beth, go get your dad, please. I don't care if that's his own mother in that ship. He's just not getting away with having the women do all the work here...no sir."

"All right, Mom."

Fifty-Four

At the Slovak Monastery

Thousands of miles away, somewhere inside the stone walls of a centuries-old Slovakian refuge, known as the Red Monastery, Zeke and Alyssa began to regain consciousness. They had spent hours in a long, artificially induced sleep.

As Zeke opened his eyes, rays from the mid afternoon sun were angling downward, beaming into his room through small, barred windows located near a high ceiling. *Is this some kind of prison?* he wondered, still feeling a bit dazed and unsure of what had happened to him. Sitting up on his bed, Zeke looked himself over. *Huh…no injuries. I feel fine.*

But where was Alyssa? The last thing he could remember was Alyssa standing next to him and a very bright light being shone at them both. Then everything faded to total darkness. He now felt very much alone, afraid for his family, worried about Alyssa, and with a growing list of unanswered questions.

He found himself in a rather spacious, medieval-looking chamber, with natural-colored stones of varying magnitudes lining the walls and rendering a look of antiquity to those quarters. A casual glance around the Spartan-looking room revealed a cavernous fireplace, centered on the wall opposite the small windows. The fireplace sat as the focal point in the otherwise unornamented chamber. Next to his bed, there was a large wooden armoire and a rustic-looking set of table and two chairs. Aside from these items, the room looked peculiarly empty.

Curious to figure out his whereabouts, Zeke stood up from his bed and walked over to the old, wood table, positioned against the wall beneath the high windows. He climbed up on one of the chairs and then stepped onto the tabletop, trying to get a view of the outside. Unable to get a satisfactory look, Zeke stood on the tip of his toes, despite the evident instability of the ancient table, and stretched upward in order to gain a better view. Just then, the table gave out, and Zeke came down with a loud crash.

"Ahhh!" he screamed.

As he lay on top of the collapsed table for a brief moment, he soon felt the slightly delayed punishment from the fall. "Oh man, that hurts," he voiced out loud. Fortunately for him, however, except for a stinging sensation on his right hand and a painful bump on his right ankle, he seemed to have sustained no serious injuries. His Aikido training had enabled him to instinctively react and break his fall on his side, protecting his head and vital organs, but the hard surface beneath him did not give like the Aikido mats, and he could definitely tell the difference.

At that moment, from behind the far wall from where his bed sat, Zeke heard a female voice calling out with an echo.

"Zeke? Are you there?"

Upon hearing it, Zeke immediately stood up and walked, slightly limping, across to the wall on that darker side of the large chamber.

"Alyssa? Is that you?"

"Yeah. It's me," she replied.

Then, with concern in her voice, she asked him, "What was all that noise? Are you okay over there?"

"Mostly," he answered. "Don't worry about it... How are *you* doing? I'm so glad to hear your voice."

"I feel a little sluggish...like I've been sleeping for days. But, otherwise, I'm fine," replied Alyssa. "Where are we?"

"My guess is as good as yours," Zeke replied, "but this looks like some sort of holding cell to me...or something of the sort."

As he stepped away from the wall, he saw on a dark corner what looked like a connecting door between their rooms. Zeke said, "Hey, I think I know why we can hear each other so well... There's a door to your left. I think it links our rooms together."

"Wait...I see it too," Alyssa said. She started making her way over to the metal door.

"See if you can unlock it from your end, and I'll do the same here," he suggested.

"I'll try..."

As each of them slid back a locking iron rod and flipped open a single door latch, Zeke swung the door toward him, revealing Alyssa's pleasant smile.

"Hi there!" Alyssa said, happy to see Zeke.

"Hey," he responded in matched exhilaration. Alyssa then stepped through the arched opening and into Zeke's room.

"What *is* this place, I wonder?" she rhetorically questioned. "Do you remember how we got here?"

"Um...not exactly," he said. "The last thing I remember is... Well, we were in the basement of my house and...the cogs...they came in," Zeke recalled.

"That's all *I* can remember, too." Then, with urgent thoughts of getting out of there, Alyssa asked, "Have you tried your door, yet?"

"I haven't."

"Well...wanna do the honors?" she proposed.

As both of them moved carefully toward the wide, arched wood door of Zeke's room, they listened for what or who might be behind it. Other than the hushed howling of the wind being squeezed through the narrow space between the bottom of the massive door and the ancient cobblestone floor, they could hear absolutely no activity.

"Okay, Alyssa," Zeke whispered. "Hang on. Here it goes..."

"I'm scared, Zeke," Alyssa told him.

Then, lifting the old, looped metal lever, which served as the door handle, Zeke pulled the heavy, squeaking door.

"It's not locked!" he said, surprised.

The door opened up to a dimly lit interior hallway. Walking out into it, the two teens quickly glanced both ways. There was no one in sight! To their left, they could see a series of other doors along both sides of a seemingly endless stony hallway. Several feet down to their right, the narrow gallery appeared to end at a halfway open wrought iron gate. Fresh air seemed to be blowing in their direction from the gate.

"Follow me," Zeke told Alyssa. She immediately grabbed tightly to Zeke's left arm. As they neared the gate, Alyssa squeezed Zeke's arm harder.

"Ouch," he cried, his voice reverberating throughout the span of the long, curved hallway ceiling.

"Shhh! Someone will hear us," Alyssa whispered.

"But, you're cutting off the circulation in my arm," he complained.

"Sorry…I can't help it. I'm so scared…" she whispered.

Finally arriving at the iron gateway, they proceeded to walk through it and into an airy but enclosed marble colonnade, yellowed by time. The majestic-looking walkway appeared to lead down to an outside courtyard. Continuing a bit further, they came upon the first clue as to their location. To their right, on the lengthy, straight wall of the colonnade, they read the phrase, "*Ora et Labora*," writ large. Zeke, recognizing the words form his partially classical homeschooling training, exclaimed, "That's Latin! I'm pretty sure it means, '*Pray and Work*'… This place is probably an old convent, or something."

"A convent? What's that?" Alyssa asked, unfamiliar with the antiquated, religious terminology.

"Well, in the past, a convent was an institution where religious women would live and work in complete devotion to The Name," Zeke explained. "But such places haven't been around for a long time. I wonder what this is being used for now."

Just as Zeke had finished saying that, two women coming out of another, connecting corridor, suddenly appeared, walking in haste onto the colonnade and turning in the teens' direction. The young duo froze in their tracks.

"Uh-oh," Zeke uttered.

The women, looking to be in their thirties, were each wearing a plain white robe with a simple, white linen headdress. As they passed by the petrified youth, these women smiled softly, and one of them said in Slovak, "*Vitajte u nás y Červenom Kláštore* [Welcome to our Red Monastery]." Unable to understand a single word, Zeke and Alyssa looked at each other in bewilderment. Realizing that the women posed no apparent threat to them, they proceeded toward the sunny courtyard.

As the young pair approached the open space at the end of the colonnade, the indistinguishable mumbling of a yet unseen crowd grew louder. Finally reaching the courtyard, Zeke and Alyssa were taken aback to see a large number of people gathered around a series of stone tables. These were arranged in rows all throughout the open patio floor, which contained a faded, continuous mosaic design, displaying a once colorful flowered motif. Evidently, all of these people were eating a meal together. Having lost all sense of time, however, Zeke and Alyssa were clueless as to what mealtime this was supposed to be.

Upon closer examination, the two observed that there were several children, teens, and many adults present in an ethnically diverse crowd. There were also other women, perhaps nuns, Zeke imagined, dressed like the ones they had just seen walking by in the colonnade. There were, as well, many men who looked to him like monks, dressed in long white, hooded habits and scapulars. For Alyssa's sake, Zeke took a moment to bring her up to speed on the strangely garbed characters. All in all, as the two of them casually perused the lively courtyard scene, they figured there must have been three to four hundred people gathered there.

At yet another elongated table, they saw, seated by themselves, a group of about a dozen old monks with long, white beards, also enjoying a meal together. Built in the mountains of northern Slovakia Province, they would later learn, the monastery had been secretly housing these twelve, very special men. They were ancient scribes who, by the hand of The Name, had been kept living in almost hermitic seclusion for centuries, waiting for such a time as this, when the events of the dark reign of Allianz were set into motion.

Puzzled to witness this congenial scene, and not sensing danger of any kind, Zeke and Alyssa proceeded toward the gathered throngs and were immediately met by more robbed women presenting them with some food and drinks in a foreign language, "*Dáte si niečo na jedenie alebo pitie? Nech sa páči.* [Would you care for something to eat or drink? Please help yourselves]," they offered.

"I think they're serving us food and something to drink," deduced Alyssa.

Then, taking some hard-crust, artisan bread and whole fruits, in addition to clay cups filled with what looked like grape juice, the two youth thanked the servers and then looked for a place to sit down. As they walked among the crowd, Zeke and Alyssa gathered that these were actually family units seated together, all of which seemed to be speaking in varied, foreign tongues. Moving a bit further down an outermost row of tables on the edge of the courtyard, and finally hearing English for the first time there, the young pair stopped and addressed one of the families whose language they could understand.

"You speak English," Alyssa said, with noticeable relief in her voice. "May we join you, please?"

"Absolutely," responded an adult woman in the group. "Did you just get here?"

"Actually, ma'am, we don't even know where *here* is," replied Zeke.

"Don't worry about it. We didn't either, when we first arrived." Then she added, "Welcome to the Red Monastery. You happen to be in a castle and monastery compound, nestled in the mountains of north-central Slovakia Province," the motherly looking lady informed them, to the teen's utter bafflement.

"You've *got* to be kidding," replied Alyssa, in astonishment. Then, catching herself, she said, "I'm sorry. I don't mean to sound so crude, but…"

"Oh, that's perfectly all right, dear. We know exactly how you feel."

"How can this be? That's impossible," Zeke exclaimed.

"No, not really," said the well-meaning woman, "but we all had the same reaction when we first got here and found out where we were."

The woman then introduced herself, "Hi, I'm Mrs. Julia Morris… and this is my husband, Joe, and our children, Rebecca and Sarah. We're from the Province of Canada and, like you, we've also been brought here because of the dreams," she explained. "You're going to be just fine. We're safe here… Where are your families?"

"Whoa! This is totally weird," Alyssa reacted, in dismay. "I guess you want to know who we are, huh?"

"We'd be delighted, honey," said Mrs. Morris.

"My name is Alyssa Lorentz...and this is Zeke Christensen. And by the way, we're not related...just friends."

Then Zeke asked the attentive lady, "What do you mean, dreams?"

"Spirit dreams," Mr. Morris interjected, as he stood up to greet the young duo. "Nice to meet you two."

"Thanks, uh... Excuse me, but...are you saying that this is not a cog prison?" Zeke asked, needing clarification.

"Far from it, son," Mr. Morris replied. "If you're here, chances are that you, too, or someone in your family, have received Scripture dreams and, like us, you've been brought to this place by a man named, 'The One Sent,' or at least that's what they call him around here. We haven't actually met him, yet. But we understand that it will happen soon.

"Really?" Zeke replied.

"Yes. But he's sort of a mysterious figure. When he's not off somewhere in the world retrieving dreamers and their families, he's usually behind closed doors, spending his days in private prayer... literally for hours on end."

"This all seems so unreal," Zeke said, "like some strange dream I'm having."

"Believe me, Zeke," replied Mr. Morris, "we've all been there."

"Speaking of dreams," said Zeke, "may I ask what portion of Scripture you've received?" to which Mrs. Morris immediately answered, "The *Evangel* according to John began coming to our youngest daughter, Sarah, about a month ago... You?" she asked in return.

"Isaiah," said Zeke. "I seem to be working my way through the entire book in my sleep."

"Praise The Name! That's wonderful, Zeke... Now, what about you, Alyssa?"

"No, ma'am. As you can see, I'm an implant. I've only recently become Spirit-sealed."

"There's nothing wrong with that, honey. You have truly been blessed, and we're so glad you have come to faith in the Anointed One," Mrs. Morris told her.

Then, Joe Morris said, "Now look around you... Each of these families here, coming from various parts of the world, has been brought here for the same reason...the dreams. You were among some of the last ones brought in by 'The One Sent,' and I believe the time is very near, when the Word of Truth will again be reunified," he explained. "We've been told that this is the reason why we're all being assembled together."

"Wow, I wish my family were here to see this," Zeke remarked. "This is truly amazing."

"You mean, you two are here alone?" asked Mrs. Morris.

"Afraid so, Ms. Julia," replied Alyssa.

"Oh, you poor things! Don't you fret. We'll help you get settled, eh?"

As they all sat down together, Alyssa mentioned seeing the old, bearded fellows.

"Who are they? I've never seen men who look like them before."

Then, Joe Morris said, "We know little about them. But we've been told that these men truly are from of old and have been appointed by The Name the task of overseeing the reunification of the Word of Truth. We rarely hear them speak. And if they do, it is usually amongst themselves."

"Wow. That's so fascinating," said Alyssa.

"Just stick around for a while, dear. Meet some of these families and hear their amazing stories. A number of them can speak at least some English, and I believe there's at least one other family here from the American Province. I tell you, it just keeps getting more and more interesting, that's for sure," Mrs. Morris commented.

Fifty-Five

Morph-ship Ride to Croce Cavern

Once aboard *The Weber*, the Christensens and I strapped ourselves down and shoved off for a brief underwater jaunt that would take us to my mountain hideout. As our transport submerged, the lights dimmed inside its cabin, to a collective gasp by my new and a bit unsettled shipmates. The underwater visibility through our small windows was poor that day, as I navigated largely by instruments, leaving much to one's imagination as to what might possibly be lurking in the murky aquatic world outside. From the look of anxious fascination I read on my passengers' faces, I interpreted that by now the Christensens felt themselves fully immersed in a sort of Jules Verne-like adventure scenario. Certainly feeling a wee bit frightened and quite out of their element, they were hardly able to say much, as they appeared busy, soaking in the amazing and for them unprecedented submarine experience. I allowed them a few indulging, if mostly quiet, moments and then opted to break the silence with an appropriate touch of nostalgia.

"So, Tanner-san... It's such a pleasure to see you and your family well. It feels like old times, again... I do hope we'll be able to catch up on each other's lives, despite our preoccupation with the troubles at hand."

"Indeed, Sensei. Indeed."

A short while later, we descended into deeper waters and headed toward the ascending wall of rock located on the far side of that remote lake. The Christensens began to relax and unwind some, and the conversation began to flow.

"*The Weber*, huh, Sensei? That's quite a name," Christensen said to me, rather out of the blue.

"Ah, yes...very a propos, wouldn't you say?" I replied, as I continued our naval navigation. "After all, Weber's classic sociological writings and the 'ideal types' he famously proposed, blew wind on my academic sail for decades... Still today, more than a century old, Weber's yet on-target social analyses and his intuition cautioning us about the dangers of modernity and the overly rationalized social order, continue to challenge and stimulate me, as I think about the state of affairs we find ourselves in."

"His 'iron cage' figure immediately comes to mind, especially as we sit in this...uh...well, what exactly *is* this complex machine? A submarine? An amphibious transport?" Christensen inquired.

"Both, actually...and much more. It is a state-of-the-art, stealth-constructed, and supersonic-capable **morph-ship**, powered by **HQAM Energy**," I told him.

"What kind of energy is that?" he asked.

"It stands for **Hyper-Quaking Anti-Matter Energy**. But, really, you're asking the wrong fellow. However, from what I gather, this is an abundant source of unseen energy that is all around us and is present everywhere in the observable universe. This transport is able to harness this energy for its use, while it moves through land, air, and water. It never needs to be fueled or powered up any other way. It's truly quite ingenious."

"That's just unbelievably awesome!" Christensen yelled out.

"Quite right, Tanner-san," I concurred and elaborated, "The morph-ship was originally conceived for military ends, to function capably and without radar detection on land, under and over water, in the air, and underground. There's not much this beauty can't do."

"This thing must really zoom, if you made it here all the way from north Brazil so fast..." Christensen pointed out.

"I can tell you from painful experience that the supersonic acceleration in this morph-ship is enough to knock the air right out of your lungs, if you're not prepared for it," I told him.

"A supersonic morph-ship?" said Bethany. "That sparks!"

The Dreamers of Allianz

Then, in unbridled curiosity, little Holly asked, "It sure does spark! What exactly do you have to do to get one of these?"

"Well, I can't really answer that, young one. I simply started out as a college-teaching sociologist, and then…due to circumstances quite beyond my control, I eventually became a top-secret agent in the Brethren Resistance," I replied, struggling to capture in simple terms the last three decades of my life.

"Wow!" Holly cheered.

Claire, wondering about the transport she had seen the night before, asked, "Did the Resistance issue this one ship to you only? Or are there others like it?"

"Well, Chiara, through a somewhat convoluted process, I was appointed to help assemble a top-level, covert research group, which was commissioned to design and develop highly advanced gadgets and transports, like this one, as part of the Global Exodus agenda. The ship we're now in, is one of two prototypical morph-ships in existence, and I have had the privilege of being among those who were singularly trained to test drive it, before its mass production plans were ultimately shelved, due to the prohibitively high costs involved. I even got to name this one…"

"And where's the other one?" Claire inquired, strongly suspecting she had seen it just hours before.

"I understand that, as of late, the other prototype, *The Redemption*, is based in Slovakia Province and has been making Resistance sorties out of there for the past few weeks. In fact, I'm quite certain that it was used to carry your son and the young lady, Alyssa, to the Red Monastery," I indicated.

"I knew it! I knew I had seen a ship like this before," Claire responded, then adding, "Oh, Dr. C., there's so much I want to ask you about."

"That's not at all surprising to me, Chiara. At this point, however, I'm afraid I can only offer you an abbreviated version, in the way of explanation about the recent happenings. However, I can tell you that the Lord has charged and equipped an Ethiopian brother by the name of Elias-Negash, who generally goes by the name of 'The One Sent,' with a very crucial task, which involves your son and a plurality of other youth and children."

"I'm not sure what you mean, Sensei," Christensen said. "What task is that?"

"That of bringing together the Spirit dreamers, for the purpose of reunifying the Word of Truth," I answered.

Immediately, Claire made the connection and remarked with excitement, "Oh, my gosh, Tanner! That's what Zeke's dreams were all about..."

It took Christensen a moment to leave his light stupor and personally connect the dots, so to speak. But momentarily he shouted out, in total awe, "Rescuing His Word? That's incredible! How great is our Lord?"

"Tan, I had such a strong feeling that Zeke's dreams had to be coming from The Name. He was working through our son..." Claire offered in utter wonderment.

Then, I pointed out, "True...and not only through your son, my friends, but also through dozens of other young people all around the world..."

"But why?" Bethany chimed in. "Why is this happening? And why now?"

"Impossible to say for certain, young lady," I replied. "But there's no question in my mind that The Name is on the move, and mightily so. For when the Word was first given to us in antiquity, it was for the purpose of drawing all of humanity to Himself, to enable the great ministry of reconciliation which He initiated, first through His promise to the patriarchs of the faith, then through the prophets' pronouncements to His people, then personally and universally through the earthly ministry, death on the cross, and resurrection of the Anointed One, and lastly through the Spirit-empowered work of the Apostles and the entire community of the saints, which is us. But in these latter days, just as the light of the Word of Truth seems almost completely extinguished in the world, He initiates its reintegration. And I have to believe that it is for another great purpose."

"Reestablishing and edifying the universal Church, perhaps?" Asked Christensen.

"Certainly, yes. But I suspect this has even more to do with those who remain outside the Body," I replied, referring to those who remained spiritually lost.

"In what way, Dr. C?" said Claire.

"My thinking is...one more season of sowing the *Evangel* throughout Allianz...and then, the Great Harvest."

Such an idea was almost too great for the Christensens to fully fathom. They immediately fell into a kind of ecstatic silence, as they pondered the truly remarkable way in which The Name had been sovereignly and so personally acting again in history to bring about His highest purposes for humanity. It was the inquisitive drive of the youngest among us that finally broke through the high-energy silence.

"So...a secret agent, huh?" Holly squealed with excitement.

"Quite so, I suppose," I said.

"Wow, that's spark-a-rama!"

As we finally approached our underwater dock, a large, oval hatch was automatically opened to allow the morph-ship to enter into our hideout. Upon completing our slow entry, the hatch closed behind us, and subsequently most of the water in the docking chamber suddenly rushed away via powerful vacuum pumps, leaving just enough water to keep our ship afloat.

"We're here," I announced.

"Where exactly *is* here?" Claire asked.

"Well, I like to think of it as my Smoky Mountains cabin hideaway..."

"An underwater mountain cabin? That's quite unique," Christensen remarked.

"Not underwater, Tanner-san, but underground... Welcome to the *Croce Cavern*, my humble abode."

After exiting the morph-ship onto an auto-retractable plank and then into a short cylindrical tunnel, we walked through a couple more safety hatch doors and then accessed the great room of the cavern.

"This is truly remarkable, Sensei," Christensen marveled upon seeing the cavern's coral, beige, and green colored limestone interior walls. Against that natural backdrop, soft ambient lighting revealed a sharply contrasting, eclectic mélange of high-tech intelligence gathering and communications equipment, integrated with a cozy living-room space, accented with a warm country-Italian décor. Adjacent to the living-room was my as-of-late rather underused Japanese-style Aikido dojo.

"Awesome! Your cavern sparks!" cheered Holly.

At that, Christensen inquired, "Croce Cavern, huh? Named after you, Sensei?"

"Yes, but only serendipitously so, Tanner-san. As you walk through the cave, you will observe how it was formed in the shape of a cross. We happen to be standing on its top tip. And since my last name means 'cross' in Italian, I thought 'Croce Cavern' was a fitting name."

"It does have a nice ring to it," Christensen replied.

"Well, friends…please make yourselves comfortable. We won't be staying here long. This evening, after a time of prayer, we will be departing for Slovakia, to reunite with your son and the others. Get some rest. I've got a nice catch in the freezer that I will be preparing for our lunch. Even the girls will love it."

"I hope so," Holly whispered in Bethany's ear.

"Same here. But I'm actually ready for the taste of some real food," Bethany confessed.

Fifty-Six

Horn and Dariah in North Africa

The Federation's A-999 carrying Horn and Dariah circled over the Mediterranean Sea. While preparing for landing at the Tunis Inter-Provincial Airport, Dariah contemplated just how to prove her loyalty to Allianz. Difficult as the task might now seem, especially considering how distant she was from her own post and authority domain in the American Province, Dariah knew that convincing Horn would take bold and resolute action on her part. Perhaps this visit to North Africa would allow her some time to reconfigure her approach to upholding the Allianz Code and punishing dissident challengers of the established order. Pensively staring out her window, she searched for a breakthrough idea that would bring relief to the tenuous situation in which she found herself, especially in relation to Horn.

At the same time, however, there was a certain feeling inside Dariah that troubled her in a different way. The persistent prodding of a once unshakable altruistic governing ethos, now struggling to compete with her all-consuming concern for self, reminded her that she was different from Horn. Unlike her perceptions of the Prosecutor General, the paramount directive in her way of ruling was not self-promotion or worship, but a devotion to duty and status-based honor, as the American Marshall and Commander. The realization that her motives for emboldened action on behalf of Allianz suddenly had more to do with saving her neck than with a reasoned, ethos-based calculation of what objective conditions called for in her estimation, gave her an ulcerating feeling in her gut; one that brought up the bitter taste of self-betrayal. As the aircraft was commencing a final approach into the district of Tunis, the existential question that began to eat away at Dariah's core was, *What's to define who I am?* Though a hauntingly persistent specter, this question would have to remain unanswered, for a clear answer to what agonized her in the prelude to her tour of Allianz's most ambitious and monstrous undertaking, eluded even her best efforts.

As seen from the air, there was almost nothing within one's view of the surface below that was not blue sea or covered by sand. The rapid desertification process in that part of the world had significantly transformed the once beautiful landscape edging the Tunis Bay. Previously world-renowned for their characteristic white-stucco homes with bright blue doors and windows, the towns of Sidi Bou Said and Carthage, for instance, now lay mostly covered in sand and almost totally abandoned. The only fully functioning urban area was central Tunis, itself. The still prominent Carthaginian Roman ruins, Horn and Dariah's final destination for that day, could be seen from the air, near the seashore and just down the hill from the Tunisian Marshall's palace, overlooking the Mediterranean.

A peculiar sight on the desert floor caught Dariah's eye. It was the widespread presence of what looked like small, white, pyramid-like protrusions pointing upward through the sandy surface. They were thousands of neatly aligned energy emitters, engaging directly with the CyberSat network of satellites. It was now late afternoon, and soon the official aircraft would be landing on the arid and sun-scorched northernmost tip of the African continent.

Upon their arrival and reception by the Tunisian Allianz authorities, an official convoy led Adammus Horn and Marshall Dariah directly to the entrance of the ancient ruins of Carthage, the main entry point into the Great Catacombs project. Dariah rolled down her window to breathe in some fresh air. The wind carried inland the salty sea air, which Dariah felt opening up her sinuses as it rushed in through her nostrils and settled heavily in her lungs.

Now beyond the gates of the Carthage ruins compound, Horn and Dariah stepped out of their vehicle and were met by the Tunisian Marshall and Commander, Mr. Wail Medina. Upon Horn's own recommendation, Medina, a native of Tunisia and himself a great and outspoken supporter of Horn, had been handpicked by the Allianz Council of Regents to oversee the Great Catacombs project. Having previously served ably under Horn, as his Deputy-Secretary General in the now defunct United Commonwealth Organization, Medina's proven allegiance to Horn earned him his appointment as Marshall and Commander of the highly strategic Tunisian Province.

"Welcome, Mr. Prosecutor General and Marshall…Vigor to Allianz," Medina greeted them. "Our expanding facilities are ready for your viewing and inspection."

"Excellent, Marshall Medina. We have been eagerly awaiting this moment. Have we not, Marshall Dariah?"

"Absolutely," Dariah replied tensely. "But if you gentlemen don't mind, I would like to take a few moments to contact the Deputy-Marshall and my staff in Washington, D.C. for a provincial situation update."

"Certainly, Marshall," answered Horn. "Mr. Medina and I have some business we need to tend to while you contact your aids."

"Mr. Prosecutor General," said Medina, "if I may, before we proceed with our official dealings, I must inform you that we have received an urgent communiqué from His Transcendence, High Sage Andrus, who has requested a private visualization with you, at your earliest convenience. Evidently, you were beyond his visualization reach while in the air. He's currently finishing a two-day visit to Damascus, to oversee plans for some new Transcienz projects."

"Very well, then… If you would show me to a private room, I will contact him at once," Horn said.

"It would be my pleasure, sir, to take you and Marshall Dariah to our recently completed conference complex, just a few floors below ground level," replied Medina. "I think the both of you will find it extremely suitable for your privacy needs. Please, follow me to our Crystal-Shuttle Incline for our picturesque descent to Level V."

Fifty-Seven

Anxiously Waiting

As the Christensens and I concluded our meal at the Croce Cavern, I gave them a tour of the rest of the facilities, and then we sat down to enjoy some coffee and hot chocolate back in the great room. Having already provided each other with a brief update over lunch, of the personal trajectories and events that had shaped our lives over the past decade or so, I felt it was now time to refocus our attention on our imminent, supersonic voyage to the Red Monastery. I told Christensen that he would experience a "baptism by fire," so to speak, as my co-pilot in *The Weber* during our trip, this time by air.

"I want you to learn to maneuver it expertly, Tanner-san," I said. "It may prove vital to our efforts from here on out. Your pilot-training will no doubt come in handy."

"I'll definitely give it my best shot, Sensei."

I then walked them over to my intelligence gathering station and addressed Claire and the girls, saying, "As for you ladies, I need you to assist me in deciphering these intercepted Federation messages. I have finished uploading them into the ship's information system. My concern is for the success of our operations in Slovakia. The work of the Resistance there will take time and must proceed unhindered. But I fear that the Federation may be gaining on us faster than I thought. Our only chance is to try and stay a step, or preferably more, ahead of them. If they discover our location and come after us, we could be in for a ghastly time. These messages contain about five day's worth of recent intelligence data gathering. We'll only have about three hours to digest them. That means we've got our work cut out for us."

"We're ready. Right girls?" said Claire.

"You bet!" they exclaimed.

"When do we start our secret spy work, Dr. C?" Holly asked.

"Soon, my eager little friend. First, I need you to get well rested. You would be wise to catch up on some sleep, while I finalize our preparations. We cast off at 5 p.m. sharp."

"I'm exhausted, but I don't know if I can relax enough to fall asleep. I can't wait to see Zeke and Alyssa…I'm so anxious to know they're truly well," Claire said.

"In that case, Mom," Bethany wisely observed, "sleeping is exactly what you do need. It'll refresh you. I'll pray for you."

"You're right, Beth. Thank you, honey."

Fifty-Eight

Andrus' Warning

Five levels beneath the ruins of Carthage, inside the Great Catacombs complex, Horn and Dariah now tended to official Allianz business, each in the privacy of their own conference room. While Dariah was being briefed on commonplace aspects of her administration's workaday world, with her aids having no news to speak of when it came to intelligence on Resistance activity in the American Province, a divergent scenario was unfolding for Horn that was far from ordinary. In a room adjacent to Dariah's, Horn listened intently to Andrus' startling disclosure that presaged – though obscurely so – the high stakes endeavor the Resistance was about to carry out, in what they would soon discover was a remote, central region of Europe.

"Your Grace, there are great stirrings in the spiritual realm," Andrus revealed, speaking from the district of Damascus, Province of Syria. "The anguished voices of our beloved ancestors cry out for swift intervention against the forces that prepare even now for a great offensive against them and all of Allianz."

"Andrus, your divinations about more Resistance gatherings in the pipeline are no news to me," Horn countered. "I hope this *urgent* visualization is not a waste of my time during this visit, truly a watershed moment in the history of Allianz."

"No, my beloved in the winding path. It is not. For I assure you, what is about to be unleashed most likely goes far beyond the localized or even regional significance of the Brethren Gatherings. If I am reading these transcendent utterances correctly, what is soon to take place has the potential of casting a great and terrifying shadow over the entire *kosmos*...and it must be stopped at all costs, or Allianz will suffer immensely."

"Then tell me at once, man... What and where is it?" Horn said, exasperated.

"Despite all of my summons, I cannot say for certain. These indistinct warnings have tortured my mind for days, now," said Andrus. "But one peculiar name have I discerned among all of the messages from beyond. It blows in the spiritual winds and repeatedly echoes in my divine meditations..."

"What the hell is it?" Horn asked impatiently.

"The Red Monastery."

"The Red Monastery? What is that, Andrus?" Horn responded.

"I regret to say, Your Grace, that I am unable to offer you any more than this," said Andrus, very apologetically.

"Then I will marshal every resource at my disposal to locate and destroy whatever this is. CyberSat's Data-Realm must certainly contain clues that can direct me to its whereabouts," Horn told Andrus. "I *will* find the Red Monastery, and I will..."

Just as Horn was uttering these words, Dariah stepped unannounced into the room.

"The Red Monastery? Did you say...the Red Monastery?" she asked.

"Yes, Misha. It is being used as a Resistance stronghold, and something big is brewing there. We must find out exactly what and where it is," Horn said.

"No need, Horn... I know exactly what you are talking about."

"What do you mean? How can you know of it?"

"When I was a little girl," Dariah recounted, "my father would tell me, over and over again, the story of how, when he was ten years old, he and his family escaped from Iran soon after the Islamic Revolution of 1979. They crossed over the dangerous and mountainous border into Turkey on horseback. There they were met by a man who dealt in human trafficking, and who, for almost all the money they had, took them and other refugees in the back of a truck, over several days, across most of Turkey, to the Sea of Marmara, which they then crossed by passenger boat with the last bit of money they had in their possession."

"Go on," Horn said, following Dariah closely.

"Well," Dariah continued, "as my father told me, his family settled temporarily in Istanbul, while his mother and father worked nights until they saved enough money to continue on their voyage to their desired destination...Austria. Then his mother, whom I never met, fell suddenly ill and eventually died of pneumonia. Soon thereafter, my grandfather took my father and his four siblings into Bulgaria and some years later Romania, where they came under intense discrimination and attacks in Bucharest by the security police, under dictator Nicolae Ceausescu. Running away, they found temporary refuge in the old Sucevita Monastery, in that country's Northeast region."

"Would that be the Red Monastery?" Horn asked.

"Not quite yet," Dariah calmly answered, fully enjoying her moment of control over Horn. She then went on, "Unable to remain there indefinitely, a visiting friar from the former Czechoslovakia agreed to take them back with him to his country. They were given provisions for their long journey through the southeastern tip of the former USSR, now Ukraine Province, where they paid border soldiers to allow them to pass through, into Czechoslovakia. The friar brought my father and the rest of his family to live near the Polish border, in an ancient mountain castle and monastery, where they stayed for two years, until the fall of Communism, when they were able to move across into Austria. During the ten years my father lived in Vienna, he met and eventually married my mother, herself a Soviet refugee, before they emigrated together to the former United States, where I was born a San Franciscan, in GDM-Minus-23.

"Touching story, darling. But what does all of this have to do with Red Monastery?" Horn asked her.

"Listen carefully, Horn. The place where my father and his family stayed at for two years, in the Slovak mountains near Poland, was called *Červeny Klástor*... In Slovak, that means, Red Monastery."

"Yes! You've done well, Misha. You've cracked it for us," Horn commended her with an insinuating grin. "Remind me to thank you more appropriately, later on."

Dariah nodded, hesitantly.

As Horn prepared to end his visualization with Andrus, he said, "And many thanks to you, Your Transcendence. You have been most helpful, and your loyalty to Allianz will again not go unnoticed or unrewarded."

"You are most kind, Your Grace. And may the stars align to bring you good fortune in North Africa." Andrus then said to Dariah, "And I shall look forward to seeing you again, Marshall, in person...tomorrow."

"Tomorrow? Will you be coming to North Africa, as well?" Dariah inquired.

"Most certainly not, Marshall," Andrus replied. "I am to leave Damascus tomorrow for a brief visit and lecture at the D.C and New York Transcienz Halls. The Prosecutor General has graciously arranged for your Federation plane to carry me to D.C., as well. I believe you will enjoy your brief stopover in Damascus. It will be a pleasure to join you on your trip back to the American Province."

"Very well, Your Transcendence," said Dariah, suddenly experiencing an acutely disarming feeling of undesired surprise.

Having ended the visualization with Andrus, Horn knew that this was the most propitious opportunity to test Dariah's commitment to Allianz. In the wake of this crucially important visualization with the Transcienz' High Sage, Horn gave Dariah one last chance to prove herself to his satisfaction, and he asked her point blank, "What will it be now, Marshall? Dereliction of a duty you find too onerous to execute against these poor subversives? Or an overwhelming display of the might of Allianz, to shatter the Resistance into pieces, once and for all? I am making this your call, Marshall."

In silence she briefly collected her thoughts and then austerely replied, "Horn, I say this not to merely save my career...but so that you will never again question my loyalty to Allianz."

"Hmm...a clear demonstration of your resolve. I can't wait. My mouth is watering, already..." Horn said.

"Take...them...out," Dariah resolutely uttered. "I want to see an all out aerial bombardment on this Resistance stronghold. Take no prisoners this time... And I also vow before you, here and now, to drastically intensify my own offensives against the Community of Brethren in the American Province. You can consider all of them goners, as far as I'm concerned. In fact, with your permission, this very day I will order the systematic and widespread seizing and destruction of all remaining property known or suspected to belong to the Resistance in my territory. This should put an end, once and for all, Horn, to your doubts about where my loyalties lie."

"...Or your name is not Misha Dariah?" Horn added, in self-amusement.

"Or my name is not Misha Dariah," she repeated.

"I must say...I have never felt so proud of my beautiful Misha as I am right now," Horn told her. "This certainly calls for our own private celebration...tonight, after our long awaited tour."

"What about the assault on the Resistance in the Slovakia Province?" Dariah inquired.

"Leave that to me...and to CyberSat," he mysteriously replied.

Fifty-Nine

What's a *Sociologer?*

While Horn and Dariah commenced their Great Catacombs project tour, the Christensens and I took our positions inside *The Weber* and cast out to nearby waters.

"Now brace yourselves..." I said. "Tanner-san, you and I are taking this baby straight up... Engage!" I exclaimed, as we transitioned the morph-ship into aerial mode for a head-spinning sea-to-air take off.

The elevated G-forces being exerted upon our bodies made us sink back into our seats, as we lifted up out of the water and into the dusk hues of the southeastern American skies. We were en route to Slovakia, under the protection of our super-speed transport's stealth capabilities.

"This is unbelievable!" Christensen yelled out. "I have never flown anything like this."

"If you're like me," I said, "you'll soon find yourself irreversibly spoiled by the sheer power, agility, and special features of this magnificent machine."

"I believe I'm already there!" Christensen replied.

Minutes later, the Atlantic shores were already in view. We reached cruising altitude and leveled off at 60,000 feet, amid fast-forming, mezzo-atmospheric, electrical storms, which caused significant turbulence. The occasionally violent air mass dislocations were enough to bring fear into the hearts of most air travelers and even some seasoned pilots yet unacquainted with that harsh airborne environment. Despite their astounding force, however, these storms had proven no match for the exceptional stability and fortitude of *The Weber*.

Once past the expected adjustment period, the Christensens took it all in stride. Upon our reaching cruising altitude, I handed all the controls over to Christensen, who thoroughly enjoyed the unmatched navigational experience. This allowed the ladies and I to move to the back of the morph-ship to begin our intelligence work. We then began to plow through and dissect the substantial amount of intelligence data. While working, Holly's curiosity peaked. She asked, "So, Dr. C... What exactly is a *sociologer*?"

"You mean, a *sociologist*, honey," her mother corrected her.

"Yeah...that."

"Well," I answered, "at his or her core, a sociologist is one who protects good social institutions and questions and debunks evil social structures."

"Say *what*?" replied the nine-year old, thoroughly perplexed.

"I beg your pardon, little one... Let me try that again," I pleaded. "Let's see... Have your parents ever told you stories about the Old Testament?"

"Sure they have," she answered. "There's the story of Adam and Eve's fall from grace, Joseph's beautiful coat, Queen Esther's courage, Elijah being fed by ravens, all the other prophets..."

"There you are, then...the prophets," I said. "Some in the past have compared sociologists to prophets, like those of the Old Testament."

"How do you mean?" Bethany joined in.

"Well," I replied, "as my sociologist friend, Dr. V, would say, the prophets of old were a voice of righteousness to their people. They saw how society was going awry from precepts of The Name and how the powerful rulers were profiting from the evil system. The Name charged His prophets with blowing the horn, as it were, on the problematic situation at hand. The prophets warned the people about the tragic consequences that would come upon them if the people and the government didn't turn things around and realigned their lives and culture with The Name's will."

"Like Jonah did in Nineveh, right?" Holly offered.

"That's precisely right. As another great sociologist, Dr. H, taught me, a sociologist has this same type of calling…to denounce social evil and work within his or her profession, out of a sense of vocation, to try and set it straight, to the glory of the Name."

"Pretty cool," Holly said, then adding, "Maybe I'll want to be a sociologist, when I grow up." To that, I replied, "With your genuine curiosity and boldness, I bet you would make a great one, little friend."

"Thanks, Dr. C. You're a real sparking dude," she said.

"Holly!" Claire called her attention. "Use your manners, please."

"Oh, that's quite all right," I said. "I've never been called a *sparking dude* before, and I rather fancy it… Now it's best that we get back to work."

Sixty

Inside the Great Catacombs Project

Back inside the Crystal-Shuttle Incline and accompanied by a sizeable security entourage, Horn, Dariah, and Medina descended to Level XX to view the almost completed Phase I of the Great Catacombs. Covering roughly sixty-six thousand square-miles of the incomprehensively vast, dry aquifer system lying beneath Northwest Sahara, this portion of the Great Catacombs was the final stop of the Carthage-originated shuttle. Subsequent construction phases would include the Nubian Aquifer System shared by the provinces of Chad, Egypt, Libya, and Sudan in Phase II. Phase III, the final one, would cover the Iullemeden Aquifer System, extending under Niger, Nigeria, Mali, Benin, and Algeria. Hands down, the Great Catacombs project was to be the most ambitious and diabolically conceived enterprise during Allianz's reign.

As they were gently lowered deeper, level by level, diagonally down toward the farthest reaches of the Phase I facilities, it was possible for one to view, through the clear enclosure of the shuttle, some of the project's activities taking place throughout each layer of the enormous secret establishment. Floor after floor revealed hordes of scientists, chemists, biomedical experts, a diverse multiplicity of engineers and technicians, medics, and even cog personnel, among other supporting cadres busily running every detail of every aspect of this most multifarious operation, so critical to the future of the Federation. Also visible from the shuttle, were shipments of machinery, specialized equipment, and parts of all sizes, which were carried to the lower levels by powerful moving belts, resembling a large, super-sized assembly line. The whole operation was indeed a masterfully planned and executed undertaking.

Upon the shuttle's arrival at Level XX, the illustrious visitors were taken through a tight and multi-layered electronic and manned security apparatus to another transparent, glass-covered transport that carried them to the main observation atrium. Medina's highly technical explanations and descriptions of the utterly colossal engineering feats that stood behind the materialization of the project, were lost in Horn's subdued but internally ecstatic anticipation and Dariah's helplessly tense apprehension.

"Any questions before we disembark at the atrium?" Medina inquired of his guests.

None were asked.

Reaching the observation atrium, they all stepped out of their transport and onto a large and luminous reception lobby. Moving past the reception area, where their badges were duly checked and scanned, the group proceeded to the back of the atrium, where a tall and semicircular dark glass wall obscured the panoramic view to the Great Catacombs gallery. As the visitors continued toward an observation deck behind the glass walls, sliding double doors automatically opened, revealing an astonishing scene.

Dariah's jaw dropped. Feeling completely beyond words, she could hardly clutch the balcony's railing and stare at the magnitude of what was before her. *I can't believe this*, she thought, as Horn said, "Not in my wildest... This is truly... I mean...I'm beyond words. This is truly an astounding spectacle to behold!" His eyes scanned the vastness of the immense gallery, which extended outward as far as the eye could see, seemingly in every direction.

"My gosh, Horn. All those bodies out there..." Dariah said, struggling to wrap her mind around what her face clearly registered as an unspeakably macabre scene.

"If you'll permit me, Marshall Dariah," Medina interjected, "these are not bodies. They are not dead. These gigantic, tilted wheels, lined in rows that extend for two hundred and fifty miles, can hold up to a thousand permanently dream connected individuals, each. These dreamers are being kept very much alive…only in an uninterrupted Transcienz Dream State."

"Behold, darling," Horn told Dariah, "the hallowed ground of Allianz…where the core energy that powers our system and empowers us is kept flowing, ensuring that both our present and our future are secured *ad infinitum*… And where the soul of CyberSat and the very heart of the Federation become immortalized."

"I feel sick, all of a sudden. If you would, please excuse me…I need to go sit down," Dariah said. She turned and quickly began to move in the direction of the double doors, back toward the atrium, to sit down.

"Marshall Dariah…all you all right? Do you need a medic?" Medina yelled out with concern, as Dariah exited the observation deck.

"Let her be, Marshall Medina. It's probably jet lag getting to her. I'm sure she'll be fine presently," Horn disingenuously spoke, on Dariah's behalf, suspecting that what was affecting her was more than mere physical sickness. Nothing, however, not even Dariah's annoying and disappointingly disgusted disposition toward Allianz's greatest accomplishments would deter Horn from thoroughly savoring the delectable sense of triumph he was experiencing, as he gazed at the awesome and unmatched display that was the Great Catacombs gallery. It was truly, in his own words, "a watershed moment."

Sixty-One

Analyzing Allianz

After four hours in the air, we were nearing our descent into Slovakia Province, so I returned to the controls of *The Weber*. Christensen took the opportunity to ask me about some of my sociological musings regarding Allianz and its phenomenal success in neutralizing almost every dissident group and attaining world hegemony.

"Sensei, I've been meaning to ask you about something…"

"If it's about my hat and smoking pipe look, I'll have you know, Tanner-san, that at my age a man gets pretty set in his ways, especially when it comes to his props," I declared. Then I continued, "I rarely ever light up anymore, you know. And if I ever do, I am strictly *Clintonesque* about it. I don't ever inhale. I just fancy the sweet, leathery perfume it leaves in the air. It reminds me of my father and grandfather."

"No, no…that's fine, sir. It's not about that, at all… I've actually been meaning to pick your brain about how you explain the way things have changed so much over the last decade," Christensen said.

"That's quite a complex subject, Tanner-san, and I doubt we would have enough time to do it proper justice," I said. "Is there any specific issue you'd like to discuss?"

"Well, I'd be interested to know about the Federation's silencing of so many system challengers over the years," he specified.

"It's rather simple, really," I explained. "You know, Tanner-san, Allianz figured out a long time ago, that the way to deal with most opposition was not to bomb them or destroy them politically. Instead, the Federation made a strong move to integrate them into mainstream society.

"How did the Federation do this?" he asked.

"At first, mainly through economic integration, via the Cognit Forehead Implant and the bracelet. Allianz literally threw money at the problem. Not bombs...money. It was not the dissident leadership, per se, that they went after, but rather these groups' constituencies...the masses."

"Fascinating, Sensei..."

"It's brilliant, indeed. You see, most of the time, and here I would have to exclude the Community of Brethren Resistance and very few other anti-system movements around the globe, it is the leadership that is strongly ideologically committed, not the rank-in-file in these groups. The common people merely want a better life. For them, it is mainly economics before politics. Then, some extremist ideologues preaching religious nationalism and other political banners show up and sell their vision to the disaffected masses, promising them a new, utopian reality. But from the outset, all the people want is a significant improvement to their plight, not be career or professionalized militants."

"And then, along comes the advent of mass assimilation into Allianz..." Christensen followed along.

"Precisely. What that did, is it pulled the rug, so to speak, from under these ideologically inflexible leaders. The people realized that they really did not aspire to be political radicals. They just wanted a dignified and satisfying life." I continued, "Meanwhile, the challenger movements themselves, in their majority, were also enticed to become integrated. Once integrated, these movements assimilated. Once assimilated, they accepted the new institutions. Once institutionalized, they internalized the routinization of the system's ways. Once routinized, they became conventionalized. Once conventionalized, they simply ceased to exist as opposition movements. Eventually, they faded into political insignificance, and their causes fell into the abyss of social oblivion... Hence, the death of so many formerly anti-Federation movements."

"That's incredible," responded Christensen.

"In theory, yes," I replied. "However, as you know, the package offered by Allianz was not simply economic assimilation. Allianz has enticed humanity with the most powerful force the world system has ever devised"

"What's that?"

"False consciousness," I said. "That is, most of humanity has become convinced that Allianz has its best interest at heart, and that if they would only assimilate, all of their troubles would cease."

"But of course, that leaves out the truth about their spiritual condition," Christensen added.

"Correct," I said. "And that's why we're here…to take back to the world the *Evangel*."

"So, is this what happened in the case of the terrorist groups that proliferated in the early part of this century, but then seemingly fell off the face of the earth?" Christensen asked.

"Well, in that case, the strategy was slightly different," I elucidated. "Allianz invested heavily in new hydrogen technology, which ultimately supplanted worldwide petrol dominance in as little as a decade. Declining demand for oil resulted in sharply declining revenues, to the point where the oil money that had been funneled into funding terrorist activity globally dwindled away. Without significant flows of cash, terrorist cells eventually collapsed."

"Naturally."

"At the same time, mass assimilation toward the implant protocol, and consequently the new economy and job market, became a more attractive option for the affected populace than supporting terror campaigns that promoted populist claims. Therefore, public support for these groups also dried up. It was a head spinning, one-two punch combination by Allianz. Again, brilliant," I concluded.

"So, Dr. C," Claire inquired, "other than the Resistance, who else is out there opposing the Federation?"

"That's an empirical question that I can only take a guess at," I replied. "I know of a small number of peaceable, religious groups. I also know of some radical environmental and animal rights groups. Any others would be pure speculation on my part. But even some of these have shown some signs of compromise, succumbing under the pressure of Allianz."

"I can believe that, Sensei," Christensen said. "There have been some among us who have gone out from us and into the Allianz world system."

"True, Tanner-san. But then I wonder if they were ever really with us."

Our conversation continued right up until we initiated our descent into Slovakia, when I announced to the Christensens, "Take your seats, friends. It's going to get bumpy for a short while. But soon, the Red Monastery will come into view."

Sixty-Two

Rejoined

At the Red Monastery, it was evening, and the air was electrified with excitement. The families there gathered were told that on the following morning they would come together for a worship service, in which they would commune at the Lord's Table. They were also informed that the One Sent, whom no one had yet met, would lead the ceremony. Most importantly, they were notified that the Word reunification process, the very reason they were all brought there in the first place, would begin then, soon after a lunch banquet, given in celebration of the glorious occasion.

Zeke and Alyssa prepared to head to their individual rooms, after having met a great number of other youth, children, and their families. Although the leadership at the monastery was aware of our imminent arrival, having been sent a message from me stating that the rest of the Christensen clan was onboard *The Weber*, we had decided, despite ourselves, to let the young pair be surprised with our coming. Completely unaware of our ever closer proximity to them, Zeke and Alyssa spent a brief time in joint prayer and then wished each other a good night.

"I wonder what my mom's doing right now," Alyssa said with sadness in her voice. "I miss her so much."

"I know, Alyssa. I can't stop thinking about my family either, especially my dad. I wish they were all here to see this amazing thing that's about to happen," Zeke said.

"Do you think we'll ever see them again?" Alyssa asked.

The Dreamers of Allianz

"I think so. I know so," Zeke affirmed. "But for now, it's nice just to imagine that they're probably safe, back home."

"I hope I can sleep," said Alyssa.

"Me, too."

"Can I get a hug?" she requested.

"Sure."

The two of them then hugged innocently. At that moment, each other was all they had. A strong bond was truly beginning to form between them.

"That was nice. Good night, Zeke."

"G'night, Alyssa."

The two of them had not been asleep, each in their own room, for more than an hour, when they heard the voice of Mrs. Morris in the hallway, right outside their rooms. Whatever it was, she sounded extremely animated, as she knocked on the youngsters' closed doors.

"Kids…kids, wake up [knock, knock]. I've got a little surprise for you…" she announced.

"What?" answered Alyssa, startled and feeling quite sleepy. "Is that you, Ms. Julia?"

"Yes, honey. Please open up… You, too, Zeke."

The two teens got up and walked to their respective doors almost exactly at the same time. As they each opened their doors, they could not believe their eyes.

"Surprise!" they heard, as they rubbed the sleep off their eyes. In utter disbelief, they both shouted, "Oh, my gosh!" when they realized that it was really the Christensens.

"Mom, Dad, girls… You're here!"

"Yes, we are Zeke. We're really here, sweetie," Claire cried out.

"Alyssa!" said Bethany, giving her friend a warm embrace.

"Beth, I just can't believe it, girl…" Alyssa said back to her friend.

"We're all together, again," exclaimed Holly. "One big, happy family. That includes you, too, Alyssa."

"Oh, thanks. You're such a cutie pie, Holly."

"Yes, yes. All in a day's work, for a secret *sociologer* agent, like me," Holly replied.

"Hi, son," Christensen greeted Zeke.

"Dad! It's really you! You're all right!"

"I'm fine, son. It's so good to see you. We've come a long way, thanks to Dr. C."

"Dr. C? Your old Sensei? Did he come with you? I've *got* to see him," Zeke told his dad.

"All in good time, Zeke," said Christensen. "He's busy, right now, talking with the leadership here. But you can see him in the morning, after we all get a good night's sleep. The old man will be with us at the worship service, tomorrow."

Sixty-Three

Horn Denied

It was now very late that same evening. Horn and Dariah were meeting privately over drinks in a luxurious lounge on Level III, just outside their lavishly appointed sleeping quarters.

"Care to tell me what that was all about down there?" Horn inquired of Dariah.

"I just felt dizzy and nauseous, all of a sudden."

"Is that all? Somehow I don't see jet lag as being the sole cause."

"Horn, look. It's late. This has been a big day for the both of us, and I'm really beyond tired. Can we leave this conversation for another time?" Dariah replied emphatically, "Please?"

"A huge day, Misha," Horn said to her. "That's why I was hoping for bit of celebrating and reconnecting, just the two of us…for old times' sake."

"All right. Kill me. Just kill me right now and get it over with," she responded, feeling absolutely weak, spent, and unable to deal with Horn's impertinent proposition.

"What is this, Misha? You talk as if I've unearthed a grotesque cadaver or something, instead of what I've actually done, which is to invite you have a nice night together."

"I can't Horn…I just can't, all right?"

"You know, darling. We'll both be leaving tomorrow. You'll be headed back to D.C., and I to Paris, from where I'll be coordinating the attack on the Resistance stronghold as evening falls. Am I asking too much to spend a bit of time with you, before we depart and go our separate ways, for who knows how long?" Horn insisted.

"Once again, Horn. I...I can't."

Convinced that Dariah's malaise was a consequence of what she had witnessed down in the Great Catacombs gallery, Horn moved to try and diffuse some of her apprehensions. He figured that casually talking about it might have a normalizing effect on the whole subject, and that it would help Dariah feel more willing to accept his eager request. But his zeal for meeting his own intense needs, or rather his depraved sensual addiction, had in past kept him from coming across genuinely and compassionately. Would Dariah again see through his twisted, perverted charade of seduction?

"Perhaps it would help you feel better, darling, to remind you that those people down in the catacombs, permanently dream connected, are the least of your worries," Horn argued. "Believe me, they're better off being there, and they're definitely worth more to us comatose than dead. At least they've been kept alive and without pain." Horn continued, "Most of the initial batch contained elderly victims of the cancerous plague that CyberSat was programmed to conveniently concoct, in order to rid the world of that vile and insolent generation. Precipitating the depletion of the ozone layer was the easiest way to target that problematic geriatric cohort, and you were fully on board with that, need I jog your memory?"

"*Was* I?" she remarked, trying to convey disinterest.

"Yes. In fact, you were. But that's not all you were in accord with, darling. You also supported and benefited from the opportune trials and arrests of those who stood in your way politically. So, some of our catacomb dwellers also happen to include a whole host of crooked politicians, and a myriad of criminals and apprehended insurgents who opposed you, as well. As I've already told you, Misha, these are the throwaways of society. Many of them recipients of the very justice you've administered as Marshall. So please, do *not* tell me that now you're suddenly developing a *conscience* about them and refusing *me* in the process," Horn said, indignant.

"Refusing you? No, Horn. Not you...it's what you've become."

"Whatever it is, it's royally *pissing* me off, darling... Either you're *mine* tonight, or I'll make your career as barren as that sandy Sahara, above us!" Horn threatened.

"Suit yourself," Dariah countered.

"*Try* me. I just might."

"Horn, does the word *despicable* have any meaning in your vocabulary?"

"Does the word *pleasurable* have any in yours?"

"Goodbye, Horn," she uttered in disdain. "Maybe you know what *that* means."

"*Fine*, Misha. *Go ahead!*" Horn said irately, as Dariah left him and headed with determination toward her quarters.

Nervously, Horn tossed back the rest of his drink and tried to deliver the last, angry word, hollering at the top of his lungs, "But know this, darling. This is the *last* time you turn me down! When I reign supreme in Allianz, you'll come crawling back to me, begging for me to restore our, our...whatever the hell this is!"

To this Dariah responded, yelling out from down the opulent grand corridor, "Remember, Adammus, *darling*. It's personal...not business."

"Uh...I think you mean, business, not...Ahh! *Forget you!*" He bellowed, violently throwing his empty glass against the hallway wall, pulverizing it as it shattered into a thousand tiny shards of glass, the count of his accumulated frustrations and disillusionments with Dariah. Still, he conceded, thinking, *You've got to love a woman who won't allow herself to be easily conquered or deciphered...* Goodbye, Misha," Horn uttered to himself. "One of these days...."

Sixty-Four

"The One Sent"

Early the next morning, the Red Monastery was abuzz with everyone expectantly waiting for the great gathering to begin. Slowly, families began to trickle into the bucolic monastery's main chapel. Before long, there was a sustained stream of people, and the momentum built steadily until the normally idyllic chapel ambiance was a hustling and bustling stage for a festive encounter of nations, with standing room only. Familiar melodies spontaneously filled the air, as different language groups took turns singing verses of well known hymns and choruses of the faith; precious snippets of a bygone era, now being briefly but intensely relived in an unlikely, isolated mountaintop location. Even the rarely vocal resident Slovak nuns and monks enthusiastically joined in as best they could on the multilingual all-sing.

As we continued in our joyful noise-making unto the Lord, we must have heard singing in scores of tongues: Bahasa Indonesia, Chinese, Korean, Farsi, Arabic, Turkish, Maltese, Slovak, German, Afrikaans, Bantu, Sudanese, French, Portuguese, Spanish, English, and even Inuit and Mayan, among countless other languages. A dear old friend of mine, a Brazilian pastor who baptized me into the faith as an adult, used to call such multi-ethnic services in his church, "Heavenly Sounds," for he imagined this type of scene to be a common and frequent occurrence around the glorious throne of the Almighty. In a way, he was quite right.

The Dreamers of Allianz

Time seemed to stand still for us, as we joined our voices in corporate praise. We hardly noticed that a couple of hours had passed, so enthralling was the whole experience for the jubilant crowd. Even the youngest among us eventually found ways to entertain themselves, as they played peacefully together, up and down the lateral corridors of the chapel, somehow managing to communicate well amongst themselves, as children had always been able to do in their own special way. In that place and time, filled with the presence of The Name, His people celebrated that which He had done for us, which enabled us to come together. For as the Word of Truth clearly proclaimed, The Name so loved the world that he gave His one and only Son, that whoever believes in Him shall not perish but have eternal life. Amen.

Suddenly, still in mid jubilee, we heard the distant sound of a bell coming from outside the chapel.

"*Eles estão vindo!* They are coming!" a young sister in the back euphorically cried out in her native Portuguese, as she looked outside and saw a small procession headed toward the chapel.

The tolling of the bell grew louder, as the single line of robed men drew nearer to the chapel. Following the hand bell-ringer at the front of the slow moving procession, were the twelve old scribes, identifiable only by their long, white beards hanging beneath the hooded ceremonial scapulars they wore. Finally, walking behind the scribes and in front of the last monk in line, there was a dark, grey-haired man. He wore what appeared to be a long, white, knee-length shirt, which covered most of his white trousers. Draped over his shoulder and arms, and coming to a point in both the front and back, well below the waist, he wore a white, cotton-knitted, poncho-like covering, traditionally worn by Ethiopian men. He was "The One Sent," and he was finally appearing before the entire group of families he had been divinely commissioned to assemble together at the Red Monastery.

Entering the chapel, the procession moved to the front, where the twelve scribes took their seats behind the altar. There was now complete silence in the chapel, punctuated only by the intermittent, resonant sounding of the hand bell. Finally, the Ethiopian man stood before the congregation and began to speak in Ethiopian. Though the words out of his mouth were foreign to us, through the Spirit they were intelligible to everyone who heard them. It was as if we were partakers in a wondrous moment, straight out of the pages of the Pentecost account.

"My dear brothers and sisters, the peace of The Name be with you," he said, as he addressed the assembly. He smiled brightly and introduced himself, "My name is Elias-Negash. You have known of me only as 'The One Sent,' but now that I have nearly accomplished my mission to bring you out of the world and into this sacred assembly, I am elated to finally meet you as your friend, and I now greet you in The Name and in the blessings of our Lord, the Anointed One, and through the Spirit of Truth, who indwells us." He then continued, "I am a humble servant of our Lord, from the ancient land of Ethiopia, where for decades I have been a pastor and evangelist, chosen and ordained by The Name to declare the *Evangel* and to make disciples among my people until, in the fullness of time, He equipped and beckoned me to endeavor this great gathering, for the glory of His Name."

Following Elias-Negash's introductory speech, we entered into a time of corporate prayer, petitioning the Lord for His constant, impenetrable panoply of protection over us, and that, once reunified, His Word would go out again into the world with great power, so that many would believe unto Spirit-sealing.

"For even now, Allianz presses down hard on the Community of Brethren throughout the entire world," Elias-Negash prayed, "and spiritual darkness consumes the hearts of men."

He then shared from memory a portion of Scripture that I vaguely recognized as being from 2 Corinthians:

"The god of this age has blinded the minds of unbelievers, so that they cannot see the light of the gospel of the glory of the Anointed One, who is the image of The Name. For we do not preach ourselves, but the Anointed One as Lord, and ourselves as your servants for His sake. For The Name, Who said, 'Let light shine out of darkness,' made his light shine in our hearts to give us the light of knowledge of the glory of The Name in the face of the Anointed One. But we have this treasure in jars of clay to show that this all-surpassing power is from Him and not from us. We are hard pressed on every side, but not crushed. Perplexed, but not in despair. Persecuted but not abandoned. Struck down, but not destroyed. We always carry around in our body the death of the Anointed One, so that his life may also be revealed in our body. For we who are alive are always being given over to death for his sake, so that his life may be revealed in our mortal body... All this is for your benefit, so that the grace that is reaching more and more people may cause thanksgiving to overflow to the glory of The Name... For our light and momentary troubles are achieving for us an eternal glory that far outweighs them all. So we fix our eyes on what is unseen. For what is seen is temporary, but what is unseen is eternal. Amen."

Elias-Negash then proceeded to consecrate the bread and the cup, and we all communed together at the Lord's Table. If at any moment I felt the Lord's pleasure and anointing over us, it was then, as we followed in the holiest of church ordinances, in remembrance of him who died for us, that we might have life. Then, as a final corporate gesture that would again serve to identify us as a community of saints, Elias-Negash prompted us to join our hands and our voices as we prayed in the model the Lord taught, together and in all the different languages there represented. That was indeed a most fitting collective action moment, which to me transcended both prayer and symbol to somehow morph into a determined battle cry for the Resistance.

"...For Thine is the Kingdom, the power, and the glory, forever and ever, Amen," we all proclaimed, as a great and thunderous applause broke out inside that centuries-old place of worship.

At the closing of our service, Elias-Negash transitioned into a time of instruction for the eager audience, as he laid out the specifics of the process the Spirit dreamers would follow, later that afternoon. They would soon participate in the long awaited reintegration of the Word of Truth, under the watchful and meticulous care of the twelve scribes. He explained how each youth or child, in the order prescribed by the ancient scribes, would take their place inside the *Verbum Dei* Chamber, a booth-like device that would capture and record both the voice and brainwave activity of each Spirit dreamer, as he or she slept and uttered the words from each canonical book. By using this incredible tool of divine providence, the entire process, from Genesis to Revelation, was expected to take about forty days. Most intriguing, however, was the fact that this particular machine, whose origin and construction were not of human but rather of angelic making, would be able to produce a version of the Scriptures in the Allianzi language, as well.

Quite clearly, we all felt we were in for an adventure of biblical significance. What none of us expected, however, in the midst of all the anticipation and unbridled excitement, was the impending devastation that was to come upon that locale.

Sixty-Five

Allianz Unleashed

On a Federation plane routed to D.C. by way of Damascus, Dariah sat alone. She had hoped to be able to experience significant relief, finally being free from Horn's vexing, caustic presence. Yet, to her chagrin, relief wholly eluded her. She still found herself struggling, unable to overcome primal emotions of raw hatred and disgust for the very person for whom she had once felt a consuming passion. Somewhere in her heart she still desired to keep set apart the old Adammus from the one she now knew. For by now, her contempt for Horn had intensified to its highest level, and she felt she could no longer personally stomach his insincerity, his arrogance, his self-exultation, or his condescension. And to top things off, she would soon have to reach down deep inside to generate enough patience and strength to suffer the High Sage Andrus as a traveling companion all the way to their final destination, several long and no doubt mystically-filled hours away. She wondered how her nerves would be able to sustain yet another insufferably entitled personality.

Dariah knew she had to find a way to measure her devotion to the system against her personal struggles with high-powered Allianz players. If she did not still believe whole-heartedly in the system, she desperately wanted to. Allianz had fashioned her into a highly educated, superbly trained Federation officer of the highest caliber. Allianz allowed her to escape her humble, immigrant family beginnings in San Francisco. On that account, she had long ago resolved in her mind to serve Allianz with deep devotion. Perhaps that was why she was able to feel justified in delivering her newest and most thoroughly devastating blow to the American Resistance. A couple of hours before she boarded the plane out of Tunis, she had given direct orders to her subordinates in D.C. to engage in a dramatic, province-wide repressive operation that would effectively wipe out the Resistance's ability to operate. In a bold and unprecedented move, she also authorized the use of overt, lethal force, as conditions necessitated.

"I'm sorry, Mr. Christensen, if by any chance you're still out there," she uttered to herself, in heavy-hearted contemplation.

While it was afternoon in Europe and North Africa, it was early morning in the American Province, and the brightness of the new day was eerily darkened by the sinister shadow of evil now blanketing the utterly dismayed members of the American Resistance. A full, frontal assault against the Community of Brethren was underway in every region of the province, but especially in the South and Southeast.

In West Tennessee, John and Shen-il Waters held each other, as they watched in horror and distress the gruesome scenes on their televisor; scenes of violent destruction perpetrated against their community by the hands of cog forces, under Dariah's maleficent orders. Somewhere in the distance, but probably not too far off from their own neighborhood, the Waters could hear the screeching sounds of cog transport sirens, bringing right into their home and into their hearts the real vulnerability of their situation at that moment.

"John, I'm so afraid," Shen-il wept.

"Fear not, He said," John replied. "Remember, Shen-il. 'Though I walk through the valley of the shadow of death, I will fear no evil, for You are with me. Your rod and your staff, they comfort me.' Hold tight to that promise, like you're holding on to me right now. He's here with us, though the hour is dark."

"But what do we do, John?"

"We'll remain at home…and wait."

"What about all the others? Should we not be with them right now? All of us, together?" Shen-il asked.

"At this time, the sheep stand a better chance for survival just being scattered…"

For the first time ever, Believers throughout the American Province literally began to look up for a sign in the sky that the time had come for their presence on the earth to be withdrawn.

Sixty-Six

Reunification Interrupted

Upon his arrival from North Africa, Adammus Horn wasted no time following through with his plans to annihilate the Resistance stronghold in Slovakia Province. From his command center in the Allianz Palace, he prepared to orchestrate the most devastatingly incisive and concerted attack ever to be carried out against the worldwide Community of Brethren. Before long, all elements of his diabolical plan were in place. At 16:00 hours, Paris time, the operation commenced. Guided by CyberSat, a squadron of unmanned Federation jet fighters and a bomber aircraft departed from a strategically selected air base in Frankfurt, Germany Province. The squadron was scheduled to reach the skies over the Red Monastery, their intended target, in exactly 28 minutes.

Meanwhile, in the Slovak mountains, the first child was being put into the *Verbum Dei* Chamber, which was located in a rarely seen room inside the Red Monastery compound. Her name was Helena, she was from Brazil Province, and she was only eight. With her family present, she was about to make history, as she proudly and courageously took her turn as the initial dreamer, in a long line of youth and children, appointed to participate in the momentous Word reunification process. Within minutes she was fast asleep inside the chamber. The twelve ancient scribes formed a circle as they sat around the device. They displayed uncharacteristic enthusiasm, brought on chirpily after centuries of patient waiting. Everyone present in the room listened for the divine utterances to begin. I was there also and found myself fighting back my own myriad of sentiments – awe, elation, relief, and liberation.

A few more short minutes elapsed. Suddenly, the words from the book of Genesis began to flow out from the young Brazilian girl's mouth:

"No começo Deus criou os céus e a terra...[In the beginning God created the heavens and the earth...]." Helena's words, though in a foreign tongue, were understood by all.

At that moment, Elias-Negash fell prostrated with his face down on the stone floor and worshiped The Name, gently sobbing and quietly praying in heartfelt thanksgiving. All of a sudden, it was as if the words from the Scriptural book of Ezekiel were breathed into his own consciousness: *And I will sanctify My great name, which has been profaned among the nations, which you have profaned in their midst; and the nations shall know that I am God...when I am hallowed in you before their eyes.* Elias-Negash then realized in great awe that, in reunifying His Word, The Name was also reclaiming His own name, "God," in His Church, and in the world. The Ethiopian's mission was now almost completed.

For several more minutes, little Helena continued in her native Portuguese dream oration.

"...'You will not surely die,' the serpent said to the woman. 'For God knows that when you eat it your eyes will be opened, and you will be like God, knowing good and evil.' When the woman saw that the fruit of the tree was good for food and pleasing to the eye, and also desirable for gaining wisdom, she took some and ate it. She also gave it to her husband, who was with her, and he ate it..."

All at once, an alarm sounded. It seemed to be coming from somewhere outdoors. In fact, it was a radar alarm, being emitted by both morph-ships, which had been brought under the covering of a rudimentary, makeshift hanger. Intuitively, I knew this was not a good sign. In fact, for the first time in a long while, I was struck by a kind of fear that one only feels in the presence of true evil. The scribes, now agitated and throwing their hands up in the air, looked around perturbed, signaling that the disturbance was severely hindering the Word reunification process.

"Dr. C," Elias-Negash called out to me in broken English, snapping me out of my fright-induced paralysis. "What is happen?"

"I will check on it right away, Negash" I responded. Rushing outside and toward the hanger, I saw Christensen running toward me.

"Sensei! Is something wrong?" he yelled out.

"Yes. Follow me!" I told him.

Entering *The Weber*, I immediately accessed the radar screen, the alarm still sounding. My worse fears were confirmed. Scores of enemy warplanes were heading toward us. They would reach us in a matter of five minutes tops.

"Oh Lord!" Christensen exclaimed. "We've got to warn everyone!"

"Tanner-san," I said, "I will go up in *The Weber*. I've got to buy us some time until everyone has gone underground."

"Underground? You mean…"

"Yes…the Global Exodus is upon us." I then instructed him, "Now, you go and alert Elias-Negash immediately. He'll know exactly what to do."

"Sensei. I can fly this thing. Why don't you let *me* go up, instead?" he pleaded.

"First, do what I ask you, son," I told him. "Then, come back and take *The Redemption*. We'll make contact when your morphship's in the air."

"Yes, sir."

Sixty-Seven

Out of Damascus

In Damascus, Andrus and a small entourage of Transcienz Sages had just come onboard the Federation's plane. Andrus was led directly to the sumptuous private compartment reserved for the highest Allianz dignitaries, where Dariah was sojourning.

"Please join me, Your Transcendence," Dariah invited him.

"You're invitation is very kind, indeed, Marshall Dariah," replied Andrus.

"I think you will find that you will lack nothing here. We are truly traveling in style," she said, trying to make light conversation.

"I have no qualms with luxury," he said. "I find that it only enhances the senses. Would you care to join me in some wine, Marshall?"

"No, thank you, Your Transcendence. But, please, be my guest."

"Lovely."

"This is most likely a very brief stop. The extended layover was cancelled, since we're under a severe weather alert. We'll be in the air shortly," she told him.

"Very well," Andrus replied, as he poured the wine, quite obviously overfilling his goblet.

Then, with his hand trembling a bit, he brought the crystal chalice up to his lips, spilling the red liquid around his mouth and all over his purple gown.

"Oh, look. Clumsy me," he uttered.

"Let me help you with that," Dariah said, walking over to the banquet spread and fetching a cloth napkin to hand to Andrus. "You look nervous, Your Transcendence."

"You've noticed… Yes, well…I do prefer to have both my feet on the ground, if you know what I mean," he said.

"U-hum," Dariah acknowledged, secretly chuckling inside from hearing so great an irony coming from the consummate mystic. *Feet on the ground? Please!* she thought to herself.

"But I'll be fine, Marshall. I've got my pills with me," said Andrus. "I'm much better off sleeping through these unpleasant disturbances."

Sixty-Eight

The Red Monastery Attacked

At the Red Monastery, panic was in the air. While I lifted off inside *The Weber* to try and intercept the Federation's warplanes, Christensen worked valiantly to mobilize the entire group of families and monastery residents. Finding his own family and Alyssa, Christensen explained that he would need to fly the morph-ship in order to help protect them. Claire and the girls begged him not to leave, but to no avail. Zeke implored to go up with his father.

"No. You need each other. Stay together. Be strong for each other…and for me. And pray that we'll be together again soon. I love you all," he said. He then hugged each of them goodbye and departed hastily toward the morph-ship.

Meanwhile, Elias-Negash was leading the ancient scribes and multitudes of families through the compound and toward the concealed access way down to their subterranean escape route. Leaving everything behind, including the *Verbum Dei* Chamber, they would, if successful, travel slowly on foot for two days, through underground passageways, until reaching a cavern sanctuary, located nearly two miles beneath the earth's surface.

Once in the air, Christensen and I made contact.

"Tanner-san," I said, "my instruments indicate that these aircraft are auto-piloted by CyberSat. We've got an advantage over them. We will be able to see them, but neither they nor CyberSat can see us. Our morph-ships are fully cloaked."

"Copy that."

"Now listen. I want you to activate the ballistic program on the morph-ship. It engages by jointly sliding all the way forward the red and gold levers, to your right. You'll then see the firing buttons light up and activate right away on your control handle."

"Done... Yes, I see them," Christensen confirmed.

"Good...cause here they come," I announced.

"Wow," Christensen uttered, audibly disheartened, as the enemy squadron came within sight. "There are so many of them..."

"Remember," I told him, "we've got to deter them and buy ourselves some time. Take out the closest ones first. And may The Name...Our God...be with us."

The aerial confrontation began dramatically, with both morph-ships firing missiles directly at the first line of incoming Federation aircraft. About a dozen frontline jet fighters exploded in mid air, resulting in a spectacular, fiery display. A new wave of enemy aircraft immediately followed, this time firing away at whatever their invisible menace happened to be. Christensen and I maneuvered our morph-ships expertly, eluding their threat, while effectuating the greatest possible amount of damage to the sizeable Allianz squadron. Yet, we had to be parsimonious with our weapons use, knowing we would need reserves for our principal target, the powerful bomber.

Soon, our sights were set on the massive and well-armed bomber airplane, which intrepidly advanced toward the Red Monastery's location. But to our extreme vexation, we witnessed the swift formation of a complete, defensive curtain around the bomber, comprised of a large number of jet fighter escorts. That protective layer now stood between our target and us, as we tried but failed to lock our dwindling arsenal of ballistic projectiles onto the bomber.

We had no time for a well thought out and orchestrated assault plan. The Red Monastery was in great peril, as it would not withstand its imminent bombardment. My instincts then kicked in.

"Tanner-san, remember your *randori* principles in Aikido," I alerted Christensen, referring to the multiple-man attack drills we conducted in our training. "Position your morph-ship such that you're angled the long way relative to your intended targets, visually establishing a line of planes, one flying behind another, from where you are. Then fire away at the first one in that line. We want to generate a sort of 'domino effect,' as you hit and blow up more than one jet fighter at a time. Hopefully, that will give me the opening I require to lock onto the mammoth bomber and destroy it."

"Got it, Sensei! Here I go."

With few seconds to spare before the squadron reached bomb-deploying range, Christensen managed to create the opening I needed, and I concentrated almost all of the firepower I had left in my morph-ship to take out the bomber airplane. I had time for only one clear shot at it. I had to perform impeccably. I desperately depended on God's availing grace.

"Yes, Sensei! You did it!"

"Good work, Tanner-san. Praise the Lord! It's not all done, yet. We've still got plenty of trouble up here. Don't lose your focus."

We marveled as we watched the condemned bomber fall, at it was sent hurling down through the air, until it crashed against a nearby mountain range.

The counter-attack continued for several more minutes, until most enemy aircraft had been disabled or destroyed. Our only hope was that our air campaign would afford our friends on the ground the time they needed to safely escape. But, unfortunately, our sense of time was impaired by the pressing situation at hand, and we could only guess at what might be happening down below.

At the Allianz Palace, in Paris, Horn was immediately updated on the strange and absolutely unexpected situation. An Allianz General informed him, "Mr. Prosecutor General, we are incurring heavy aircraft losses."

"What? Why is this happening, General? Where is it coming from?" Horn demanded an explanation.

"Sir, we're unable to detect the source of these defenses. We're basically shooting at ghosts out there, trying to defend ourselves in the air," answered the high cog officer.

"What about CyberSat-enabled detection?"

"Negative, sir. CyberSat cannot pinpoint the source of the counter-attack, either."

"Then release the bombs and get it over with...now!" Horn ordered.

"Unfortunately, sir, our bomber aircraft has been shot down."

"This is preposterous!" he yelled out, pounding his fist on the table in front of him. "I'll handle it!" he said, as he stormed out of the room, leaving the cog General baffled.

Now in his private office, Horn quickly accessed CyberSat through his PSS. Within seconds, he had generated a close up, visual confirmation of the exact Resistance hideout location, positively identifying his target. Then, a hauntingly dreadful thing unfolded. Horn proceeded to close his eyes. Suddenly, he inhaled forcefully. Slowly, then, he exhaled. His entire body began to shake profusely, as if experiencing an extreme seizure of some kind. Hunching over slightly, his eyes rolled up into their sockets. Horn then reopened his eyes, revealing only the whiteness of his ocular orbs. His face turned a vivid red and became strangely disfigured, barely recognizable. White knuckled, as both of his hands balled into a fist, Horn began to murmur something that sounded like an ancient incantation. He then applied pressure to his forehead, deeply stroking his Cognit Implant with both hands, partly covering his devilish-looking face.

In an instant, a bright beam of green light was projected through space, originating from CyberSat and aimed directly onto the site of the Red Monastery. Suddenly, there was a massive explosion, which ultimately leveled the entire compound. Absolutely nothing could have withstood such a powerful, formidable blast.

Still in the air, both Christensen and I veered our morph-ships directly back toward the source of the explosion, to our horrified reactions.

"No!" Christensen cried out, seeing the expansive, mushrooming cloud of fire and smoke rising straight out of the ground, right above the monastery compound.

"Tanner-san, we've got to get out of here!" I told him over our communicator.

"Sensei...the monastery!"

"It's gone, Tanner-san! Everything's gone, now!" I cried out. Then I said, "I fear the *Verbum Dei* Chamber has been totally destroyed! It's a catastrophe! Just pray that everyone has made it out safely!"

"What now, Sensei?"

"Follow me!" I instructed him.

Within seconds, our two morph-ships had made a sharp turn. Transitioning into marine mode, we took a nose-dive into a nearby lake.

A short time later, Horn sat alone in his darkened office. Now back to his normal self, he reflected on the bizarre and surprising events that had transpired over Slovakian skies. What was left of the Allianz warplanes had been ordered back to their base. Although the reasons behind the almost complete destruction of the Federation's squadron were still obscure to him, Horn was nonetheless pleased with the final outcome of the operation against the Resistance. He had succeeded in thwarting the dangerous, clandestine operation Andrus had so fervently warned him against. In a self-congratulating tone, the Prosecutor General contacted his top officers, inviting a select few to a triumphal gathering at his mansion, later that evening. Horn knew he had achieved a great and possibly final victory over the Resistance, that afternoon. Furthermore, the reports on anti-Resistance operations, coming to him out of the American Province, were also greatly satisfying. Dariah had actually delivered as she had promised, and that was reason enough for him to convince himself to excuse her recent faltering resolve as Marshall and Commander, as well as her graceless coldness toward him as the beautiful Misha.

Sixty-Nine

Going Underground

Sometime later, Christensen and I arrived at an underground clearing and rested our morph-ships there. We had managed to access it aquatically by following a network of underground lakes, finally emerging inside a large cavern. I calculated that within an hour or so the first pilgrims from the Red Monastery might reach that location, if they had managed to escape unharmed. The cavern had been specifically mapped out to provide the first freshwater respite along the tortuous journey to the sanctuary, deep beneath the surface of the earth.

We had received no news from Elias-Negash or anyone else since the mass exodus, and we anxiously awaited contact with them. Were there casualties from the enormous explosion? Had the dreamers survived? Was anyone badly hurt? What about the scribes? Would they be able to endure the long trek on foot? Christensen's thoughts and prayers were especially with his loved ones. We both sat down by the calm cavern waters. Christensen looked downcast, and despair began to overtake him.

"What if we failed everyone? What if this was all for nothing?" he lamented. "What if they all perished? Claire? The kids? Everyone else?" He needed answers, and my silence only increased his agony. "How can you just sit there so calmly?" he challenged me.

"Tanner-san, I understand your anguish," I tried to console him. "Don't mistake my silence for a lack of concern. I am greatly troubled, as well, but…"

The Dreamers of Allianz

"But you don't understand... Everything I love in this world I left back in that monastery! Why did this have to happen? They did nothing wrong! How could The Name allow this tragedy? We came so close!" Christensen struggled to the point of tears, as the rugged cavern walls loudly echoed his grief.

"Tanner-san... You've been at this almost as long as I have. We must never forget that God's ways are higher than ours. Keep your center, son...or your imbalance will lead you to shipwreck your faith. Don't give up just yet," I exhorted him.

"But...what if this is the end of man?" Christensen asked, still discouraged.

"The end of man?" I questioned him. "The end of man is to end in God. Everything else is simply process. I urge you, my son, stand firm. We'll get there."

"But we saw it with our own eyes! The explosion..."

"Tanner-san, this was not an unexpected development," I told him. "When we first arrived at the Red Monastery, I met with Elias-Negash and the scribes, and we discussed this eventuality at length. We knew things could go wrong, and that Allianz had everything to gain from preventing the Word reunification process."

"But even if the dreamers and the others miraculously escaped that blast, how can we possibly go on with the work of the Resistance under this kind of repression?" Christensen asked.

"We'll start over."

"Do you have any strategy, at this point?"

"No...more like a tactic," I answered.

"What's the difference?"

"A strategy involves a pre-established, well laid out plan, going from A to B to C. That, I regret to say, we don't have. But a tactic, on the other hand, means having a primary goal in mind, and being willing to account for flexibility in redirecting our efforts as we meet challenges along the way, in order to reach the intended goal."

"So, what's your tactic?" he asked.

"It will take time...perhaps even years. But we can achieve the same results without the *Verbum Dei* Chamber...assuming we still have the dreamers, the scribes, and hopefully all the others. The scribes will copy the Scriptures by hand, as book by book the dreamers relate them. It's our only hope, now. Meanwhile, the Community of Brethren will 'disappear' in underground sanctuaries all over Creation. Once there, we will undergo training, to be able to go out again and re-sow the Word into world, when the appointed time comes."

"When will this happen globally?" Christensen asked me.

"Soon. If all goes well, and I pray that it does, we should be seeing the first signs of the monastery refugees in a matter of minutes. Then, you and I will leave here in the morph-ships and will make a sign in the heavens that will announce the Global Exodus to the worldwide community of Believers. I have a distinct feeling that they are already looking up for the sign to be given, for darkness is truly overtaking the world."

Minutes later, the echo of voices began to reverberate through the cavern. They were coming. They were almost there. Slowly, and in separate groups, the Red Monastery refugees began to arrive. Finally, after several gut-wrenching moments, Christensen's family appeared out of the dark tunnel leading to the underground clearing. Spotting their father, the Christensen children ran to him, as Claire watched gladly and in profound relief.

"Kids, Alyssa, you're all right! And here comes Mom!" he exclaimed.

"We're fine, Dad. Mom's a bit frazzled, but she's okay," said Bethany.

"Yeah, and best of all," said Holly, "everyone in the monastery got out safely."

"That's incredible!" Christensen cried out. "Thank you…God."

"Dad," Zeke said, "the *Verbum Dei* machine…it's gone!"

"I know, son. Everything will be all right."

Within minutes, we were all gathered together again. The scribes sat down to rest by the water. Elias-Negash then addressed the crowd, again in Ethiopian.

"My brothers and sisters… All over the world, the People of God will be retreating, as we're doing, into the safe covering of underground sanctuaries for a lengthy time of physical and spiritual preparation." Once again, through the help of the Spirit of Truth, we were all able to understand his Ethiopian language. "The

Global Exodus is commencing, and though it will take time, we will achieve our mission to fully reintegrate the Holy Scriptures, which were robbed from us and from the world by Allianz. I pray that God will superintend all aspects of our lives, as we labor for Him and for His ultimate glory. His hand of protection is over us all." He then puzzled us, as he announced, "You will go on from here without me. I will leave you for a time, for there is one more I must bring in before my mission is complete. May He bless all of us, as we seek Him each day, throughout the trying times to come."

Elias-Negash then sought Christensen and I to delineate the plan for the universal signaling of the Global Exodus. Our time of respite, basking in the glory of the deliverance we all witnessed, was all too brief. Once again, we said goodbye to our friends and loved ones and departed, Christensen and I in *The Weber*, and Elias-Negash alone in *The Redemption*.

Epilogue

Dariah's Conversion

Now en route to the American Province from Damascus, Dariah and Andrus sat across from each other. CyberSat had predicted unusually strong, weather-related turbulence, and throughout the aircraft the *"Fasten Seatbelt"* sign had been flashed. Andrus was sweating copiously in dread of the airborne mayhem he anticipated.

"Are you all right, Your Transcendence?" Dariah asked, noticing how nervous and worried Andrus appeared.

"I'll be fine, Marshall, thank you…as soon as I take my pills," he replied, busily searching in his handbag for his medicine case.

Within minutes the airplane had entered a gigantic, high altitude weather system, and was shaken fiercely amid the thick, dark clouds. As a Marshall, Dariah had traveled extensively by air over the past decade and was used to occasional bouts of severe turbulence. Yet even she admitted that this particular disturbance seemed abnormally violent.

"This is a bit rough…even for me, Your Transcendence," she said.

"Can anybody do anything about it?"

"Hardly," she replied. "We're in an auto-piloted aircraft. Unless CyberSat reroutes us, which does happen from time to time, we're in for an exciting ride."

"Marshall…I suppose you find it odd that a spiritual man, like myself, and leader of a global metaphysical path at that, would be troubled with such fears…" Andrus commented.

"The thought did cross my mind," she said, "but I suppose you're only human."

"And mortal..." he added.

"Of course... I'll tell you what, Your Transcendence. I will contact D.C. to see if there's something that can be done to get us out of this uncomfortable, unsteady route," she proposed.

"That would be most kind and considerate of you, Marshall Dariah," Andrus responded, now feeling very nervous indeed.

As Dariah operated her PSS, trying to reach D.C., a major shake up hit the aircraft. It repeatedly bounced up and down, losing and then gaining back altitude in a disorienting manner, which caused the lights to flicker intensely.

"Wow, this *is* getting bad..." she uttered, while Andrus let out shrieks of terror.

The vibrations and the noises from the slightly twisting fuselage increased, and the plane rolled sideways and then back under the pressure and force of the air mass dislocations. It was an ongoing, harrowing ordeal, and both Dariah and Andrus wished they had not gotten on their flight. Feeling convinced that their aircraft was in serious trouble, Dariah frantically operated her PSS, but without success.

Suddenly, a bright flash, like that of a close-up lightening bolt, lit up the cabin. Dariah then saw a ball of white fire roll down the length of her cabin compartment. Instantly, all power was lost. As the emergency lighting came on, Dariah dropped her PSS and hung on to her seat with all she had. By now, Andrus was already under the sedating effects of his drugs, and his body flopped about in his seat. In one final, dreadful jolt, the airplane's fuselage was breached, and everything began to fly, as oxygen masks were dropped down throughout the plane.

Eyes closed, Dariah screamed, "help!" Suddenly, she felt herself gasping for air. The airplane was now splitting in half, throwing everything and everyone in it into a terrifying freefall.

Dariah, still attached to her seat, was sent plummeting down. But then, everything stopped. *Am I dead?* she wondered. Opening her eyes, she could see nothing but the purest, softest whiteness, and she floated freely in uncommon peace, as if she had entered a different dimension. *Maybe I am dead*, she thought.

Suddenly, there appeared before her a blindingly bright light, and she heard a voice, calling her name.

"Misha," the voice said, although she was not at all certain she had actually heard it, except in her own head.

Yes? she replied in her own mind.

"I Am the Lord, Who speaks to your spirit... I know your works, and they are detestable to Me. You've seen the evil that inhabits the earth and destroys My people and My living legacy. Why do you serve it?"

How can I fight it? she replied, still in thought.

"Come into the light."

If I leave, Horn will have me killed, she rationalized.

"You are already dead. But I will give you new life, a new name, and a heart to serve only Me."

Yes, Lord. But what must I do? she asked in her mind's voice.

"In time, it will be revealed to you. But know this, Horn's ambitions are even greater than attaining absolute power. He will be possessed to subjugate all of humanity under the weight of evil devastation. In hatred against Me, the evil one, who controls Horn, seeks retribution against humans. Humans are My highest creation, even above the angels themselves. Therefore, by oppressing humanity he shakes his fist in the face of I Am. But his days are numbered and his punishment already prepared. Although My image is upon Horn, his father is the Enemy, and his mother, Great Rebellion."

I understand, Dariah replied.

"Now, go. And serve Me alone."

I will, Lord.

As these last words still lingered, echoing inside her head, she woke up, shocked and surprised to find that she was back in the same aircraft she had witnessed being destroyed in the storm. But instead of turbulence, there was now a quiet calm in the air. The storm had passed, at least for the moment. Dariah refocused her gaze and saw Andrus, who was passed out before her, still buckled in his own seat. His head was drooped to one side, and he snored loudly, with drool running down the left side of his mouth; a rather undignified image for so high and exalted a Transcienz guru. Dariah wondered, *Was I hallucinating?*

The Dreamers of Allianz

Upon arrival in D.C., Dariah left Andrus behind and ordered an individual transport for herself. Highly concerned, her aids pleaded with her against such an unusual and risky decision. She then drove herself directly to the White House, despite continued pleas by her staff, who profusely admonished her about the sudden and peculiar color change in the atmosphere. The sky had mysteriously turned a resplendent shade of red, covering the early evening moon like blood.

That evening, Dariah felt strangely compelled to seek out the Believers she knew. The Christensens immediately came to mind, though she feared for the fate of Tanner Christensen and his family when she thought of her own cog forces' overwhelming attack on the Resistance.

Later that night, after wrestling with these confounding emotions, Dariah informed her staff that she was taking a personal leave; some time off to go be by herself. Refusing security detail, Dariah flew her own private transport back to West Tennessee, in search of members of the Children of the Promise group. Though it was quite late, she searched for them in every place she could think of. She went to the Christensens' home, to the charred remains of their gathering place, and to the Waters' residence. When no one could be found, Dariah concluded that they were gone, all of them. Strangely, it appeared that the Believers had completely vanished from the face of the planet. But where had they disappeared to? And why was the night sky still bizarrely tinted with red?

At 4 a.m. the next morning, Dariah checked in at a local hotel under a name not her own. Lying in that strange bed, she felt completely alone, like the only person left on the face of the earth. As she fell asleep, she received another divine visitation, and things finally began to come together in her confused mind. Still, it was all so surreal, and by now she questioned her own sanity.

Late the next morning, the American Marshall flew off to California, back to her roots. Over and over again, intense anguish overtook her, and she desperately craved relief. When evening fell, she stood on the Headlands, in Marin County, overlooking the magnificent Golden Gate Bridge. The glistening downtown lights of San Francisco appeared not far behind it. They were illuminant reminders of the life, the glory, the world she was leaving behind. Dense fog was beginning to roll in from the open seas. Below her feet, the high, steep cliffs descended far down to the entrance of the bay. She knew that to plummet from that height would mean certain death. The end had come for Marshall and Commander Misha Dariah. She closed her eyes, squeezing out tears. The gusting evening breeze felt cool on her wet face, and she lingered there, hoping for courage to go forward. Then, as she took a deep breath, she suddenly heard a voice behind her gently say, in a strange yet understandable tongue:

"Petra... Are you ready?"

"I am," she replied, acknowledging her new name and surprising herself with her sudden, calm certainty and complete abandon.

Taking the unknown man's dark hand, she climbed into the low-hovering morph-ship. The ship's inscription was partially obfuscated in the softly glowing lights. Lifting off, *The Redemption* contoured the sides of the Headlands' cliffs and then flew downward in the direction of the city lights, passing under the luminous, orange bridge, now almost fully immersed in the increasingly dense, white fog. Then, turning sharply upward, the morph-ship flew over the bridge in the space between its towering supports and headed out to sea. Clearing past the foggy bay, it dove down and plunged into the dark ocean, its blue lights soon disappearing beneath the troubled Pacific waters.

Allianz Timeline

Midnight
GDM • The Great Digital Meltdown takes place.

GDM-1 • Beginning of Provisional Mandate year for the Allianz Government.
• Launching of the CyberSat network of satellites, under Project Red Dragon.
• The first specialized Cognit Forehead Implants are applied on an initial, elite cohort.
• A post-digital information and communication system, based on the PSS, is introduced.

GDM-2 • Installation of a permanent Allianz Federation government.
• Official approval of the Allianz Code.
• Worldwide "Imagine" campaign begins for universal conformity with the Allianz Code.
• Beginning of mass conversions to the Implant Protocol and the Cognit Bracelet system in commercial establishments.
• Commercialization of PSS information/communications platform.
• Worldwide apostasy sharply increases.
• Path of Transcienz is declared the official metaphysical path.
• Introduction of the Medallianz as the official monetary unit of exchange.

GDM-3
- Founding of the Worldwide Resistance movement.
- The Global Exodus plan is unveiled for the Resistance.

GDM-4
- Allianzi is declared the official world language.
- Religious and religion-affiliated institutions are ordered shut down.
- All broadcasting begins to be done in Allianzi.
- The medical establishment aggressively promotes newborn implants.
- Construction of the Resistance's Global Exodus infrastructure begins in earnest, with donations by wealthy Believers.

GDM-5
- Beginning of the cataclysmic cancerous plague.
- Climate-related destruction of paper-based products begins, including religious texts.

GDM-7
- Allianzi Language is declared the educational *Lingua Franca*.
- Medical treatments are readjusted to the new cell cyclosis patterns, due to Cognit Implant activation.
- Total Federation control of agriculture and food supply begins.

GDM-9
- *Les Invalides* II Program is instituted.

GDM-12
- Worldwide Federation crackdown of Resistance intensifies.
- The Great Catacombs Program is initiated.
- New wave of interactive CogniToys hits the market.

GDM-13
- Beginning of *Dreamers of Allianz* story plot.
- Zeke Christensen begins receiving Spirit dreams.
- Federation crackdown of Resistance intensifies in the American Province.
- Dozens of Believer families mysteriously vanish across the globe.

Cast of Main Characters

Claire Christensen – Claire is Tanner Christensen's wife and the mother of his three children. In her late 30s, Claire is a stay-at-home mom. Against the assimilationist policies of the Federation, she has been defiantly homeschooling her children. She also mentors many of the youth in the "Community of Brethren," and has had a strong influence on an implanted teenage neighbor girl named Alyssa.

Bethany Christensen – As the middle child and eldest Christensen daughter, Bethany is 14-years old and has already been playing an important part in youth mobilizations for the Resistance in the South, the Children of the Promise. She is gifted with a beautiful singing voice and natural ability to witness to other youth. Bethany befriends Alyssa, an implanted teen, who lives in their neighborhood.

Holly Christensen – At nine-years old, Holly is the youngest Christensen child. When she was born, the medical establishment had begun strongly pushing infant implantation, and her parents were nearly led to accept it. Holly is the family's little clown and brightens any room simply by entering it.

Tanner Christensen – Christensen, as he is referred to in the story, is the head of the Christensen family. He has three children with his wife, Claire. At 41, Christensen is a gifted "techy" and has a graduate degree from MIT. He has been working as an air traffic controller at the Memphis Inter-Provincial Airport. By night, however, he is also a leader and logistics tactician for the southern Resistance and helps coordinate local operations in that region. John "The Baptist" Waters is his closest friend. Christensen's relationship with his mentor, Dr. C, goes back to his college years, at Faith&Knowledge University, where Dr. C also served as Christensen's Aikido teacher, or Sensei.

Zeke Christensen – Zeke is the eldest of the three Christensen children. As a "regular" 16-year old, his main interests are sports, particularly soccer, which he's talented at. Zeke has also trained in Aikido with his dad. Recently, he's been a recipient of the Spirit dreams.

High Sage Andrus – A flamboyant and charismatic guru, Andrus is the recognized High Sage and world leader of the Path of Transcienz. He spends most of his time traveling and lecturing at Transcienz Halls around the world. When back in Paris, Andrus teaches in the Grand Hall of Transcienz, where his quarters are temporarily located, while the new and colossal headquarters in Rome are being built. Andrus is a trusted and influential adviser to Adammus Horn and the Allianz Federation's Council of Regents.

Arkadaş – An up-and-coming young leader among the Community of Brethren in the Province of Turkey, he was last seen being taken away by cogs, during a Federation blitz at a Brethren Gathering in Istanbul.

Dr. C – The story's narrator, Dr. Angelo Croce, is in his mid-to-late 60s, wears a clipped, white beard, and his trademark continues to be a skipper's beret worn backwards and a smoking pipe, though he rarely ever lights up anymore. A former sociology professor and spiritual mentor of Christensen's, Dr. C was also his Aikido master in college. They have kept in touch for years. However, since the closing of the denominational university where he once taught, his specific whereabouts have become unknown, as he moves around the world in concealment helping out the Resistance. He appears in person toward the end of this book and is instrumental in the Community of Brethren's move underground.

Marshall & Commander Misha Dariah – The top administrator and head of Cog operations in the American Province, Marshall and Commander Dariah has become increasingly aware of the Resistance in the South. At 36, she is highly astute and expertly trained in tactical operations. She believes in the system and exercises her authority with an iron-fist and nerves-of-steel in order to guarantee order and conformity with the Allianz Code. She is a former love-interest of Prosecutor General Adammus Horn. A former MIT graduate, she met Christensen when he was her T.A. at MIT.

Tomazo DiPaoli – Born in the former Italy, Tomazo DiPaoli is a valuable brother in the Resistance. A world-traveling, freelance photojournalist, he is a theologian and a former priest. On his left eye, he wears a black patch and uses his only good eye for his expert photography. His interests in metaphysics have taken him to many of the sites across the globe where ancient religious establishments are being transformed into Transcienz Halls. Lately, he's been documenting this process in Istanbul and reporting back to Christensen on a regular basis. He attends and assists in Brethren Gatherings wherever his travels take him.

Elias-Negash – A mysterious character who appears at the end of the novel, Elias-Negash is first known as "The One Sent" and plays a significant role in the course of events involving the global Resistance movement. An Ethiopian, Elias-Negash is foreshadowed in a dream Christensen has had, in which he is told that a helper will be sent.

Adammus Horn – As the young and ambitious Prosecutor General of the Allianz Federation, Mr. Horn, 39, has been given credit for bringing a horde of allegedly corrupt former world leaders to trial, under the Supreme Juris Court. A well-regarded Allianz Code policy adviser, with great charisma, his power and influence have been increasing within the Federation and in the public's view. He and Dariah share a romantic past.

Alyssa Lorentz – A 15-year old implanted neighbor girl, Alyssa's Cognit Implant has not yet been activated. Alyssa has taken an interest in the Christensen family, helping them during some tough times. She has befriended Bethany Christensen and has developed a fondness toward Mrs. Christensen, who has been a strong witness to her in the faith.

John "the Baptist" Waters – John, age 32, is a gifted young evangelist and a caring pastor, whose sensitivity and talent for reaching into people's souls has been resulting in many becoming Spirit-sealed and baptized at the local Brethren Gatherings of the Children of the Promise group. John is Christensen's most trusted friend. He is married to Shen-il, whom he met while living and ministering in Southeast Asia.

Shen-il Miang Waters – As Pastor John Waters' wife, she hails from Southeast Asia. Although she is relatively new to the Community of Brethren in the South, Shen-il leads worship at the Brethren Gatherings with her expert piano playing. She is 30 years old and has also been Bethany's voice teacher. Well acquainted with religious persecution in her native Java Island, Shen-il is known as the cautious and skeptical one in her group of Believers.

Allianz Glossary

Age of Reason: Precisely estimated by the Resistance to be 12-years old; the age at which implanted children are able to willfully choose to assimilate and activate their Cognit Forehead Implant.

Aikido: "The Way of Harmony with Energy." A Japanese art of self-defense, founded around the mid 20th century by Master Morihei Uyeshiba, called *O'Sensei*. Aikido utilizes principles of timing, leverage, and an attack's momentum to redirect its energy and subdue an opponent.

Allianz: See Allianz Federation.

Allianz Broadcasting Network (ABN): The state-sponsored broadcasting medium.

Allianz Code: The legal-rational system of political authority; the body of laws and regulations upon which the entire Federation is ordered.

Allianz Federation: The new world order; the single-government, global Federation, headquartered in the district of Paris, Province of France.

Allianz Federation Council of Regents: The principal executive governing body of the Allianz Federation; made up of ten council members.

Allianz Federation General Parliament: The legislative branch of the Allianz Federation government; made up of 200 Allianz Nobles.

Allianz Federation Marshall and Commander: The leader of an Allianz Federation province; the equivalent of the President and Commander-in-Chief under the superceded world order.

Allianz Federation Police Force: The main law enforcement institution in the Allianz Federation; made up of cog units.

Allianz Federation Press: The state-sponsored printed medium.

Allianz Federation Supreme Juris Court: The judiciary branch of the Allianz Federation government.

Allianz Nobles: 200 individuals who make up the General Parliament.

Allianz Palace: The central headquarters of the Allianz Federation; located in the district of Paris, Province of France.

Allianz Prosecutor General: The powerful, independent counsel of the Federation, who has been responsible for litigating against and imprisoning a vast number of former, democratically elected world leaders.

Allianzi: The new and official world language.

Anointed One: The Christ; the Messiah; the second person of the Trinity.

Brethren Gatherings: The corporate worship meetings of the Community of Brethren Resistance cells.

Children of the Promise: A fast growing Community of Brethren cell; located in the district of Midville, in West Tennessee.

Code Challengers: Those who oppose the Allianz Code and Allianz as a world system.

Cogs: Police officers; the principal law enforcement body of the Allianz Federation.

Cog Blazer: A variable-strength weapon used by cog forces.

Cognit Biotechnology: The technological platform which integrates the Cognit Forehead Implant and all other Cognit-based components used by individuals, institutions, and the Federation.

Cognit Bracelet: A device used for making any and all purchases with medallianz units of exchange under the new, worldwide Cognit-based system of commerce.

Cognit Detectors: Used in public and government facilities to scan and identify implanted and non-implanted individuals in the population.

Cognit Forehead Implant: A new technological advancement that, if implanted and activated, enables its users to assimilate into the new Allianz society.

Cognit Implantation: The procedure through which a Cognit Forehead Implant is administered to an individual.

Cognit Implant Activation: The willful initialization of the Cognit Forehead Implant; the necessary step in assimilating into Allianz society once someone is implanted.

Cognit Implant Outlets: The trendy establishments, often located in shopping complexes, where Implant Technics perform the implantation, activation, and subsequent programming of the Cognit Forehead Implant.

Cognit Implant Palm Extension: Part of the Cognit Bracelet system; located at the center of one's left-hand palm.

Cognit Implant Platform: Part of the machinery used to perform implantation.

Cognit Implant Program: The Cognit software used to activate and operate the Cognit Forehead Implant.

Cognit Implant Protocol: The body of laws and bylaws which regulate the Cognit Implant program under Allianz, and which establishes the parameters for one's participation in the Allianz society.

Cognit Links: Cognit pathways connecting one's implant and bracelet to CyberSat.

CogniToys: Interactive gadgets displaying incredibly realistic images and feel, which offer a wide array of sport modalities and other activities; marketed primarily to Allianz teens.

Cognit Technological Protocol: The myriad of core and peripheral infrastructure requirements imposed on all sectors of society, which make all industry sectors compatible with the Cognit-based technological reality.

Community of Brethren: The global underground Church; the anti-Allianz, Resistance movement.

CyberSat Data-Realm: A vast information database, accessible only by top Allianz Federation officials, in which all Cognit-based information is stored about the entire dominion of Allianz.

CyberSat Network of Satellites: The constellation of four main satellites and numerous other new-generation, secondary satellites which compose the CyberSat system.

CyberSat System: The powerful, satellite-based intelligence and administrative information gridiron.

D.C. Allianz Marshall Air Base: The main official air base of the American Province; located in Washington, D.C.

Dream Connected: The state in which Transcienz dreamers enter into when seeking the exhilarating effects of Transcienz.

***Evangel*:** The message proclaimed by the Community of Brethren that brings Spirit-sealing, or reconciliation with The Name, to those who hear and accept it.

FlightPak: A transport contraption worn on one's back that causes one to levitate and move about several feet above ground.

GDM Calendar System: A new date system which was created after the Great Digital Meltdown and which begins in calendar year GDM-1.

Global Exodus Plan: The escape plan conceived as a last resort by leadership cadres in the worldwide Community of Brethren Resistance movement; to be implemented upon the advent of the darkest hour of persecution by Allianz, at which point a global sign occurs in the heavens.

Global Provinces: Former nation states, now members of the Allianz Federation; governed by a Marshall and Commander.

Grand Hall of Transcienz: The headquarters of the Path of Transcienz, temporarily located in the district of Paris, Province of France.

Great Catacombs Program/Project/Gallery: The most secretive Allianz undertaking involving a massive number of permanent dream connected individuals; built on the site of enormous North African aquifers, with its entry point being the ancient city of Carthage, Province of Tunisia.

Great Digital Meltdown (GDM): The catastrophic result of the devastating Minotaur Virus attack on the global digital gridiron.

Great Allianz Directive: The master plan of the Allianz Federation, involving the use of the Path of Transcienz followers to generate power for the entire CyberSat system.

HealthScan: A medical examination done on implanted individuals.

H-Pak: The hydrogen-based fuel cell pack which powers most transports in Allianz.

Hyaline Televisor: A thin, crystalline monitor which broadcasts Allianz's officially approved network programs.

Hyper-Quaking Anti-Matter Energy (HQAME): The secret but abundant source of energy which powers up the Resistance's morph-ships.

"Imagine" Propaganda: Used by Allianz to publicize the benefits of assimilation into the Cognit Implant Protocol.

Implants/Implanted: Human beings who have received the Cognit Forehead Implant.

Implant Technics: The trained specialists who oversee the implantations.

***Les Invalides* II Program (LI-II):** A prototype of the Great Catacombs Project; located in Washington, D.C., and part of the Allianz Forces Medical Research Hospital Complex.

Medallianz Units of Exchange: The official currency in Allianz.

Minotaur Virus: The name given to the wireless, part electronic, part electromagnetic virus that brought the digital age to a catastrophic end.

Morph-ship: An advanced, highly versatile, secret transport; designed and developed by the Resistance; only two in ever made; uses Hyper-Quaking Anti-Matter as an energy supply.

Non-Implants (N.I.s): The term used by Allianz cogs to refer to non-assimilated humans.

Path of Transcienz: The official world metaphysical path in Allianz.

Personal Sat Spec (PSS): Communication and data processing devices based on holographic imaging.

Project Red Dragon: A top-secret aerospace project which developed and launched the CyberSat network of satellites into orbit from an undersea base, located in the Red Sea.

Resistance Movement: See Community of Brethren.

Secret Cogs Units: Allianz's secret police forces.

Spirit Dreamers: Those who receive the Holy Scriptures in Spirit dreams.

Spirit-sealed: The new spiritual condition of those who hear and believe the *Evangel*.

Supreme Juris Council: The highest judiciary branch in the Allianz Federation government.

Sword of the Spirit: Another term for the Holy Scriptures.

The Name: The term used by the Community of Brethren to refer to the One, True, Triune, and Living God.

Transcienz Dreamers: Those who seek Transcienz Halls in order to experience Transcienz Dream States.

Transcienz Dream States: The result of being Transcienz Dream Connected; produces an invigorating and increasingly addictive sensation in those who experience it.

Transcienz Hall/s: The locations where the teachings of the Path of Transcienz are disseminated, and where followers become dream connected.

Transcienz High Sage: The top leader and guru in the worldwide Path of Transcienz.

Transcienz Sage/s: The body of Transcienz teachers and servants under the High Sage.

Trash Scanning: The process of inspecting refuse as it is picked up by robotic trash transports.

United Commonwealth Organization (UCO): The leading international body of nations under the former world system.

***Verbum Dei* Chamber:** The peculiar, booth-like machine designed to reunify the Word of Truth, and also translate it into the Allianzi language.

Visual Coordinates (Visuals): The set of numerical addresses used for communication via the PSS.

Water Baptism Seal: The practice required of new members of the Community of Brethren to publicly and obediently acknowledge their new condition of Spirit-sealing.

WormRail Underground Transport System: A rapid, tram-like, transportation system which links regions within a province.

Word of the Spirit: The Holy Scriptures.

Printed in the United States
99746LV00003B/103-120/A